Further Up and Further In

A literature-based unit study
utilizing C.S. Lewis'
The Chronicles of Narnia

DIANE PENDERGRAFT

EDITED BY MARGIE GRAY

Cadron Creek Christian Curriculum
4329 Pinos Altos Road
Silver City, NM 88061

Published by:
Cadron Creek Christian Curriculum
4329 Pinos Altos Rd
Silver City, NM 88061
First printing © 2002
ISBN 0-9652511-4-4 (paperback)
Second printing © 2006
ISBN 0-9652511-6-0 (spiral bound)

Design and layout by Howell Graphic Design
www.howellgraphics.com

About the Front Cover Photo:
The front cover photo was graciously supplied by the talent and kindness of my lifelong friend, Richard Ziriax, who took the photo on a recent trip to Alaska. Thank you Richard.

About the Back Cover Photo:
The back cover photo was taken by Mary Jo Mason, part-time nurse, starving artist, and proprietor of Picture This Photography in Thermopolis, Wyoming.

About the Author:

Diane Pendergraft was born in Oregon and via a circuitous route through Montana, Iowa, Germany, and Colorado, now lives in Thermopolis, Wyoming.

She and her husband Ken have homeschooled their two sons and one daughter for seven years. Diane was active in a homeschool group in Colorado for six years, co-teaching a geography class, a high school literature class, and frequently leading discussions for book clubs. She also helped start an adult book discussion group that has been together for five years. Diane believes that the unit study approach to literature equips students for a lifetime of learning.

Acknowledgments:

Curt, thanks for editing this book. Ken, thanks for the years of hard work, sacrifice, and faith that God would fill in the gaps that made it possible for me to stay home and educate our children.

About the Illustrator:

Patty Ann Martirosian is originally from Santa Barbara, California. She holds an associates degree in Liberal Arts from Santa Barbara City College and majored in Deaf Studies at California State University, Northridge.

She started her career as an artist by painting oil portraits of her husband and his fellow officers. Paying tribute to heroes of World War II, she painted a retired Medal of Honor winner and contributed the painting to his Commemorative Hall of Fame in Fort Benning, Georgia.

She is married to an Army officer, homeschools five lovely children, and enjoys art and poetry.

About the Editor:

Margie Gray is the author of *The Prairie Primer*, a literature-based unit study using the Little House series. She is also the author of *Where the Brook and River Meet*, a literature-based unit study on the Victorian Era. Margie has been published in Bill and Diana Waring's *50 Veteran Homeschoolers Share . . . Things We Wish We'd Known*. She and her husband, Owen, home educate their five daughters and one son in Silver City, New Mexico.

Acknowledgments:

I would like to thank the Lord who has enabled me to do more than I thought possible. He is the great Provider. He has given me an encouraging, helpful husband.

This work would not have materialized without the services of Howell Graphic Design, who not only did the cover design, but also formatted this book. Erin Hall capably assisted the task of editing. Patty Martirosian graciously illustrated the text. Thanks to my twins Jessica and Karissa who tested the study and to my family who missed me while I worked. I am grateful to the numerous homeschoolers across the country whose enthusiasm for this project spurred its completion.

TABLE OF CONTENTS

INTRODUCTION

> " These commandments that I give you today are to be upon your hearts. Impress them on your children. Talk about them when you sit at home and when you walk along the road, when you lie down and when you get up."
>
> Deuteronomy 6:6–7 NIV

Further Up and Further In has been created to help parents instruct their children in academic subjects and godly development. The Narnia books by C.S. Lewis provide a springboard for growing in the knowledge of our Lord in the settings of World War II England and the fictional world of Narnia.

Further Up and Further In is designed for students in grades fourth through eighth; but as with most unit studies, it can be adapted for use with those younger or older. It covers a variety of academic studies including history, mythology, geography, science, literature, practical living, health and safety, cooking, and even a little art and music. *Further Up and Further In* is a well-rounded scholastic program needing only math, grammar, and spelling curricula to complete the student's course work. Much of the work can be done independently with some oversight, guidance, and assistance by the parent. Suggested activities can and probably will be changed by the parent. Above all, *Further Up and Further In* emphasizes studying the Word of God. It is hoped that through this study the student will learn the character of the great I Am and our relationship with Him.

Using *Further Up and Further In*

Resources Required

The page numbers in *Further Up and Further In* correspond to the January 1995 printing of the Scholastic edition of the Narnia books. This applies to all seven of the Narnia books used in this study which are as follows:

The Magician's Nephew
The Lion, the Witch and the Wardrobe
The Horse and His Boy
Prince Caspian
The Voyage of the Dawn Treader
The Silver Chair
The Last Battle

You will need access to the Internet and/or a good set of encyclopedias, a dictionary, a Bible, a Bible concordance, and a thesaurus. The online dictionary at <http://dictionary.reference.com> is useful, especially for hard-to-find words. Much of the suggested reading will be found in the Recommended Reading Appendix. Larger selections will need to be obtained from the library. You may also want to check your local library for suggested videos and audiocassettes.

Additional Resources Recommended

These materials are used several times during the curriculum.

- *Genesis: Finding Our Roots* by Dr. Ruth Beechick. Arrow Press. ISBN 0-940319-11-X.
- *Surprised By Joy: The Shape of My Early Life* by C.S. Lewis. Harcourt, Brace, Jovanovich. ISBN 0-15-687011-8.
- *Poems* by C.S. Lewis edited by Walter Hooper. Harcourt, Brace and Company. ISBN 0-15-672248-8.
- *Tales from Shakespeare* by Charles and Mary Lamb. This resource is also available online.

Organization

Units: There are seven units in *Further Up and Further In*—one corresponding to each of the seven Narnia books. *Further Up and Further In* follows an average of a book-a-month schedule. When a chapter is covered each day there will be an additional eight weeks left in your school year, but we would like to emphasize that you should follow a plan best suited to your family's pace. Some chapters may have more activities than one could do in a day. The extra eight weeks will give you time to explore these ideas and still finish in a year.

It is recommended that the books be studied in the order presented in *Further Up and Further In.* Many times studies will refer to previous assignments. Thus activities tend to build on one another.

It is a good idea to skim through the entire curriculum at the beginning of the year to prioritize which materials you want to purchase to enhance the studies. (Be sure to look at the Resource Appendix for help in finding resources and prioritizing.) Skimming will also help you to preview the field trips ahead of time, allowing you to be on the watch for certain once-a-year community activities such as a Renaissance Festival.

Planning Guides: Each unit is divided into four sections. Each section generally covers four chapters. At the beginning of each section is a Planning Guide that lists the information and items that need to be gathered for the section's activities. Suggested resources for the information and items are given along with occasional field trip or video possibilities. Space is allotted throughout the Planning Guide for you to note your own suggestions for resources, field trips, or memorization. Use the Guide pages to prepare for the week ahead.

A list of materials you will need will be provided before each book to be studied so if you choose, you will only need to make one trip to the library or store. An effort has been made to keep the materials as simple and inexpensive as possible and all are optional. Parents, please preview any suggested reading material before assigning it to your child. Nothing objectionable has been deliberately recommended; however, opinions differ as to acceptable reading material for children. Remember, no one knows your children as well as you do.

The chapter number in which each assignment is given is included after each item so that you can review each assignment before making a purchase or looking for a book. If you have difficulty finding a resource, please refer to the Resource Appendix.

Books go in and out of print. Some of the books suggested in this study are out of print. *The Narnia Cookbook* is one of them. An effort has been made to supply many of the recipes listed in the Narnia books in the Activity Appendix. I wanted to see what *The Narnia Cookbook* looked like so I obtained it from interlibrary loan (ILL). If you would like to do ILL for this book or another book for the study, tell your public librarian, who will give you a request form. The more information you know about the book, the better. As a minimum, you need to know the author, title, and publisher. Sometimes they also request the ISBN. If you do not know this information and the book is in print, your librarian can direct you to a books-in-print catalog. Generally the library will check its other branches first for an ILL request, then check outwards in your state, and finally extend its search to the country. Once the book arrives at your library, you have about three to four weeks to check out and use the book. There is usually a stiff fine for not returning an ILL book promptly. In most cases, the library also puts a limit on the number of books one can ILL in a year. It is costly in time and postage if the book must be ordered out of their system.

Chapters: Each chapter corresponds with the reading assignment in the Narnia books. The first assignment is to learn the chapter's vocabulary words and read the chapter. The activities, which are based on the chapter, follow reading the chapter and the vocabulary section. A week in *Further Up and Further In* consists of four days of assignments. Use the fifth day of the week to catch up on any reading, unfinished activities, field trips, or projects. The suggested time a student should spend on each chapter and its activities is an average of two to three hours. More than that and the chapter extends into another day.

Vocabulary: Not only are there assigned vocabulary words to study for each chapter, but also activities such as fill-in-the-blank sentences, crossword puzzles, and cooking assignments to help the student learn the vocabulary words. There are answers to the fill-in-the-blank sentences and crossword puzzles in the Answer Appendix.

Comprehension and Critical Thinking Questions: Sometimes comprehension and critical thinking questions are included for parents to ask students. These questions should be answered orally and in complete sentences. If an answer is given in the Answer Appendix, then the question will be followed by "See answer in Answer Appendix" or "See Answer Appendix." Parents are encouraged to read the books so the question and answer exchange can lead to the development of good communication and thinking skills. Let the dialogue with your child during this time be relaxed and enjoy getting to know their opinions and their skills in logic and observation.

The comprehension questions and critical thinking questions differ in that the reading comprehension questions have an objective answer which may be found in the Narnia series, while the critical thinking questions are either deduced or inferred.

Activities: The activities cover academics and Bible studies that relate to the chapters or pages read. An academic category is given in the margin next to each assignment to help you choose, record, or balance your child's studies. *Choose those activities that are time, age, ability, and interest appropriate for your child.* Many of the activities may take more than one day to complete depending upon your family's interest and time allotment. Make note of any activity that is inappropriate due to season of the year or the readiness of your family and complete it when the time and conditions are more appropriate.

Frequently, there are more activities assigned in a day than one student could possibly complete. If the activities are interesting and important to you, slow your pace and take time to explore. If more than one student is using *Further Up and Further In*, have each student pursue a different activity. At the end of the week, have them share what they have learned. There will be activities you will want your student to skim over and others into which you will want him to delve deeper. Some of the written assignments you may choose to go over orally, especially if you have a student for whom writing is tedious or if there are more writing assignments for that day than you want the student to do. *Remember to adapt to time available, age, ability, and interest.*

A column with icons is present throughout the activities. These icons are there to readily show you which assignments require time spent in reading, researching, doing hands-on activities, etc.

The icons:

Read . . . . 📖

Write . . . . ✏️

Discuss . . . . 📜

Find out—research . . . . 🗝️

Hands-on activity—drawing, cooking, making a model, field trip . . . . ✋

Watch a video. . . . . 👓
Listen to a cassette. . . . . 📼
Memorization. . . . . 🦁

Not all activities requiring an answer from the student have answers in the Answer Appendix. For those that do have answers you will see the question followed by "See answer in Answer Appendix" or "See Answer Appendix."

Topics Covered
in *Further Up and Further In*

In the Subjects Covered Appendix there is a complete listing of topics covered in *Further Up and Further In*. The list is broken down into subject areas only. You will find that your child learns progressively. That is, he can be exposed to a topic superficially at first and later acquire more in-depth details and understanding. Still later, the student may develop mastery of that subject. Each step in progressive learning, introduction, development, and mastery, is necessary for the child to assimilate and add to his store of knowledge. Some of the topics in *Further Up and Further In* you may just want to briefly introduce to your child. Other topics your child may be ready to master.

In mathematics, concepts build upon previously mastered skills. Subjects such as history, science, or Bible, however, can be presented in a varied order. You need not always follow a prescribed, rigid sequence. For example, the study of ants is not a prerequisite to the study of grasshoppers. Nor does it truly matter if a child learns about insects in the third grade or in the sixth. The key to learning, at any age, is to be introduced to a specific topic, to be given the tools to develop the new information, and to be allowed the time and further exposure to master the subject area. Your child will be learning and learning how to learn.

Additional Curricula Needed for
a Rounded Year's study

• A separate mathematics course.

• A separate grammar course, particularly if the student is not proficient in grammar. *Shurley Grammar* is my recommendation. If you have not used this before you may need to drop down one or two grade levels. See Resource Appendix.

• Spelling. *Spelling Power* is the suggested program of choice. See the Resource Appendix.

Making the Most
of *Further Up and Further In*

Bible: Almost every chapter has at least one Bible activity. Use a Bible version your child is comfortable reading, but not one that is too easy or in which the meaning is unclear. Many of the studies will require the use of a Bible concordance. My favorite Bible concordance is online. The keyword may be typed in and the online concordance will bring up all the verses with that keyword. The verses may be skimmed quickly for the topic that the student is looking for, and if the student wants to read the verse in context of the chapter, that may be done with a click of the mouse. This process markedly speeds up Bible research.

The most successful method in teaching the Bible studies is to preview the scriptures beforehand and allow the Spirit of God to quicken them to you. If certain scriptures come alive to you, you can in turn give your child fresh "meat and milk from the Word." One of the best ways to encourage a child to taste the Word is for the parent to feed them what they themselves have been "chewing on" or thinking about. If you share with your children "living words," they will experience the fact that God's Word is relevant and meaningful to our daily lives.

Also, because of differing attention spans and assignments, there may be more verses given than can be absorbed. By previewing the scriptures, you can choose to use only those that will emphasize the point you wish to make. Some scriptures are doctrinal by nature.

These are listed without comment so you can help your child interpret the Word of God according to your belief. Sometimes, real life is such that there may be little or no time to meditate on the scriptures before presenting them. In this case, you and your child will discover the Word of God together.

Older and more independent students may do many of the assignments alone. It is important to set aside a time for discussing what your child has gleaned from their Scripture reading.

Bible Memorization: *Further Up and Further In* encourages Scripture memory. The verses selected for memorization will aid your student in processing the information contained in *Further Up and Further In*, give them wisdom for life, and encourage character building. If Scripture memory is not already a part of your student's life, let me encourage you that Scripture memorization is obtainable. The more verses that are memorized, the more trained the mind becomes to memorize. Joshua 1:8 says, "This book of the law shall not depart out of thy mouth; but thou shalt meditate therein day and night, that thou mayest observe to do according to all that is written therein: for then thou shalt make thy way prosperous, and then thou shalt have good success." The skills learned in Scripture memorization improve one's ability to learn any new course of study. Memorization is one of the great tools of learning that has been downplayed for too long in education.

Scripture memorization offers its own rewards, but give your child rewards for memorizing. Perhaps let him quote his memorized section at the dinner table, then serve his dessert first. Offer monetary rewards for large passages of Scripture learned. Praise him when he sees how the Scripture he memorized is applicable to life or his studies.

There are many different ways to memorize. When chapters are memorized, people generally begin by reading the chapter over daily until parts are familiar, then start breaking it down into smaller parts. Verses can be copied, then quoted aloud and checked by a parent or sibling.

Writing: *Further Up and Further In* has a variety of writing assignments. Only through frequent writing can a student improve his skill. Using additional helps, such as *Write Source 2000*, can aid you in learning the teaching skills necessary to successfully improve your child's writing. For instance, the first time a paragraph is assigned go over the section on "Writing a Paragraph"; perhaps the next time a paragraph is assigned, review the section on paragraph unity. When planning your week have your writing handbook nearby. Jot down the writing handbook pages you want to cover with the writing assignment. Be sure to encourage your child in the editing and writing process. This will serve to motivate them to learn the rules of punctuation, spelling, and grammar.

In correcting your child's writing it is important to be stingy with the red pen. Over-critical instructors have produced many a writer's block. Prioritize one or two skills you want the student to improve and correct those. Leave the others for another time or another paper.

Hands-on activities: These activities add the needed spice, variety, energy, and enthusiasm to your schooling. Sometimes pooling energy and resources with another family who is doing *Further Up and Further In* will make it practical for your family to complete more of these. The hands-on learner's comprehension will increase as more of these activities are done. Do them as time and energy allow.

Art: The drawing assignments in *Further Up and Further In* will increase the comprehension of the reading material, as well as increase retention and contemplation of difficult subject matter. It will allow the student to strengthen his nonverbal communication abilities. The book, *Drawing with Children*, by Mona Brookes can help you sharpen your child's drawing skills. Each month as you begin a new Narnia book, try to concentrate on learning a different art skill. Focus on skills such as lines, shapes, overlapping, perspective, shading, color, color tone, and positive and negative space. Use different media to achieve variations in effects: colored pencils, markers, watercolors, charcoal, tempera, and metal tooling. Experiment with combinations for different results.

Organizing Your Notebook

Students will need one large three-ring binder with at least ten dividers or they may choose to keep their work (or some sections of it) in individual notebooks. Throughout the study each subject section will be referred to as a notebook, i.e. plant notebook, vocabulary notebook, etc. Students should file all completed work in the appropriate notebook.

Section 1, Vocabulary: The vocabulary notebook should have separate pages for words beginning with different letters of the alphabet so that when students are finished with *The Chronicles*, they will have their own glossary. The vocabulary words will always be listed first in each chapter assignment. Before reading the chapter, students should look up the words in a dictionary and write them, along with a definition, in their vocabulary notebook.

Section 2, Plants: Unlined paper will work best for the plant section.

Section 3, Animal Notebook: Unlined paper will work best for the animal section.

Sections 4–10, Books: One section corresponding to each of *The Chronicles of Narnia* books.

Web Sites

Further Up and Further In may be used without the assistance of a computer, although using the Internet to do research will help develop research skills and make it easier to obtain information. If you do not have access to the Internet in your home, many libraries have Internet capabilities. Usually they will allow you to print Web pages for later study at home. At <www.CadronCreek.com> on the Research Links page, there is a list of links for *Further Up and Further In* you may find helpful during your study. Please inform us if a site is no longer working or has changed. It is important to monitor your child while research is being done on the Internet since pornography and witchcraft may be encountered on the Web.

In the Resource Appendix there are some Web sites which might be used daily in completing the assignments. Although the sites work as of the writing of this book, Web sites frequently change addresses, servers go down, etc. If a particular Web site cannot be found, use one of the search engines to find another site on the topic or see if the <www.CadronCreek.com> Web page has an updated Web address for that site.

We hope you will be as blessed by using this curriculum as we have been by the process of its creation. Let the adventures begin.

THE MAGICIAN'S NEPHEW

⧗ PLANNING GUIDE – CHAPTERS 1-4

Gather These Items:

1. *The Magician's Nephew* by C.S. Lewis. Any edition will do, however, any page numbers given correspond to the January 1995 printing of the Scholastic edition. This applies to all seven of the Narnia books used in this study.

2. One notebook for vocabulary notes and one each for plant and animal notes. Or use one large three-ring binder with dividers. Unlined paper will work best for the plant and animal notebooks. (For more information on notebooks, see "Organizing Your Notebook" in the Introduction.)

3. Set of encyclopedias.

4. Dictionary.

5. Bible with references.

6. Bible concordance—preferably an exhaustive concordance.

7. Basic art supplies—pencils, paper for drawing, crayons, or colored pencils. Also:
   • Contact paper for lamination, Chapter 1.
   • Water color paints or acrylics, Chapter 4.
   • Butcher or computer paper for a mural, Chapters 3 and 4.

8. "The Speckled Band," a short story by Sir Arthur Conan Doyle, Chapter 1. (The old Sherlock Holmes movies starring Basil Rathbone would also be a good introduction to the Sherlock Holmes stories.)

9. Books featuring the Bastables by Edith Nesbit, Chapter 1. These books are: *The Five Children and It; The Phoenix and the Carpet; The Story of the Amulet; The Treasure Seekers;* and *The Wouldbegoods.* These books can be found online at <www.classicreader.com>.

10. *Treasure Island* by Robert Louis Stevenson, Chapter 1.

11. Biography of a scientist, Chapter 2.

12. One chapter of Proverbs each day, Chapter 2.

13. Solargraphics (photo) paper kit, Chapter 2. See Resource Appendix.

14. *Into the Forest,* a food chain game, Chapter 3. Make your own or purchase one. See Resource Appendix.

Suggested Information to Gather:

Encyclopedia or books about:

A good encyclopedia will probably cover these topics well enough for a general overview. The chapter in which each is suggested is given so if you decide you would like to study a topic in greater detail, you will have a complete list to take to the library or bookstore. This will apply to the research topics listed for each of the seven Narnia books.

Almost any subject may be researched on the Internet if you have access to a computer. Simply begin a search with your topic typed inside quotation marks. (Note to parents: *Please supervise your children if you decide to use this method.*)

1. Vacuum cleaner invention, Chapter 1 (History).

   ....

2. India, Chapter 1 (Geography).

   ....

3. Photography, Chapter 2 (History).

   ....

4. Atlantis, Chapter 2 (History/Science).

   ....

5. Solar system, Chapter 2 (Science).

   ....

6. Biographies of scientists, Chapter 2 (History/Science).

   ....

7. Balance of nature, ecology, food chain, Chapter 3 (Science).

   ....

8. Sound waves, Chapter 4 (Science).

   ....

Suggested Videos:

1. A movie that shows a mime, such as *Mime over Matter,* or a Red Skelton video, Chapter 1.

2. *Treasure Island*, Chapter 1.

3. The old Sherlock Holmes movies starring Basil Rathbone, Chapter 1.

Suggested Field Trips:

1. Visit a photography studio and watch photos being developed, Chapter 2.

Suggested Memorization:

1. I Corinthians 10:13, Chapter 1.

2. Philippians 4:8–9; Galatians 5:22–23; Ephesians 4:20–24; and Proverbs on controlling anger, Chapter 2.

3. Romans 5:19, Chapter 4.

Notes:

✎ WORKSHEET/CHAPTER 1

Character List

Keep track of the characters as they appear. Decide what or whom you think
each represents. You may not be able to tell right away.
Remember that not everyone represents something or someone.

Characters   Symbolic Meaning

Polly

Digory

Uncle Andrew

Aunt Letty

WORKSHEET/CHAPTER 4
People Affected by Digory's Mistake

Character   Consequence   Good or Bad

_____   _____   _____

_____   _____   _____

_____   _____   _____

_____   _____   _____

_____   _____   _____

_____   _____   _____

_____   _____   _____

_____   _____   _____

_____   _____   _____

_____   _____   _____

_____   _____   _____

_____   _____   _____

_____   _____   _____

🐾 SOUND STUDY WORKSHEET/CHAPTER 4

1. _____ is the name applied to the number of crests passing through a place per second.

2. A _____ is the high point on a wave.

3. A _____ is the low point on a wave.

4. _____ is the height of a wave.

5. The _____ is the distance between two neighboring crests or troughs.

6. _____ is the SI unit for frequency.

7. A _____ is equal to 1,000,000 hertz.

8. The shorter the wavelength, the _____ the frequency.

9. Can all matter conduct sound waves? _____

10. In which will sound waves travel faster, solids or liquids?

    _____

11. In which will sound waves travel further, liquids or gases?

    _____

12. In which will sound waves travel faster, liquids or gases?

    _____

13. _____ are substances which trap sound waves.

14. The unit for measuring loudness is the _____.

15. A _____ is a place with no matter.

16. The _____ are the three smallest bones of the body.

17. _____ is how high or low a sound is.

18. The thicker the vibrating object, the _____ the pitch.

19. The tighter the vibrating object, the _____ the pitch.

20. Can a sound of zero decibels be heard by people?

    _____

21. In which will sound waves travel further, solids or liquids?

    _____

22. The warmer the conductor, the _____ sound waves will travel.

23. People can perceive sound waves from _____ to _____ hertz.

24. The shorter the vibrating object, the _____ the pitch.

25. Prolonged exposure to sounds over _____ decibels can cause hearing loss.

26. What is the function of the ossicles?

   _____

27. What is the function of the pinna?

   _____

28. The _____ _____ is another name for the ear drum.

29. The _____ is a long, curled, fluid-filled canal lined with microscopic hair cells.

30. The _____ is the external, fleshy portion of the ear which is trumpet-like in shape.

31. An _____ is heard when sound waves bounce off of something and return to the ear.

32. In normal air, sound travels at about _____ miles per hour.

STUDY GUIDE – CHAPTERS 1-4

Vocabulary:

Begin a notebook for vocabulary words. Use separate pages for words beginning with different letters so when you are finished with *The Chronicles,* you will have your own glossary. You will need more than one page for some letters of the alphabet: A (2), B (2), C (4), D (3), E (2), F (2), G (2), H (1), I (2), J and K (1) together, L (2), M (2), N and O (1) together, P (4), Q (1), R (2), S (4), T (2), U and V (1) together, W (1). Vocabulary words will always be listed first in each chapter.

🔑 **Look up the words in a dictionary before you read the chapter and write them, along with a definition, in your vocabulary notebook. If your handwriting is large, allow yourself more pages than suggested above for each letter.**

✎ Skim the chapter for *coiner.* Write at least one sentence from this chapter containing this word under its dictionary definition. Follow each sentence with a citation enclosed in parenthesis. (A **citation** is a note which either gives the source of information used in the text or adds useful information.) Use the following format: Author (first name then last name), <u>title</u> (underline the title), city where the book was published: publishing company, year of publication, page cited. An example: (C.S. Lewis, <u>Of Other Worlds</u>, San Diego: Hartcourt, 1994, 29).

✎ Using your vocabulary words, fill in the blanks. The answers may be found in the section entitled Answer Appendix.

1. The _____ worked hard in his new country.

2. The mime entertained the crowd with his _____.

3. It was a _____ attempt to pull the boats across the snow drifts.

4. My grandmother is very _____ and cannot travel.

5. Many women take care of their _____ elder brothers.

6. The _____ went dry during the drought.

7. The Communist reeducation camps encouraged many _____ Vietnamese to enter Thailand.

Vocabulary Words:

immigrant

cistern

emigrant

bachelor

coiner

feeble

pantomime

vain

Read Chapter 1 of *The Magician's Nephew.*

Assignments:

Art   1. Watch a video or a live performance of a mime.

Bible

2. Although Polly, at first, did not trust Uncle Andrew, she was strongly tempted by the beauty of the rings. Giving in to the desire to have the rings began a series of events that would affect many people besides Polly.

Who in the Bible was tempted? In Genesis 3:1–7, we read that Adam and Eve gave in to temptation, and sin entered the world through them. Every human has been tempted from then until now. Even Jesus was tempted. Read Matthew 4:1–11; Mark 1:12–13; and Luke 4:1–13.

When we are tempted, we can take comfort from the Scriptures. The author of Hebrews tells us that Jesus, our High Priest, understands our weaknesses because He faced all of the same temptations we do; but He did not sin: Hebrews 4:15. Because He has gone through the same suffering and temptations we have, He can help us when we are tempted: Hebrews 2:18.

Where does temptation come from? Read James 1:13–15 and I Timothy 6:9.

Resisting temptation makes us stronger: James 1:2–4. We will be blessed for enduring: James 1:12. We can resist by praying. Read Matthew 6:13; Luke 11:4; Matthew 26:41; and Mark 14:38. The Lord knows how to deliver us out of temptations. Read II Peter 2:9. A way of escape will always be provided.

   Memorize I Corinthians 10:13.

   Make a bookmark exhorting yourself to resist temptation. Laminate it using contact paper.

History

3. C.S. Lewis opens *The Magician's Nephew* by telling us the story is about something that happened long ago when your grandfather was a child.

According to C.S. Lewis' outline of Narnian history, Digory was born in 1888 and Narnia was created in 1900.

Look up *Lewis, C.S.* in your encyclopedia.
  • When was C.S. Lewis born?
  • When was this book written?
  • How old was C.S. Lewis when he wrote this book?
  • When was your grandfather a child? If possible, interview your grandfather or grandmother and find out what significant historical events were happening when they were children.

   Write about your interview with your grandparent.

4. Read in your encyclopedia: History
   • How were ink bottles, fountain pens, and sealing wax used?
   • When was the vacuum cleaner invented?
   • Who invented it?

5. In the second paragraph there are two clues this book is fiction.   English
   C.S. Lewis speaks of the Bastables and Sherlock Holmes as though they
   were real people.

 If you do not know who these fictional characters are, read some books
   about them. "The Speckled Band" by Sir Arthur Conan Doyle is a
   good introduction to Sherlock Holmes. Stories about the Bastables were
   written by Edith Nesbit.

   Treasure Island by Robert Louis Stevenson is mentioned also. Read the
   first chapter of this book as an introduction. Would you like to read more
   or watch the video?

 Watch *Treasure Island* and/or a Sherlock Holmes movie.

6. An **allegory** is a story in which people, things, and actions represent   English
   ideas and truths. A **parable** is a type of allegory. Jesus taught
   with parables.

   Read John 10:3–16.

   Who is the Good Shepherd? What truth did Jesus express through the
   parable? In *The Magician's Nephew*, not every character or object has a
   moral or religious meaning, but you will recognize some representations
   as you read.

   In a letter to a fifth grade class written May 29, 1954, C.S. Lewis said
   he was not trying to write allegorically. He did not attempt to represent
   Jesus as He really is in our world by a Lion in Narnia, but imagined
   a land like Narnia and what would happen if the Son of God, as He
   became a Man in our world, became a Lion there (*Letters to Children*).

   Use the worksheet following the Planning Guide to keep track of
   the characters as they appear. Decide what or whom you think each
   represents. You may not be able to tell right away. Remember that not
   everyone represents something or someone.

   How did C.S. Lewis differentiate the Narnia series from an allegory?

7. Using pantomime techniques, demonstrate a scene from this chapter for   Reading
   your parent.   Comprehension

English   ⊙━   8. Knowing the parts of a book can help you find information easily and quickly. The title page is usually the first printed page in a book.
- Find the title page of *The Magician's Nephew.*

With your instructor find:
- the full title of the book
- the author's name
- the publisher's name
- the place of publication.

My copy does not have the place of publication on the title page, but on the copyright page. The copyright page follows the title page. Here you will find the year the copyright was issued; this is usually the same year the book was published. Tell your instructor the copyright year. Check the copyright date for all seven Narnia books. In what order were the books written? There is also Library of Congress information. Included on this page is C.S. Lewis' full name.
- What does the C.S. stand for?
- In what year was C.S. Lewis born?

The following page is a dedication page.
- To whom is this book dedicated?

Sometimes a preface comes before the table of contents and gives you an idea of what the book is about, who may have been involved in writing it, and why it was written. Other names for the preface include foreword, introduction, or acknowledgment.
- Find a book that has a foreword and show it to your instructor.
- Find the table of contents. The table of contents shows you the major divisions of the book and their corresponding page numbers.
- How many chapters does this book have? On what page does each chapter start?

The body of the book follows the table of contents; it is the main text of the book.

Other parts of a book, not included in *The Magician's Nephew,* are an appendix, a glossary, a bibliography, and an index. These are generally found in nonfiction books. *Further Up and Further In* contains an appendix.

Show the appendix to your instructor. An appendix provides extra information, often in the form of maps, charts, tables, diagrams, letters, or documents.
- Look in a textbook or other nonfiction book for a glossary, index, and bibliography. Show them to your instructor. Bibliographies give sources for learning more about subjects that interest you.
- What type of information is included in a glossary?

9. Digory's father was in India.

Geography

 Find India on a map or a globe. England claimed India as a colony for over 200 years. During the reign of Queen Victoria it was said the sun never set on the British Empire.

Read about India in the encyclopedia.

Vocabulary:

 Look up the vocabulary words in a dictionary before you read the chapter and write them, along with a definition, in your vocabulary notebook.

In the word **mortal**, the prefix, *mort*, comes from the Latin, *mors*, meaning death. This prefix is often a clue to the meaning of other words that begin in the same way. Tell your instructor what the words *mortician, mortify,* and *mortuary* have in common.

The word **preposterous** comes from two Latin words: *prae*, meaning before, and *post*, meaning after. Combining the words before and after gives us one word that means contrary to nature, reason, or common sense: absurd. Use the word *preposterous* in a sentence for your instructor.

Skim the chapter for *jaw*. Write at least one sentence from this chapter containing this word under its dictionary definition. Follow each sentence with a citation enclosed in parenthesis. (A citation is a note which either gives the source of information used in the text or adds useful information.) Use the following format: Author (first name then last name), <u>title</u> (underline the title), city where the book was published: publishing company, year of publication, page cited. See example, page 9.

Using your vocabulary words, fill in the blanks. The answers may be found in the section entitled Answer Appendix.

1. Goliath was _____ at the challenge of David.

2. Though he failed in his attempt, I had to admire his _____.

3. Her _____ helped her grow into a charming woman.

4. The Old West is not known for its _____ .

5. The story she told was _____ .

Vocabulary Words:

indignant

godmother

chivalry

preposterous

jaw (slang)

adept

pluck

mortal

6. Don't give me any _____ .

7. The toddler was _____ at picking up Cheerios.

Read Chapter 2 of *The Magician's Nephew*.

☀ Assignments:

Bible   📖   1. Uncle Andrew implied there were different standards of right and wrong for different people and that people who have standards are narrow-minded. God is narrow-minded about sin and has told us in His Word what is right and what is wrong. Read Matthew 7:13–14 and Isaiah 5:20. The Ten Commandments, found in Exodus 20, tell us what we should not do. Jesus summed all of them up in two commandments which tell us what we should do: love God and love our neighbor. See Matthew 22:34–40. If an action is unloving, it is wrong.

Proverbs 6:16–19 tells us seven things God hates. We can find other lists of evil behavior in the New Testament in Galatians 5:19–21. The best way to recognize wrong, however, is to be familiar with what is right. Read Hebrews 5:14. Have your senses trained to discern good and evil by practicing. Rather than memorizing lists of evil actions to avoid, concentrate on what is good.

🦁   Memorize Philippians 4:8–9; Galatians 5:22–23; Ephesians 4:20–24.

Bible   📖   2. In order to justify his cowardly treatment of Polly and his cruelty to animals, Uncle Andrew said sacrifice was required to acquire great wisdom. He was right; wisdom does not come easily. Solomon gave his heart "to seek and search out wisdom," Ecclesiastes 1:13 and 7:25; but Uncle Andrew's mistake was to seek after the wisdom of the world.

📖   Read Romans 1:18–23.

🚩   Discuss the wisdom of this world. What is it?

📖   Read I Corinthians, Chapters 1–3, to find out what kind of wisdom God wants us to seek.

🚩   Discuss the difference between worldly wisdom and Godly wisdom.

📖   Read one chapter of Proverbs every day for one month. When you finish, you may want to start over again and make it a habit to read a chapter of Proverbs each day.

Bible   📖   3. Uncle Andrew told Digory he needed to learn to control his temper. There is a place for anger. Read Ephesians 4:26. Jesus had zeal against things that were against the Lord. Read John 2:15–17. Christians must learn self-control. Read Galatians 5:23 and II Peter 1:6.

Discuss and evaluate Aristotle's statement regarding anger:

> It is easy to fly into a passion—anybody can do that—but to be angry with the right person, to the right extent and at the right time, with the right object and in the right way, that is not easy and not everyone can do it. —Aristotle

Was Digory's anger justified?

Read Proverbs 14:17, 15:18, 16:32, 19:11, 22:24, 29:22; Ecclesiastes 7:9; Ephesians 4:31–32; and Colossians 3:8.

Choose one or two of the above verses from Proverbs to memorize.

---

4. To **foreshadow** is to give hints or clues that suggest what will happen next or later in a story. Foreshadowing is an indication of beforehand and a literary technique used to create interest in the story. The mention in the first chapter that Uncle Andrew is either mad or that there is some other mystery indicates something unusual may happen. We hope it will. We are interested and we want to keep reading.   English

Discuss with your instructor other pieces of literature or movies that use this technique.

---

5. Digory did not think you could judge someone very well by how they looked in old photographs.   History

Look at the earliest photographs you can find.

Read in your encyclopedia:
- When was photography invented?
- Who is credited with the invention?
- Why is it so hard to see what people were really like?
- Why did no one smile?

---

6. Visit a photography studio and watch them develop photos. Interview the photographer about current-day technology.   Field Trip

---

7. Make an art project using solargraphic paper.   Art

---

8. Uncle Andrew said his box came from Atlantis.   English/
   - Where did the legend of Atlantis originate?   History
   - Do you think it was a real place?

Write an imaginary story about how the box made its way from Atlantis to Uncle Andrew. Use the literary technique of foreshadowing in this story.

Science 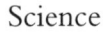 9. In this chapter, Uncle Andrew tells us there are worlds that can never be reached by traveling through space. We do not know this for sure, but we can find out how far the other planets in our solar system are from earth.
- How far away is the nearest planet?
- The farthest?
- How far away is the nearest galaxy?
- How long would it take us to get there?

Science/ History 10. Uncle Andrew was shocked Digory would suggest he could have gone into the Other Place himself to see what was there. Successful scientists and inventors are more serious about their work. Some have made great sacrifices for their work and some have even ruined their health in pursuit of their goals.

 Read the biographies of some scientists such as Marie Curie, Jonas Salk, and Edward Jenner. What kinds of sacrifices did they make to help others? This assignment may carry over into the following weeks until you feel you have covered the topic to your satisfaction.

Critical Thinking 11. **Coercion** means forcing to act or think in a given way by pressure, threats, or intimidation; to compel.

 In this chapter, who used coercion? What pressure, threats, or intimidation were used? Why did it work?

Are there people who are free from the common rules? Do the rules that apply to us apply to profound students and great thinkers and sages or kings or presidents?

Read Chapter 3 of The Magician's Nephew.

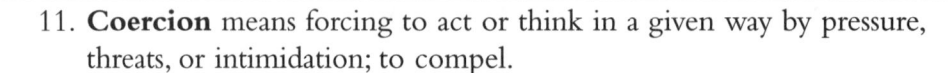 Assignments:

Science 1. The Wood between the Worlds was very much alive even though there were no birds, insects, animals, or wind.
- What would happen if there were such places in our world?
- What is the purpose of birds, insects, animals, and wind in the pollination process?
- Could birds, insects, or animals survive without each other?

You should be able to find this information by looking in your encyclopedia under: Balance of Nature, Ecology, or Food Chain.

Draw a food chain using animals that live in your area.

---

2. Play the game of *Into the Forest*. This game of 41 cards teaches about the food chain using the plants and animals of the forest and their relationship to each other. There are several ways to play, but my favorite is a variation of the game of *War* that was popular when I was a child. In this version, more respectably named *Showdown,* each player places his half of the deck face down and the two players turn their top cards over in unison. Whoever "eats" the other wins that set.

Science

---

3. **Quotation marks** are used to designate the exact words of a speaker other than the author. "My name," said the girl, "is Sally Brown."

English

Single quotation marks designate a quotation within a quotation, such as when a person is telling a story and repeats what someone else said within the story. "And the woodcutter said to the old woman, 'I'll do exactly as you say.'"

When a speech continues on to another paragraph, quotation marks are not used at the end of the first paragraph but are used at the beginning of the next paragraph to indicate that the same person is still speaking. Use quotation marks at the end of a paragraph in which the speech ends.

---

4. Read the conversation between Digory and Polly aloud. Have one person read Digory's part. Have another person read Polly's part. If there is a third person available, have him/her read the unquoted sections.

English

---

5. Digory wanted to know more before he and Polly went home: he wanted to know everything. Polly just wanted to go home. Discuss these questions with your instructor:
   • Which would you want to do?
   • Why?

Critical Thinking

Write a conversation between yourself and a person with the opposite opinion discussing what to do next in a situation. Be sure to use quotation marks correctly.

➤━◆➤━O━◆━┥◄

Chapter 4

**Vocabulary
Words:**

majestic

obstinate

Vocabulary:

☞ **Look up the words in a dictionary before you read the chapter and write them, along with a definition, in your vocabulary notebook.**

 Skim the chapter for your vocabulary words. For each word, write at least one sentence from this chapter which contains the vocabulary word under its dictionary definition. Follow each sentence with a citation enclosed in parenthesis. (A citation is a note which either gives the source of information used in the text or adds useful information.) Use the following format: Author (first name then last name), <u>title</u> (underline the title), city where the book was published: publishing company, year of publication, page cited. See example, page 9.

Read Chapter 4 of *The Magician's Nephew.*

☀ Assignments:

English

1. C.S. Lewis contrasted the silence of this new place with the silence of the Wood between the Worlds. One seemed full of life, the other seemed dead.

   ✎ Write several paragraphs comparing and contrasting types of silence you have experienced. For instance, how would you describe the silence of a library? A church? Your room at night? **Comparing** shows similarities between two or more things. **Contrasting** shows the differences. You may compare and contrast point by point, such as: "The silence in a church is peaceful, but the silence in my room at night is lonely," or by describing one example completely, and then describing the next. The concluding paragraph should tie the two together.

English

2. An **adjective** is a word used to describe or limit a noun or a pronoun. Descriptive adjectives describe or tell what kind of noun or pronoun it is. Examples: whirling shapes, arched doorways, red light. The limiting adjectives tell how many, which one, or how much. (The interrogative pronouns may be used as limiting adjectives: which, whose, and what. Numerals are limiting adjectives when they precede a noun: one, two, three or first, second, and third.) The demonstrative adjectives are this, that, these, those, and such. Sometimes the indefinite pronouns are used as adjectives: all, another, any, both, each, either, every, few, many, most, much, neither, no, other, several, and some.

Discuss with your instructor:
- How do you think C.S. Lewis wanted you to feel about Charn?
- What types of words give you clues?

List the adjectives in the chapter that support your opinion. Identify the type of each adjective you list.

Now identify the different types of adjectives you used in writing your conversation in Chapter 3, Activity 5.

---

3. In the line of ancestors, what do you think might account for the change in the people's faces? The first ones look happy, but each one in the line looks worse than the one before, until the last people look cruel. The line of ancestors presents an indication beforehand.

   What literary technique is this called? What do you think Mr. Lewis is indicating? See Answer Appendix.

English

---

4. In the room with the bell and hammer Digory was "too wild with curiosity" to think about it being an enchanted room. Do you think it was really magic that caused Digory to ring the bell? Digory did not stop to think about what the consequences of this one act could be.

   The Bible is full of people whose one act affected themselves or others. Think of some Bible characters whose one action changed things for many others.

Bible

Biblical Character	Action	Consequence(s)
Adam	Ate forbidden fruit.	Brought sin into the world. Everyone had to work for their food.

Read Exodus 20:4, 34:6; Leviticus 26:40–45; and Romans 5:12–19.

Memorize Romans 5:19, "For as by one man's disobedience many were made sinners, so by the obedience of one shall many be made righteous."

Use the worksheet provided after the Planning Guide to chart the people affected by Digory's action. Use at least five characters and ten consequences. Record how many people are affected by his action and whether it is for good or bad.

---

5. Digory wanted to know everything, but mere curiosity without discretion got him into trouble. Knowledge is important (Proverbs 10:14, 24:5), but it must be tempered by love, wisdom, and self-control.

Look up these verses: Proverbs 1:4, 2:6, 28:2; Romans 10:2–3; I Corinthians 8:1, 13:1–2; II Peter 1:5–8, 3:18.

Bible

Art

6. Draw or paint the scene from this chapter that is the most vivid to you. (Note to instructor: *The purpose of most of the drawing assignments in this book is to check your child's comprehension. If you would like to use these drawing assignments to improve his or her art skills you might want to use* Drawing With Children *by Mona Brookes or a similar art book.*)

Games

7. Play the *Quiet Game:* all players are quiet and the object of the game is to see who can be quiet the longest.

Science

8. The quietness of Chapter 4 echoes in our minds.

Read about sound and sound waves in the encyclopedia and the Recommended Reading Appendix.

There are also several Web sites that have experiments related to sound listed at CadronCreek.com's *Further Up and Further In* Research Links page.

Complete the Sound Study Worksheet which follows this unit's Planning Guide. The answers may be found in the Answer Appendix.

⧗ PLANNING GUIDE – CHAPTERS 5-8

Gather These Items:

1. *Surprised By Joy: The Shape of My Early Life* by C.S. Lewis, Chapter 7.

2. *Of Other Worlds: Essays and Stories* by C.S. Lewis, edited by Walter Hooper, Chapter 8.

3. Church hymnal or a copy of the hymn by Sir George J. Elvey and Henry Alford, "Come Ye Thankful People, Come," Chapter 8. The words may be found in the Recommended Reading Appendix. Go to the research links page for *Further Up and Further In* at <www.CadronCreek.com> to listen to the song.

Suggested Information to Gather:

Encyclopedia or books about:

A good encyclopedia will probably cover these topics well enough for a general overview. The chapter in which each is suggested is given so if you decide you would like to study a topic in greater detail, you will have a complete list to take to the library or bookstore. This will apply to the research topics listed for each of the seven Narnia books.

Almost any subject may be researched on the Internet if you have access to a computer. Simply begin a search with your topic typed inside quotation marks. (Note to parents: *Please supervise your children if you decide to use this method.*)

1. Sun, stars, Chapters 5 and 8 (Science).

   ....

2. Format of plays, *Hamlet* by William Shakespeare, Chapter 6 (English).

   ....

3. London, Buckingham Palace, and the Houses of Parliament. Also the British pound, Chapter 7, (History/Social Studies). Try searching the Internet under "London" + "Virtual Tour."

   ....

4. Time and seasons, Chapter 8 (Science).

   ....

Suggested Videos:

Suggested Field Trips:

Suggested Memorization:

1. Proverbs 16:18, Chapter 6.

Notes:

Study Guide – Chapters 5-8

Vocabulary:

Vocabulary Words:

ebony

aghast

🗝 **Look up the words in a dictionary before you read the chapter and write them, along with a definition, in your vocabulary notebook.**

🗝 Look up *ebony* in both a dictionary and an encyclopedia.

📖 With your parent discuss what information is common to both. What is different? Which source could be used for the pronunciation? Which source could be used for the parts of speech? Which source could be used for different forms of the word? Etymology? Uses for the product?

Read Chapter 5 of *The Magician's Nephew*.

☀ Assignments:

1. The sun of Charn looked much different from our sun because it was dying.

   Bible

   📖 Read about the birth and death of stars in your encyclopedia. Keep in mind God's promise in Genesis 8:22. What do Revelation 21:23–24 and Revelation 22:5 tell us about the sun?

2. The Queen said rules do not apply to her. Compare her attitude to that of Uncle Andrew in Chapter 2.

   English

   • How are they the same?
   • How are they different?

   ✏ Use at least 10 adjectives to describe the Queen's character.

   📖 Reread the story of the destruction of Charn as told by the Queen, especially the section that begins, "It was my sister's fault." The Queen excused her own actions by blaming everything on her sister.

   ✏ Rewrite the story from her sister's point of view.

>─◄◆─○─◆►─◄

Chapter 6

**Vocabulary
Words:**

sham

dabble

vain

scorn

treachery

pax

distinguished

Vocabulary:

🔑 **Look up the words in a dictionary before you read the
chapter and write them, along with a definition, in your
vocabulary notebook.**

✏ Using your vocabulary words, fill in the blanks. The answers may be found in
the section entitled Answer Appendix.

1. The _____ gentleman was our governor for many years.

2. Digory and Polly each apologized and called it _____ .

3. Judas is known for his _____ .

4. It was a _____ decision to buy another dress instead of
   groceries for her children.

5. Many get rich quick schemes are a _____ .

6. One must not _____ in witchcraft.

7. "This my long sufferance and my day of grace,
   Those who neglect and _____ , shall never taste."

   —John Milton

Read Chapter 6 of *The Magician's Nephew.*

☀ Assignments:

Bible

1. Can you "dabble" in magic without any danger to yourself? What does
   God say about magicians?

📖 Read Deuteronomy 18:9–14; Isaiah 8:19; Exodus 22:18; I Samuel 15:23;
II Chronicles 33:6; Micah 5:12; Acts 19:19; and Galatians 5:19–20.

Uncle Andrew had become a magician because he was as vain as a
peacock. **Vain** and **vanity** come from the Latin *vanus* meaning empty.
Vain, in Uncle Andrew's case, means overly proud of one's appearance or
accomplishments.

From your reading in Proverbs you have probably seen that the Bible
uses *vain* and *vanity* to mean empty or to no avail. From what you have
read about pride so far in Proverbs, tell how being overly proud is empty
and to no avail.

🦁 Memorize Proverbs 16:18.

2. You have already practiced writing a story in dialogue form using quotation marks to indicate the speaker. A different form is used for writing a play. For example, look at Shakespeare's *Hamlet*. Rather than using quotation marks, each character's name is written before the lines he is to speak. The manner in which the lines are to be spoken is usually left up to the interpretation of the actor. There are a few lines before each scene describing where the scene takes place and stage directions are inside brackets. Shakespeare used very few stage directions but there may be times when more are necessary.

English/
Art

Beginning in Chapter 6 with the line, "Where is the magician who has called me into this world?" and ending in Chapter 7 with, "Jiminy! She's loose in London," write out the dialogue in the form of a script for a play using *Hamlet* as a model.

Memorize and perform the exercise above as a short skit. This will be an ongoing project. Use as much time as you need to do a good job.

3. Discuss the following questions with your instructor:
   • After Jadis' description of how she conquered Charn, would you have taken pity on her when she begged for mercy?
   • Uncle Andrew's expression resembled that of Jadis. He had the "mark" of a magician. What do you think caused the resemblance? What is the "mark"?

Critical
Thinking

Chapter 7

Vocabulary

Look up the words in a dictionary before you read the chapter and write them, along with a definition, in your vocabulary notebook.

Using your vocabulary words, fill in the blanks. The answers may be found in the section entitled Answer Appendix.

1. The kitchen _____ had a table and chairs next to it.

2. The _____ cab's distinctive feature was the elevated driver's seat in the rear.

3. The feeble landowner sent his _____ to find a wife for his son.

**Vocabulary
Words:**

minion

bow–window

hansom

Read Chapter 7 of *The Magician's Nephew.*

☀ Assignments:

History		1. C.S. Lewis' mother died when he was 10, so when he wrote about Digory's feelings about his mother's illness he wrote from experience.
		Read about C.S. Lewis' childhood in his autobiography, *Surprised by Joy: The Shape of My Early Life*, Chapters 1–3. This is a challenging book. For younger students or weaker readers this book is best read aloud by the parents. On a page by page basis discuss what is understood and explain what is not.

History		2. C.S. Lewis said Aunt Letty was a tough old lady and that aunts often were in those days. Do you know a story about a brave woman in your family in the past or present? If you do not already know a story, interview your relatives, then write a story you have learned.

History		3. Find some pictures of Buckingham Palace and the Houses of Parliament in your encyclopedia, a picture book about London, or on the Internet. Learn something about what has taken place in these buildings in the past and what takes place in them now. Who built Buckingham Palace? Who lives there now?
		Tell your instructor what you have learned.

Social Studies		4. What are the different denominations of British money? Who is on the coins and bills? You should be able to find this information in your encyclopedia under *pound*. What is the current exchange rate? See <www.CadronCreek.com> for some links for the exchange rate. Which is currrently worth more, the dollar or the pound?

Art		5. Reread the details of this chapter after the cab crash. Using butcher paper or computer paper, make a mural of the scene.

Critical Thinking		6. Discuss these questions with your instructor:

- C.S. Lewis thought waiting as Polly did would have been easier than waiting as Digory did. Why do you think he might have felt that way?
- Do you agree?
- List some of the things about the rings about which Uncle Andrew was mistaken.

⊱━◆━○━◆━⊰

Vocabulary:

Vocabulary Word:

impertinent

Look up this word in a dictionary before you read the chapter and write it, along with a definition, in your vocabulary notebook.

Colney Hatch was an insane asylum in London, so when a bystander at the lamp-post called Jadis the "Hempress of Colney 'Atch," he meant she was crazy.

Skim the chapter for your vocabulary word. Write one sentence from this chapter containing today's vocabulary word under its dictionary definition. Follow the sentence with a citation enclosed in parenthesis. (A citation is a note which either gives the source of information used in the text or adds useful information.) If a work has been fully documented in a citation, succeeding references need only include the author's last name and the page(s) cited. An example: (Lewis 44).

Read Chapter 8 of *The Magician's Nephew.*

☀ Assignments:

1. Examine the reactions of each character to the voice. See Answer Appendix. Why do you think each person felt as they did about the voice?

   Bible

   If Jadis represents Satan, we can see why she might have understood the music better than anyone. Isaiah 14:12–17; Zechariah 3:1–2; and Job 1:6–12, 2:1–7 tell about Satan actually being in the presence of God. Although he became completely evil because of his self-will, he has seen God and knows something about what God is like. He hates God and God's creation. He knows his own future and fears God.

2. Who does the lion represent? *(Aslan is Turkish for lion. Jesus is referred to in the Bible as a lion in Revelation 5:5.)* In C.S. Lewis' own explanation of how he came to write the Narnia books, he said, "I don't know where the lion came from or why He came. But once He was there He pulled the whole story together, and soon He pulled the six other Narnian stories in after Him" (*Of Other Worlds: Essays and Stories,* "It All Began With a Picture").

   Bible

Bible/ English 3. In Chapter 2 of *Surprised By Joy: The Shape of My Early Life*, C.S. Lewis remembers his father addressing rhetorical questions to his brother and him. Read Job 38. Verse 7 mentions the morning stars singing together. Might C.S. Lewis have had this verse or chapter in mind when he imagined the creation of Narnia?

A **rhetorical question** is one to which no answer is expected.

How many can you find in this chapter of Job?

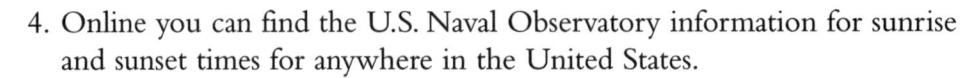

Science 4. Online you can find the U.S. Naval Observatory information for sunrise and sunset times for anywhere in the United States.

 Make a graph using the run as the months of the year. The rise should be in five minute increments. Pick one date of the month and graph the time of sunrise and sunset for each month for your area. Older students may want to compare this graph with one made of an area with at least a 10° difference in latitude. What is the shortest day of the year? The longest?

As an alternative, get up early and watch a sunrise. You can find out in your local newspaper at what time sunrise will be tomorrow. Check the time of sunrise each day for a few weeks or months. What pattern is developing? Why? If you do not know why the days shorten and lengthen, study the methods of measuring time and what causes the change of seasons.

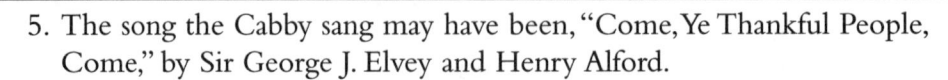

Music 5. The song the Cabby sang may have been, "Come, Ye Thankful People, Come," by Sir George J. Elvey and Henry Alford.

 Find this song in a church hymnal and learn to play or sing it. Or you may read the words in the Recommended Reading Appendix. If you would like to listen to this song, go to the research links page for *Further Up and Further In* at <www.CadronCreek.com> or use a search engine and type in the name of the song.

Critical Thinking 6. Discuss these questions with your instuctor:
  • What are some things we know about Uncle Andrew by the end of Chapter 8? Answers may vary. See Answer Appendix.
  • What are some things we know about the Cabby by the end of his speech while everyone is in the dark? Answers may vary. See Answer Appendix.
  • Have you ever seen or heard anything so beautiful you could hardly bear it? If you have, describe it.

➤·◆·○·◆·◁

⧗ PLANNING GUIDE – CHAPTERS 9-12

Gather These Items:

1. Basic art supplies—pencils, paper for drawing, crayons, or colored pencils. Also:
   • Large paper for a collage, Chapter 9.
   • Old magazines with pictures of birds, Chapter 9.

2. *Paradise Lost* by John Milton, Chapter 11. See *Further Up and Further In* links page at <www.CadronCreek.com>. For older students only.

Suggested Information to Gather:

Encyclopedia or books about:

1. Pictures of currant, lilac, wild rose, rhododendron, daisy, buttercup, and primrose plants and flowers from an encyclopedia, magazines, or seed catalogs, Chapter 9 (Science/Art).

   ....

2. Air, Chapter 12 (Science).

   ....

Suggested Videos:

Suggested Field Trips:

Suggested Memorization:

Notes:

STUDY GUIDE – CHAPTERS 9-12

Chapter 9

Vocabulary Words:

lilting

ostentatious

Vocabulary:

🔑 **Look up the words in a dictionary before you read the chapter and write them, along with a definition, in your vocabulary notebook.**

✏️ Skim the chapter for your vocabulary words. For each vocabulary word, write one sentence from this chapter which contains the word under its dictionary definition. Follow each sentence with a citation enclosed in parenthesis. (A citation is a note which either gives the source of information used in the text or adds useful information.) If a work has been fully documented in a citation, succeeding references need only include the author's last name and the page(s) cited. An example: (Lewis 44).

Read Chapter 9 of *The Magician's Nephew.*

☀ Assignments:

Bible		1. The grass spread out from the Lion like a pool. Remember that the Lion represents Jesus. Jesus is the center of creation. See John 1:1–5; Colossians 1:15–19; and Romans 11:36. The Cabby said it was time for watching and listening, not for talking.
		Read Ecclesiastes 3:1–8. There is a time for everything.
Science/ Art		2. Begin a plant notebook with unlined, white paper. In your encyclopedia or plant book, find out what currant, lilac, wild rose, rhododendron, daisy, buttercup, and primrose plants and flowers look like. Draw and color a picture of each or cut pictures out of magazines and glue them into your notebook. Where can these plants be found? Write any interesting facts you find about them.
Art		3. Cut out pictures of birds from magazines. On a large sheet of paper draw a tree and make a collage over the tree showing showers of birds.

⊳–◆–O–◆–◁

Chapter 10

Vocabulary:

🔑 **Look up the words in a dictionary before you read the chapter and write them, along with a definition, in your vocabulary notebook.**

✋ Look up today's vocabulary words in both a dictionary and the encyclopedia. With your instructor, discuss what information is common to both. What is different? Draw a picture of each vocabulary word to include with the definition.

faun

satyr

naiad

Read Chapter 10 of *The Magician's Nephew.*

☀ Assignments:

📖 1. Read "The Blind Men and the Elephant" by John G. Saxe in the Recommended Reading Appendix. How does this poem apply to the characters in this story?

English/
Bible

🖻 Describe a time when you jumped to a conclusion about something and later found out you had only part of the story.

✋ Give different family members a different verse from the list below. As in the poem, have them defend their scripture to the exclusion of others.

1. God is love—I John 4:16, "And so we know and rely on the love God has for us. God is love. Whoever lives in love lives in God, and God in him."

2. God is merciful—Deuteronomy 4:31, "For the LORD your God is a merciful God."

3. God is a consuming fire—Deuteronomy 4:24 and Hebrews 12:29, "For the LORD your God is a consuming fire, a jealous God."

4. God is God—Deuteronomy 7:9 and Deuteronomy 10:17, "Know therefore that the LORD your God is God."

5. God is Spirit—John 4:24, "God is spirit."

6. God is peace—I Corinthians 14:33, "For God is not a God of disorder but of peace."

7. God is just—II Thessalonians 1:6, "God is just: He will pay back trouble to those who trouble."

8. God is light—I John 1:5, "God is light; in him there is no darkness at all."

9. God is the Alpha and Omega—Revelation 1:8, "I am Alpha and Omega, the beginning and the ending, saith the Lord, which is, and which was, and which is to come, the Almighty."

10. God is holy—I Peter 1:16, "Because it is written, be ye holy; for I am holy."

As the poem illustrates, we need to be careful not to base our beliefs solely on our own experience with God or an isolated scripture. The Bible tells us to, "Study to shew thyself approved unto God, a workman that needeth not to be ashamed, rightly dividing the word of truth," II Timothy 2:15.

Mr. Saxe may have thought all religions held a partial truth of God, but Jesus told us, "I am the way and the truth and the life. No one comes to the Father except through me," John 14:6. As Charlotte Mason said, "How necessary then that a child should be instructed to understand the limitations of his own reason, so that he will not confound logical demonstration with eternal truth. . . ." (*School Education*, Vol. 3, The Original Homeschooling Series, 116.)

"Do you see a man wise in his own eyes? There is more hope for a fool than for him," Proverbs 26:12. "There is a way which seemeth right unto a man, but the end thereof are the ways of death," Proverbs 14:12.

Bible

2. It may be hard for you to believe that Uncle Andrew could make himself unable to see and hear what was actually going on, but the Pharisees denied Jesus in the same way. Find instances in the Gospels where the Pharisees or Sadducees could not deny that Jesus was from God, yet plotted to kill Him anyway because He was a threat to their position or did not fit into their idea of what He should be.

 Read John 11:45–12:42 and Matthew 21:23–46.

Bible

3. Compare Aslan's charge to the Talking Beasts to Genesis 1:28–31. Aslan told the animals who received the gift of speech not to go back to the way of Dumb Beasts.

 Read II Peter 2:19–22.

Discuss what can happen to people who go back to their old ways.

Bible

4. How could all of the creatures know Aslan's name before they were told?

 Read John 10:4, 5, 14, 27 and Romans 1:19–20. What is put into every man's heart?

Vocabulary:

Vocabulary Words:

sagacious

🗝 **Look up this word in a dictionary before you read the chapter and write it, along with a definition, in your vocabulary notebook.**

✏ Skim the chapter for your vocabulary word. Write one sentence from this chapter containing today's vocabulary word under its dictionary definition. Follow the sentence with a citation enclosed in parenthesis. If a work has been fully documented in a citation, succeeding references need only include the author's last name and the page(s) cited. An example: (Lewis 44).

Read Chapter 11 of *The Magician's Nephew.*

☀ Assignments:

---

1. Aslan told the animals Digory was the boy who had brought evil into his new world.

   📖 Read Romans 5:12–21. Aslan also told them not to be downcast because the evil which would come of that evil was still a long way off and he would see to it that the worst of it fell on himself.

   Aslan already had a plan to control the evil that entered Narnia at the very beginning, as though he had already known it would come. From the beginning God had a plan to save the world from sin and death.

   🗝 Using a Bible with references, start with Genesis 3:15 and follow the references to find God's promises to send a Savior.

   📖 Older students may enjoy reading Book III of John Milton's poem, *Paradise Lost,* in which he writes his idea of what the conversation between God and Jesus may have been like when Jesus agreed to come to earth and die for our sins. This poem may be found online; see <www.CadronCreek.com> for a direct link.

Bible

---

2. Compare the Cabby's attitude about being king to the reactions of others appointed by God to special tasks:

   Moses—Exodus 3–4:17   Isaiah—Isaiah 6:1–8
   Samuel—I Samuel 3   Jeremiah—Jeremiah 1:1–10
   Saul—I Samuel 10:17–24

   There are others. Do you have a favorite?

Bible

---

3. Draw a picture of the animals planting Uncle Andrew. Include all of the animals mentioned.

Art

Chapter 12

<table>
<tr><td>Vocabulary
Word:

fledge</td><td>

Vocabulary:

🗝 **Look up this word in a dictionary before you read the chapter and write it, along with a definition, in your vocabulary notebook.**

✏️ Skim the chapter for your vocabulary word. Write one sentence from this chapter containing today's vocabulary word under its dictionary definition. Follow the sentence with a citation enclosed in parenthesis. If a work has been fully documented in a citation, succeeding references need only include the author's last name and the page(s) cited. An example: (Lewis, 44).

</td></tr>
</table>

Read Chapter 12 of *The Magician's Nephew.*

☀ Assignments:

Bible

1. Fledge told Digory and Polly that Aslan probably had known they would need something to eat, but Fledge had an idea that Aslan liked to be asked. Does God need us to ask for things before He can know what we need? What can we ask for? Are there conditions for receiving what we ask for?

📖 Read Matthew 6:8; Luke 11:9–10; John 15:7; James 1:5–8; and I John 3:22, 5:14, 15.

📝 Discuss what you have learned.

Science

2. What do you know about our atmosphere?

🗝 Look in your encyclopedia under *air.* How high can you go and still be able to breathe? How much does the temperature change as you go up? Would sounds seem different?

Art   ✋   3. Draw Narnia as it looked from the air.

Critical   📝   4. Discuss the following question with your instructor:
Thinking   • Do you think there was something in the Dark?

⊱─◈─◉─◈─⊰

⧗ PLANNING GUIDE – CHAPTERS 13-15

Gather These Items:

1. *Miracles* by C.S. Lewis, The Macmillan Co., Chapter 15. Only recommended for older students.

2. *Of Other Worlds: Essays and Stories* by C.S. Lewis, edited by Walter Hooper, Chapter 15.

3. *Poems* by C.S. Lewis, edited by Walter Hooper, Chapter 15.

Suggested Information to Gather:

Encyclopedia or books about:

1. British Crown Jewels, Chapter 14 (History).

   ....

2. World leaders of the early 1900's—Vladimir Lenin, Benito Mussolini, Josef Stalin, Adolf Hitler, Hirohito, Chapter 15 (History).

   ....

Suggested Videos:

1. *The Hiding Place,* Chapter 15.

2. *Life is Beautiful,* Chapter 15.

3. Audiocassette – *Bonhoeffer: The Cost of Freedom,* Chapter 15. Borrow from a friend or see the Resource Appendix.

4. *The Miracle of the Bells,* Chapter 17.

Suggested Field Trips:

Suggested Memorization:

Notes:

STUDY GUIDE – CHAPTERS 13-15

Chapter 13

Read Chapter 13 of *The Magician's Nephew.*

✳ Assignments:

Bible   🔑   1. The rhyme on the gates of the garden said anyone who stole fruit from the garden would find their heart's desire but would also find despair. How could finding your heart's desire cause despair? Look up the following scriptures:

Desire for Wrong	Desire for Right
Psalm 112:10	Mark 11:24
Proverbs 21:25	Romans 10:1
James 4:2–3	Proverbs 30:8–9
Numbers 11	

    Compare this garden scene to the one in Genesis 3:1–7. In what ways were the Witch's tactics the same as Satan's? What kept Digory from doing the wrong thing?

    Read Matthew 16:24–26. Comment on the Witch's reasoning and compare it to the principle in these verses.

Science   🔑   2. In your encyclopedia or plant book, find out what the herb *honesty* looks like. What is another name for it? Add a picture of it to your notebook.

Read Chapter 14 of The Magician's Nephew.

☀ Assignments:

---

1. Aslan did not put new traits into Frank, he used the ones already in him.   Bible

📖 Read about the lives of Moses (Exodus), Peter (the Gospels and Acts), and Paul (Acts).

✏️ Write a paper on how God used their pasts and character traits for His own purposes. If you do not already know something about each of these people, reading about them may take some time. You may want to take a week to read about Moses and read about Peter and Paul the next week. Take notes as you read, then write the paper the following week.

---

2. The animals called Uncle Andrew, "Brandy," because that was the noise he kept making.   English

🔑 Find the meaning and etymology (word history) of *onomatopoeia*. What are some examples?

📖 Read Edgar Allan Poe's poem, "The Bells," in the Recommended Reading Appendix. How is this an example of onomatopoeia?

🔑 3. Find a picture of the Crown Jewels of Britain. How old are they?   History/
For whom were they made? You may be able to find them in your   Art
encyclopedia, a picture book of London, or on the Internet.

✋ Design a crown that you would like to wear.

📓 4. Discuss these statements: Critical
• The tree's smell "which is joy and life and health to you, is death and   Thinking
horror and despair to her." Read II Corinthians 2:16.
• "Things always work according to their nature."
• "All get what they want; they do not always like it."

➤━◆━○━◆━┥

Read Chapter 15 of *The Magician's Nephew.*

☀ Assignments:

Bible

1. The doctor said the recovery of Digory's mother was like a miracle. What is the dictionary definition of a miracle?

   Read the miracles that occurred in one of the Gospels or in Acts.

   Watch *The Miracle of the Bells.* What does Fred MacMurray say a miracle is? Older students may want to read C.S. Lewis' *Miracles.*

   Write a one page essay on miracles. Make sure you have an introductory and concluding paragraph as well as topic sentences for each paragraph.

History

2. Of what do you think C.S. Lewis was thinking when Aslan warned Polly someone in our world may find a secret as evil as the Deplorable Word?

   Aslan's prophecy stated that soon great nations in our world would be ruled by tyrants who care no more for joy or justice and mercy than the Empress Jadis. In what way was this true?

   Remember Narnia was created in 1900, our time.

   Learn something about world leaders since then such as Hirohito, Vladimir Lenin, Benito Mussolini, Josef Stalin, and Adolf Hitler. If you do not already know about them, spend a day investigating each of these leaders.

   Write at least one paragraph about each of the above leaders.

   Consider this quote from *Evangeline* by Henry Wadsworth Longfellow: "Tyrants reign with fear. Alike were they free from fear that reigns with the tyrant, and envy the vice of the republics."

   Watch videos, read books, or listen to cassette tapes that illustrate the effects these tyrants had on Europeans. See Planning Guide for a few suggestions.

Critical Thinking

3. Discuss these questions with your instructor:
   - Three times we have read "what a day that girl" [the housemaid] was having. Why do you think this was repeated? What do you think her days were usually like?
   - Do you think any of the people in the story got into Narnia by accident?

4. Read the essay, "Sometimes Fairy Stories May Say Best What's To Be Said," in C.S. Lewis' *Of Other Worlds: Essays and Stories,* edited by Walter Hooper.

Literature

C.S. Lewis said sometimes fairy stories say best what is to be said. Do you think this is true of this story? What do you think he was trying to say? Did he have more than one reason for writing this story?

5. How many people did you count who were affected by Digory's rash ringing of the bell? Was it all for bad? All for good?

Bible

6. Gregory the Great (540-605) developed a list of Seven Deadly Sins. It is characterized by its Latin acronym, *saligia,* for *superbia* (pride), *avaritia* (greed), *luxuria* (luxury, later lust), *invidia* (envy), *gula* (gluttony), *ira* (anger), and *acedia* (sloth). Dr. Don King has written about these sins in Lewis' work:

Literature/
Bible

> Great writers such as William Langland in *Piers Plowman,* Dante in the *Divine Comedia,* Chaucer in "The Parson's Tale" from *The Canterbury Tales*, and Spenser in *The Faerie Queene* all devote serious attention to these sins. It is not surprising then that C.S. Lewis knew them so well as we see in *The Allegory of Love.* Throughout this study of allegory, C.S. Lewis refers to the seven deadly sins. . . . In *Poems* he focuses an entire poem, "Deadly Sins," on each one of the seven deadly sins. —"Narnia and the Seven Deadly Sins." A version of this essay first appeared in
>
> *Mythlore* 10 Spring 1984: 14–19.

From the book *Poems* read "Deadly Sins."

Dr. King describes how Lewis presents anger in the first book of *The Chronicles:*

> *The Magician's Nephew* portrays the deadly nature of **anger**. Lewis would have us see that anger, uncontrolled rage, is another form of blindness. It turns us away from a right and whole vision of the truth, and instead leads us towards egoism, expressed by choler and revenge. —"Narnia and the Seven Deadly Sins." A version of this essay first appeared in *Mythlore* 10
>
> Spring 1984: 14–19.

Give examples of the sin of anger found in this book.

7. Review vocabulary words by completing *The Magician's Nephew* Crossword Puzzle. The answers may be found in the Answer Appendix.

Vocabulary

Complete any unfinished assignments prior to going on to
The Lion, the Witch and the Wardrobe.

The Magician's Nephew Crossword Puzzle

ACROSS

2 grow feathers

4 subordinate

7 black

8 flaunty

10 disloyalty

11 carriage

12 half man, half goat

13 absurd

14 balky

16 courage

17 rude

18 a Roman demigod

20 gallantry

21 sickly

23 unsuccessful

24 a knight of the lowest order

25 migrant

DOWN

1 holding tank

3 trifle with

5 female sponsor for a child in baptism

6 conspicuous

9 grand

12 yell★

13 mimicry

15 mythological water nymph

16 religious ornament

17 displeased

19 light movement or song

22 scam

★Not a vocabulary word

THE LION, THE WITCH AND THE WARDROBE

⧗ PLANNING GUIDE – CHAPTERS 1-4

Gather These Items:

1. *The Lion, the Witch and the Wardrobe* by C.S. Lewis.

2. A book about children who were sent away from London during World War II, fiction or nonfiction, such as Noel Streatfeild's, *When the Sirens Wailed,* Random House ISBN 0-394-83147-0, Chapter 1.

3. A cookbook of English tea recipes or *The Narnia Cookbook* by Douglas Gresham. Although not required, *The Narnia Cookbook* contains recipes for most of the suggested cooking activities in this study. This book is currently out of print but may be available in your public library, Chapter 2.

4. Mothballs, Chapter 3.

5. You will also need recipes and ingredients for Turkish Delight, Chapter 4. See Activity Appendix for two recipes.

Suggested Information to Gather:

Encyclopedia or books about:

1. World War II, London Blitz, Chapter 1 (History).

   ....

2. Silenus, Bacchus, nymphs and dryads, Chapter 2 (Mythology).

   ....

3. Seasons, Chapter 2 (Science).

   ....

4. The North Pole, Robert E. Peary, the Arctic, reindeer, and Shetland ponies, Chapter 3 (History/Social Studies).

   ....

Suggested Videos:

1. *Goodbye Mr. Chips* with Peter O'Toole, Chapter 1.

Suggested Field Trips:

Suggested Memorization:

Notes:

Study Guide – Chapters 1-4

Chapter 1

Vocabulary Word:

wireless

Vocabulary:

🔑 **Look up this word in a dictionary before you read the chapter and write it, along with a definition, in your vocabulary notebook.**

Note: In the case of this vocabulary word, Peter probably means a radio.

Read Chapter 1 of *The Lion, the Witch and the Wardrobe.*

 Assignments:

History

1. During which war did this story take place? In what years did this war occur?

After World War I, Britain, which had previously relied on its powerful navy for protection from its enemies, realized it was now vulnerable to attack from the air. As early as 1924 some government leaders who believed a second war was inevitable began to plan for the evacuation of children and mothers of small children in the event of air attacks. From June to September of 1939, more than 3,500,000 people—school children, mothers with children five years of age and under, expectant mothers, blind people, and school teachers—were evacuated from areas deemed likely targets of bombing. Many families with the means to do so made their own arrangements to send their children to places that were considered safe. The children evacuated by the government were sent to live with anyone who had a spare bed; they had no idea who they would be with or where until they got there. Some of these children ended up living with very kind families under conditions that were a vast improvement over the homes they had left. Some were abused. In any case it was a life-changing event for the children and sometimes for the hosts.

C.S. Lewis had three children come and stay with him during World War II. They had been sent out of London because of the air raids just like Peter, Edmund, Susan, and Lucy.

Read a book about children who were sent away from London during World War II. (Parents: *Please preview any book selected. Although there are several fictional books written for children on this subject, most are about unpleasant experiences.*)

2. Why was there a lamp-post in the middle of a wood? Briefly tell the story.

English

3. Draw a picture of Lucy meeting the Faun.

Art

4. Watch the movie *Goodbye Mr. Chips* with Peter O'Toole to see how life in England was affected by the war.

History

Vocabulary:

Look up the words in a dictionary before you read the chapter and write them, along with a definition, in your vocabulary notebook.

Skim the chapter for *inquisitive*. Write at least one sentence from this chapter containing this word under its dictionary definition. Follow each sentence with a citation.

Vocabulary Words:

inquisitive

anthropomorphism

Read Chapter 2 of *The Lion, the Witch and the Wardrobe.*

✷ Assignments:

1. Why did the Faun refer to the children as Sons of Adam and Daughters of Eve?

Bible

Read Genesis 3:20 and Romans 5:12.

2. Look up Silenus and Bacchus. What are nymphs and dryads?

English

You should be able to find these mythological characters in a dictionary. The encyclopedia will be a little more thorough, a book on mythology even more so. Although Christians do not believe in the gods and goddesses of old mythology, a basic knowledge of some of the major characters will be useful when reading much of classic literature.

Science

3. Mr. Tumnus told Lucy the White Witch had made it always winter and never Christmas in Narnia.

What causes winter? Is it winter everywhere in the world at Christmas time?

Use your encyclopedia or read a book to learn about the seasons if you have not already done this.

Cooking

4. What are the typical components of the meal called tea?

Find out about the history of tea and the different types. Learn about the meal and the drink.

Use a cookbook of English teatime recipes for ideas and prepare and serve tea to your family or friends.

In *The Narnia Cookbook,* the section on afternoon tea begins on page 27.

Critical
Thinking

5. Discuss whether you would have gone to tea with the first faun you met. What choices did Lucy have? What might have happened if Mr. Tumnus had turned Lucy over to the Witch?

Vocabulary:

🔑 **Look up the words in a dictionary before you read the chapter and write them, along with a definition, in your vocabulary notebook.**

🖊 Using your vocabulary words, fill in the blanks. The answers may be found in the section entitled Answer Appendix.

spiteful

sulk

gilded

1. The _____ employee damaged the equipment.

2. The Buddha's thinly _____ exterior was peeling.

3. She is prone to _____ when she does not have her way.

✋ Show your student mothballs. Have him or her describe the smell.

Read Chapter 3 of *The Lion, the Witch and the Wardrobe.*

☀ Assignments:

✋ 1. Draw the White Witch, her dwarf, and sledge. **Art**

🖊 2. Write your answer to the question, "What are you?" **English**

📖 3. Imagine your brother or sister told you the story that Lucy told her brothers and sister. What would you think? What proof would you need before you would believe it? **Critical Thinking**

---

4. In Chapter 3 we see sledges, reindeer, and a polar bear coat. The most common animals in the Arctic and Subarctic are reindeer and caribou. **History/ Social Studies**

During the late 1800's people of many nations began going to the Arctic for adventure and exploration. The first exploreres to reach the North Pole were U.S. Navy Commander Robert E. Peary and his aide, Matthew Henson.

🔑 • How old was C.S. Lewis when Peary reached the North Pole?
   • Look in your dictionary or encyclopedia: How big are reindeer? Shetland ponies?
   • In an encyclopedia or on the Internet read about the North Pole, Robert Peary, and the Arctic.

📖 Pretend you are C.S. Lewis telling his father about Robert Peary's trip to the North Pole.

>–◦<

Chapter 4

Vocabulary Words:

courtier

dryad

Vocabulary:

🗝 **Look up the words in a dictionary before you read the chapter and write them, along with a definition, in your vocabulary notebook.**

✎ Using your vocaulary words, fill in the blanks. The answers may be found in the section entitled Answer Appendix.

1. A _____ life ends when its tree is cut down.

2. There was not, among all our princes, a greater _____ of the people than Richard III.

Read Chapter 4 of *The Lion, the Witch and the Wardrobe.*

✳ Assignments:

Critical Thinking	📓	1. At first Edmund did not want to come into the Witch's sledge; but by the time he had finished all the Turkish Delight, he had changed his mind. What changed his mind? What kept Edmund from telling the truth after he had been in Narnia?
Bible	📓	2. What does the Bible say about greed and pride? You should have some idea from your reading in Proverbs. The book of James also has a lot to say on this subject.
Cooking	📓	3. If someone asked you what you like best to eat, what would you say?
	✋	Find a recipe for and make Turkish Delight. It is on page 97 in *The Narnia Cookbook.* Also see the Activity Appendix.

>+◆+○+◆+<

⧗ PLANNING GUIDE – CHAPTERS 5-8

Gather These Items:

1. You will need recipes and ingredients for Mrs. Beaver's meal, Chapter 7: fish, bread, potatoes, marmalade roll. See Activity Appendix for marmalade roll recipe.

Suggested Information to Gather:

Encyclopedia or books about:

1. Logic, Chapter 5.
   - *Introductory Logic* by Douglas J. Wilson and James B. Nance, Canon Press, ISBN 1-885767-36-6.
   - *Traditional Logic I: An Introduction to Formal Logic* by Martin Cothran, Memoria Press, ISBN 1-930953-10-0. (Reading level: seventh grade and up)

   ....

2. Bird migration, Chapter 6 (Science).

   ....

3. Beavers, Chapter 7 (Science).

   ....

4. Ice fishing, Chapter 7 (Life Skills).

   ....

Suggested Videos:

1. An instructional video on ice fishing, Chapter 7.

Suggested Field Trips:

1. Go birding, Chapter 6.

2. Go ice fishing, Chapter 7.

Suggested Memorization:

Notes:

Study Guide – Chapters 5-8

Chapter 5

Vocabulary Words:

snigger

row (noun)

disposal

Vocabulary:

🔑 **Look up the words in a dictionary before you read the chapter and write them, along with a definition, in your vocabulary notebook.**

✏️ Using your vocabulary words, fill in the blanks. The answers may be found in the section entitled Answer Appendix.

1. We tried not to _____ as we watched the toddler attempt to wash the dishes.

2. Every time those two get together, they end up having a _____ .

3. The master told his friend he would leave everything at his _____ during his absence.

Read Chapter 5 of *The Lion, the Witch and the Wardrobe.*

✳ Assignments:

Logic

1. Professor Kirke wanted to know why the children had not learned logic in their school.

🔑 What is logic?

Find the meanings of *deductive, inductive, fallacy,* and *syllogism;* add them to your vocabulary notebook.

You can learn some basic things about logic in your encyclopedia. Or, begin a logic study using one of the many books available through homeschool catalogs. See the Resource Appendix for some source suggestions.

Critical Thinking

2. Why do you think C.S. Lewis keeps repeating you should never shut yourself in a wardrobe?

▷·◁▸·○·◂·▷·◁

Vocabulary:

Vocabulary Words:

camphor

fraternize

prig

chatelaine

🔑 **Look up the words in a dictionary before you read the chapter and write them, along with a definition, in your vocabulary notebook.**

✏️ Using your vocabulary words, fill in the blanks. The answers may be found in the section entitled Answer Appendix.

1. The _____ quickly offended those at the gathering.

2. The smell of _____ is not quickly forgotten.

3. The _____ gave me a tour of her family's estate.

4. The owners of the different construction companies in town frequently _____ at the local coffee shop.

✳️ *Extra assignment:* See if your local pharmacy has any products with camphor in them.

Read Chapter 6 of *The Lion, the Witch and the Wardrobe.*

✳️ Assignments:

1. Edmund made the mistake of mentioning the lamp-post, forgetting he had lied and told everyone he had never been in Narnia. Liars have to have good memories.

Bible

🔑 Use an exhaustive concordance and look up all of the verses in the Bible in which the words *liar* and *liars* are used. Also look up all of the New Testament references using the word *lie*, meaning a false statement purposely put forward as truth.

Mark Twain said, "If you tell the truth, you don't have to remember anything." The English poet Sir Walter Scott said, "What a tangled web we weave when we first practice, to deceive" (*Marmion*, Canto Sixth, Stanza XVII).

🔑 2. Robins are considered a sign of spring. Why?

Science

✏️ Write a report on bird migration. You may use your encyclopedia or a book about birds.

🔑 What types of birds migrate through your area? At what times of year do they come through your area?

Life Skills		3. Make bird suet cakes to help your traveling feathered friends. Find recipes for bird suet in the Activity Appendix.
Field Trip		4. Plan a field trip to go birding. What will you need? What birds do you expect to see?
Art		5. Draw the four children in their fur coats in Narnia.
Writing		6. Write a story about what may have happened at the faun's house and where he is now. First make an outline of your story. Make each new heading a new paragraph.
Critical Thinking		7. How did the Witch find out Mr. Tumnus had let Lucy go? Peter said robins were good birds in all the stories, and he did not think a robin could be on the wrong side. Do you think it would be wise to judge another world by what is normal in our world?

⊱⊱⊷⦿⊶⊰⊰

Chapter 7

Vocabulary Words:

gumboots

oilcloth

festoon

Vocabulary:

🔑 **Look up the words in a dictionary before you read the chapter and write them, along with a definition, in your vocabulary notebook.**

🖉 Using your vocabulary words, fill in the blanks. The answers may be found in the section entitled Answer Appendix.

1. The sailor had on an _____ coat.

2. Modern day streamers are a type of _____ .

☀ *Extra Assignment:* **Gumboots** are rubber work boots which come up to or above the knee. Another name for gumboots is Wellingtons. These boots were named after the Duke of Wellington, Arthur Wellesley, best known for his important role in the defeat of Napoleon at Waterloo (1815). He later became prime minister (1828–1830). See if you can find a picture of gumboots and show them to your parent.

Read Chapter 7 of *The Lion, the Witch and the Wardrobe*.

✳ Assignments:

📖	1. Read Luke 2:25–35. Does this remind you of any characters in the story? See Answer Appendix.	Bible
✏️	2. Write a report on beavers and their dams.	Science
✏️	3. Have you ever had a dream such as Lewis described in this chapter? Write about it. If not, write about the nicest dream you have ever had.	Writing
👓	4. Read about ice fishing or watch an instructional video on ice fishing.	Life Skills/ Cooking
✋	Go ice fishing. If you do not catch any fish, buy some as fresh as possible. (If you are able to catch the fish, all the better.)	
✋	Cook and eat a meal like the one Mrs. Beaver cooked: fish, bread, potatoes, and marmalade roll. A recipe for marmalade roll can be found in the Activity Appendix.	

>–⊷–○–⊶–◄

Vocabulary:

🔑 **Look up the words in a dictionary before you read the chapter and write them, along with a definition, in your vocabulary notebook.**

Etymology is the history of a linguistic form (as a word) shown by tracing its development since its earliest recorded occurrence in the language where it is found. This is done by tracing its transmission from one language to another, by analyzing and breaking it down into its component parts, by identifying its cognates in other languages, or by tracing it and its cognates to common ancestral forms in an ancestral language. Example: etymology [Middle English *ethimologie*, from Latin *etymologia*, from Greek, from *etymon* + *-logia -logy*]. Knowing the etymology of a word is helpful with its spelling. Write the etymology of today's vocabulary words in your definitions.

Vocabulary Words:

stratagem

decoy

Read Chapter 8 of *The Lion, the Witch and the Wardrobe.*

☀ Assignments:

| Bible | | 1. Mrs. Beaver told Lucy she had been able to tell Edmund had been with the Witch by something in his eyes. |
| | 📖 | Read what Jesus said about eyes in Matthew 6:22–23; Luke 11:34–36. |

Bible	📖	2. In this chapter, the children heard about Aslan from the Beavers. Reread the section beginning with "Oh, yes! Tell us about Aslan!" through, "He's the king, I tell you."
	✏️	Compare what the Beavers say about Aslan with what you know about Jesus.
		Older children should find scriptures about Jesus that correspond to the Beavers' statements about Aslan.

| Games | ✋ | 3. Have you ever played a game called *Statue*? You will need at least three people to play. One person is the statue-maker. The statue-maker swings another player around by the hand carefully and lets go. The other person freezes in the position in which he falls. The statue-maker does this to all of the players. Then he judges the statues for the most interesting or funniest. The winner then becomes the statue-maker for the next round. |

| Critical Thinking | | 4. If you read *The Magician's Nephew* first, discuss Mr. Beaver's comment there had never been any of the children's race in Narnia before. Was this a mistake on Lewis' part or had the true history been forgotten by Narnians? If none of their race had been there before, how did the rhyme get started? Which book was written first, *The Magician's Nephew* or *The Lion, the Witch and the Wardrobe*? (Hint: check copyright dates.) |
| | | Can you think of any rhymes, poems, or sayings that were created for the purpose of helping us remember history or prophecy? |

>─+◆─○─◆+─◄

⧗ Planning Guide – Chapters 9-12

Gather These Items:

1. Modeling clay or ingredients to make clay, Chapter 9. See Activity Appendix.

2. *D'Aulaire's Norse Gods and Giants* by Ingri D'Aulaire, Chapter 9. This book is out of print and only available through the library system.

3. *Genesis: Finding Our Roots* by Dr. Ruth Beechick, ISBN: 0-94039-11-X, Chapter 10.

4. Plaster of Paris, Chapter 11.

5. Recipe and ingredients for plum pudding or fig pudding, Chapter 11. See pages 81 and 82 in *The Narnia Cookbook*. Also see the Activity Appendix.

Suggested Information to Gather:

Encyclopedia or books about:

1. Fog, Chapter 11 (Science).

   ....

2. Celandines, snowdrops, crocus, primrose, bluebells, larch, birch, laburnums, beech, flowering currants, hawthorn bushes, and elm, Chapters 11 and 12 (Science).

   ....

3. Animal tracking, Chapter 11 (Science).

   ....

4. Kingfisher, thrush, Chapter 12 (Science).

   ....

Suggested Videos:

Suggested Field Trips:

Suggested Memorization:

1. Ephesians 6:10–18, Chapter 10.

Notes:

STUDY GUIDE – CHAPTERS 9-12

Chapter 9

Vocabulary
Words:

turret

eerie

sledge

cat-a-mountain

Vocabulary:

🔑 **Look up the words in a dictionary before you read the chapter and write them, along with a definition, in your vocabulary notebook.**

✏️ Using your vocabulary words, fill in the blanks. The answers may be found in the section entitled Answer Appendix.

1. A puma is a type of _____ .

2. Shackleton took ponies, dogs, and a motor car to assist in hauling his _____ across the Antarctic.

3. The house's _____ was mainly for decoration.

4. The cat's cry had an _____ sound.

Read Chapter 9 of *The Lion, the Witch and the Wardrobe.*

☀ Assignments:

Bible		1. What does the Bible say about selfishness?
	🔑	You may want to use a concordance to find verses on this subject.
	📓	Is there something in which you tend to be selfish? Why do you feel this way? What can you do to change this?
	📖	Read Philippians 2:3–8.
Critical Thinking	📓	2. Why was Edmund's feeling, at the mention of Aslan's name, different from everyone else's?
Art	✋	3. Using clay, sculpt some of the statues Edmund saw in the castle. Buy clay or make your own. See Activity Appendix for recipe.
Literature		4. C.S. Lewis had a varied literary background. Fenris Ulf is a minor character in Norse mythology.
		Fenris was the son of Loki and Angerboda. Loki was blood brother to Odin and Angerboda was an ogress. Because both parents were bad, Odin thought their offspring could only be worse; but because they were his brother's children, he could not kill them. Instead, he put them each

where they could do the least harm. Fenris, the wolf, was put on an island in the middle of a lake surrounded by a forest of iron trees. As he grew and became uncontrollable, the gods decided he must be bound by magic. He was fed every day by an ogress who lived in the forest and continued to grow until Ragnarokk, the day of reckoning. On that day the earth split open and all bonds were broken; Odin and his army of gods and heroes had to fight all of the evil creatures. In the fight Fenris swallowed Odin.

📖   If you have access to *D'Aulaire's Norse Gods and Giants*, read more about Norse mythology and look for other references to Norse mythology in Lewis' books.

🗝 5. From what country did Norse mythology originate? Find this country on a map and then find Ireland, C.S. Lewis' boyhood home.   Geography

⊱┈❖┈❖┈❖┈⊰

Vocabulary:

🗝 **Look up the words in a dictionary before you read the chapter and write them, along with a definition, in your vocabulary notebook.**

✏ Use your vocabulary words in sentences. Write at least one sentence for each word.

Vocabulary Words:

frowsty

cordial

Read Chapter 10 of *The Lion, the Witch and the Wardrobe.*

☀ Assignments:

📖 1. Ephesians 6:10–18 tells about the armor of God.   Bible

🦁 Memorize this passage.

✋ Make a poster illustrating these verses.

✏ 2. A hieroglyph represents a word picture of an idea or intangible thought. Egyptian hieroglyphics are the most frequently thought of hieroglyphics. Write your name in hieroglyphics. You can find hieroglyphics or code on the Internet or make up your own. See <www.CadronCreek.com> for some hieroglyphics.   Bible/History

📖 Read about the gospel message in Chinese writing characters from *Genesis: Finding Our Roots* by Dr. Ruth Beechick, pages 35 and 55.

Bible/
History

3. Although it does not really make sense for Father Christmas to appear in Narnia, or for the animals to know about Christmas, since Jesus was not born in their world, Father Christmas may be a word picture for the joy that comes with Aslan. He may also represent the Holy Spirit, the giver of spiritual gifts. We do not know exactly what Lewis meant to express with Father Christmas, but there are a couple of possibilities. Like hieroglyphs, Lewis used certain characters as symbols of concepts. Our alphabet uses letters to represent sounds. Looking at some Egyptian or Chinese writing shows a different way of thinking; using symbols to represent concepts. In some ways the picture languages are less efficient than English, but sometimes they are more expressive because one symbol tells a whole story. One word can express an entire concept just as Lewis used Father Christmas to represent an entire idea.

 Read I Corinthians 12 and 13.

 What are some of the gifts the Holy Spirit gives? What should we desire more than these?

Writing

4. Have you ever been as tired as Lucy was but had to keep going?

 Write about that time or make up a short story about being as tired as Lucy.

English

5. A **pronoun** is a word that takes the place of a noun previously used in order to avoid repeating the noun. A pronoun referring to a person is called a **personal pronoun**.

FORMS OF PERSONAL PRONOUNS				
		SUBJECTIVE	*POSSESSIVE*	*OBJECTIVE*
SINGULAR	first person	I	my, mine	me
	second person	you	your, yours	you
	third person	he, she, it	his, her, hers, its	him, her
PLURAL	first person	we	our, ours	us
	second person	you	you, yours	you
	third person	they	their, theirs	them

The form of the pronoun used is determined by its place in the sentence. Is it the subject of the sentence or the object? Consider this sentence:

*I believed that he would help **me**.*

In the sentence above, **I** is the subject of the sentence and is a **subjective pronoun**. **Me** is the object of the verb *help* and is an **objective pronoun**. Any of the singular or plural subjective pronouns in the chart above can be substituted for *I* in this sentence:

*You/he/she/we/you/they believed that he would help **me**.*

When you need to decide whether to use **we** or **us** in a sentence, it is sometimes helpful to rephrase the sentence.

*They were glad **we/us** girls could come.*

Try rephrasing the above sentence:

*They were glad **us** could come.*

*They were glad **we** could come.*

Which seems correct? Saying the sentence out loud can help you determine that **we** is the subject of the phrase, *we girls could come,* and that it is correct to use the subjective form of the pronoun in this sentence.

Pronouns must agree. Never use a subjective form with an objective form. **I** is used with **he, she,** and **we. Me** is used with **him, her,** and **us.**

Try these sentences. You will find the answers in the Answer Appendix.

  a. Had I guessed it was (they, them), I would have hurried.

  b. The visitors sat beside (we, us) boys.

  c. Mom blamed (we, us) for the mess.

  d. I thought the culprit to be (she, her).

  e. The youngest member of the band was (he, him).

  f. It wasn't (I, me) who whispered.

  g. No one but (he, him) knew the answer.

Note: Further help with the topic of personal pronouns may be found in the Answer Appendix following the answers for this activity.

---

6. Can you imagine a voice that sounds pale? Try to think of one-word descriptions for some voices with which you are familiar.

Critical Thinking

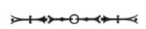

Vocabulary:

Look up the words in a dictionary before you read the chapter and write them, along with a definition, in your vocabulary notebook.

Using your vocabulary words, fill in the blanks. The answers may be found in the section entitled Answer Appendix.

1. Benedict Arnold was a _____ during the American Revolution.

2. It is _____ to smell dead animals.

3. The _____ endlessly vexed us.

Vocabulary Words:

gluttony

indulgence

repulsive

vermin

traitor

4. How many children are ruined by _____ !

5. _____ can cause one to vomit.

Read Chapter 11 of *The Lion, the Witch and the Wardrobe*.

☀ Assignments:

Science	🔑	1. Use your encyclopedia. What causes fog? What did it mean to the Witch when it kept becoming foggier?
Science	🔑	2. Find out what celandines, snowdrops, crocus, primrose, bluebells, larch, birch, laburnums, and beech look like.
	✋	Draw pictures of them, one per page, in your plant notebook. Add an interesting fact about the plant to each page.
Science	🔑	3. Look at a book about tracking animals.
	✋	Mix Plaster of Paris according to directions on the container. Pour into a plastic lid or old cookie sheet and make animal tracks in it. Make them as realistic as possible.
Art	✋	4. Draw a picture of the animals having Christmas dinner.
Cooking	📖	5. In a British cookbook, find a recipe for plum pudding. Or use the recipes for steamed pudding or fig pudding on pages 81 and 82 in *The Narnia Cookbook*. Also see the Activity Appendix.
Critical Thinking	📖	6. Why was the Witch so angry when she saw the animals enjoying the Christmas dinner? At the end of the chapter, why did she threaten to kill the next person who mentioned Aslan's name?

>─┼─◆>─0─<◆─┼─<

Chapter 12

Vocabulary:

Vocabulary Words:

pavilion

Alsatian

standard

🔑 **Look up the words in a dictionary before you read the chapter and write them, along with a definition, in your vocabulary notebook.**

✏ Using your vocabulary words, fill in the blanks. The answers may be found in the section entitled Answer Appendix.

1. The _____ was easy to train.

2. The wedding reception was held at the park's _____ .

3. The _____ was kept at great loss of life.

Read Chapter 12 of *The Lion, the Witch and the Wardrobe.*

☀ Assignments:

1. What was Aslan doing when he struck Peter with the flat of his sword and gave him a new name?	Reading Comprehension

2. Draw or paint what the children saw from the top of the hill.

    Art

3. Add pictures of flowering currants, hawthorn bushes, and elms to your plant notebook.

    Science

   Then, in your animal notebook, draw pictures of birds. Start with kingfisher and thrush.

4. Discuss the following questions:
   - How can something be good and terrible at the same time?
   - Had the Beavers ever seen Narnia without snow?
   - What does it mean that Aslan's paws were velveted?

    Critical Thinking

5. When Peter saw the wolf attacking Susan, he did not feel brave, but that did not change what he had to do.

    Critical Thinking

   Consider the following quotes:

   For courage mounteth with occasion. —William Shakespeare, *King John*

   He who loses wealth loses much; he who loses a friend loses more; but he who loses courage loses all. —Miguel De Cervantes (1547-1616), Spanish novelist

   A great deal of talent is lost to the world for want of a little courage. —Sydney Smith (1771-1845)

   The ultimate measure of a man is not where he stands in moments of comfort, but where he stands at times of challenge and controversy. —Martin Luther King, Jr.

   Courage is almost a contradiction in terms. It means a strong desire to live taking the form of a readiness to die. —G. K. Chesterton

   Valor is a gift. Those having it never know for sure whether they have it till the test comes. And those having it in one test never know for sure if they will have it when the next test comes. —Carl Sandburg

   Discuss courage and duty. Does being courageous mean you are without fear? From literature or real life, give an example of a courageous person.

>⊷•○•⊷<

⧗ PLANNING GUIDE – CHAPTERS 13-17

Gather These Items:

1. *Genesis: Finding Our Roots* by Dr. Ruth Beechick, ISBN: 0-94039-11-X, Chapter 13.

2. A book of names and their meanings, Chapter 13.

3. *Eyewitness: Knights* by Christopher Gravett, Eyewitness Books, Chapter 17.

Suggested Information to Gather:

Encyclopedia or books about:

1. Light, Chapter 16 (Science).

....

2. Knights, Chapter 17 (History).
   - *The Knight's Handbook: How to Become a Champion in Shining Armor* by Christopher Gravett. This book is currently out of print. Check your library.

....

Suggested Videos:

Suggested Field Trips:

Suggested Memorization:

1. Memorize a Code of Conduct, Chapter 17.

2. Ecclesiastes 12:1, Chapter 17.

3. 1 Peter 4:10, Chapter 17.

Notes:

Study Guide – Chapters 13-17

Vocabulary:

Vocabulary Words:
crave
audience
cheek
forfeit

🔑 **Look up the words in a dictionary before you read the chapter and write them, along with a definition, in your vocabulary notebook.**

✏️ Using your vocabulary words, fill in the blanks. The answers may be found in the section entitled Answer Appendix.

1. Columbus requested an _____ with the King.

2. A felon has to _____ many rights.

3. A diabetic will often _____ sugar.

✏️ Skim the chapter for *cheek*. Write at least one sentence from this chapter containing this word under its dictionary definition. Follow each sentence with a citation.

Read Chapter 13 of *The Lion, the Witch and the Wardrobe.*

☀ Assignments:

✋ 1. Add yew trees to your plant notebook. — Science

---

2. Mr. Beaver was outraged that the Witch would call herself the Queen of Narnia. Aslan said all names would soon be restored to their proper owners. In many cultures names are very important and when parents choose a child's name, they carefully consider its meaning. — Bible

📖 Read *Genesis: Finding Our Roots*, "Hidden Message," page 51. Research some of the meanings of the names of Bible characters and names that were changed, such as Abram to Abraham, Sarai to Sarah, and Jacob to Israel. Some Bibles have lists of name changes. A reference Bible or study Bible may be of help.

🔑 What does your name mean? Look in a book of names.

🔑 Use a concordance and read the verses in Revelation where the word *name* is used.

📖 3. When the Witch was accusing Edmund, he kept his eyes on Aslan and what the Witch said did not seem to matter. — Bible

Have we read about others doing the same thing? See Answer Appendix.

Bible 4. Who is the Accuser in Revelation 12:10? What will be his fate?

In Titus 2:3, the Greek word which is translated *malicious gossips* in some versions and *false accusers* in others is **diabolos**, the same word which is translated *Satan* in verses such as Matthew 4:5, Acts 13:10, and I Timothy 3:6. How does Satan fit the description of a false accuser?

Bible 5. Read about the conversion of the Apostle Paul and his time alone with God afterward in Acts 9. Who are some others who spent time alone in preparation for a task given by God?

Chapter 14

Vocabulary Words:

siege

whet

gibber

Vocabulary:

🔑 **Look up the words in a dictionary before you read the chapter and write them, along with a definition, in your vocabulary notebook.**

✏️ Using your vocabulary words, fill in the blanks. The answers may be found in the section entitled Answer Appendix.

1. "The graves stood tenantless, and the sheeted dead
   Did squeak and _____ in the Roman
   streets." —William Shakespeare, *Hamlet*

2. "Draw thee waters for the _____ , fortify thy strongholds: go into clay, and tread the mortar, make strong the brick kiln." Nahum 3:14

3. "If I _____ my glittering sword and mine hand take hold on judgment; I will render vengeance to mine enemies, and will reward them that hate me." Deuteronomy 32:41

Read Chapter 14 of *The Lion, the Witch and the Wardrobe.*

☀ Assignments:

Bible 1. Read about Jesus' night in the Garden of Gethsemane before His crucifixion: Matthew 26:36–56; Mark 14:32–52; and Luke 22:39–53.

Also Read Isaiah 53.

Discuss the similarities between Jesus and Aslan.

---

2. Discuss the Witch's speech at the end of the chapter. Do you think she has won? Do you think she believes she has?

Critical Thinking

---

3. Go back to *The Magician's Nephew* and reread Chapter 11. Find Aslan's prophecy that has been fulfilled in *The Lion, the Witch and the Wardrobe*.

Critical Thinking

⊱┄⊶┄⊙┄⊰┄⊱

Vocabulary:

Vocabulary Words:

vile

rabble

cavern

skirling

stead

gorse bush

🔑 **Look up the words in a dictionary before you read the chapter and write them, along with a definition, in your vocabulary notebook.**

✏️ Using your vocabulary words, fill in the blanks. The answers may be found in the section entitled Answer Appendix.

1. She was _____ and running away from the fire.

2. The _____ lacked a leader.

3. Peter Rabbit caught his coat on a _____ .

4. One must be careful not to become lost in a _____ .

5. Many of today's movie films are too _____ to have any worth.

6. The minion acted in his lord's _____ .

Read Chapter 15 of *The Lion, the Witch and the Wardrobe*.

☀ Assignments:

📖 1. Read about Jesus' resurrection day in Matthew 28; Mark 16; Luke 24:1–12; and John 20.

Bible

✏️ From the Four Gospels, compile a chronological list of all of the events of the crucifixion and resurrection. If an event is repeated in more than one account, use it only once. If an event is mentioned in only one account, add it to your list where it belongs chronologically.

✏️ Then, referring to your list, write out the events in story form.

📝 Who were the women who stayed with Jesus at his crucifixion?

Critical Thinking		2. What did Aslan mean when he said, "death itself would start working backward"?

Bible		3. When Aslan died, the Stone Table cracked. To what event at the death of Jesus does this correspond? See Matthew 27:51.

Chapter 16

Vocabulary Words:

liberate

ransack

saccharine

din

plumage

indigo

prodigious

Vocabulary:

🗝 **Look up the words in a dictionary before you read the chapter and write them, along with a definition, in your vocabulary notebook.**

✏ Using your vocabulary words, fill in the blanks. The answers may be found in the section entitled Answer Appendix.

1. The peacock's _____ is frequently used in decorating.

2. The _____ in the feather is stunning.

3. We were awed by the body-builder's _____ strength.

4. The word _____ preceeded the product by the same name.

5. I could not hear the telephone over the _____ of my toddler's banging on pans.

6. The DEA may _____ your home without a warrant.

7. Jesus came to _____ us from sin.

Read Chapter 16 of *The Lion, the Witch and the Wardrobe.*

✷ Assignments:

Bible		1. Read Genesis 2:7 and John 20:22. What were the results when God breathed?

Bible		2. Aslan invaded the Witch's castle, revived all of the statues, and let light into all of the dark places. Using a concordance, do a study of light and darkness in the Bible.
		Discuss where light comes from? What do light and darkness symbolize?

3. Without light we would not be able to see, but it would not matter because without light we would not be alive. Plants use sunlight to grow and make food. We eat animals that eat plants. Growing plants give off the oxygen that we need to breathe.

   Light from the sun keeps us warm.

🗝 Use your encyclopedia or a book about light to study light. How fast does light travel? Why do we see colors? What are the colors in the spectrum?

   Define: *phosphorescence, bioluminescence, reflection, refraction, absorption.* Write the definitions in your vocabulary notebook.

Science

Chapter 17

Vocabulary:

🗝 **Look up the words in a dictionary before you read the chapter and write them, along with a definition, in your vocabulary notebook.**

✏ Using your vocabulary words, fill in the blanks. The answers may be found in the section entitled Answer Appendix.

1. The hunter would not rest until he had captured his _____ .

2. Handel did not eat while he worked fervently on his musical _____ .

3. "All speaking, or _____ of one's mind, implies an act or address of one man to another." —South

4. "Be thou _____ for me, and fight the Lord's battles." I Samuel 18:17

5. The _____ after the inauguration went on for hours.

6. For several hours the dove did not _____ .

7. "Gad not abroad at every _____ and call Of an untrain'd hope or passion." —Herbert

8. Sir Ernest Shackleton's greatest _____ was when he brought back all his men from the Antarctic alive.

9. His wife had a _____ feeling she would not see her husband again.

Vocabulary Words:

quarry

revelry

alight

valiant

foreboding

signification

quest

score

feat

Read Chapter 17 of *The Lion, the Witch and the Wardrobe.*

 ## Assignments:

Bible 1. Aslan miraculously provided food for the group. Who in the New Testament did this? (Matthew 14:13–21)

History 🗝 2. In medieval times, how did someone become a knight? What were the qualifications? How was a knight to live?

Eyewitness: Knights by Christopher Gravett, has good pictures of armor. *The Knight's Handbook: How to Become a Champion in Shining Armor*, also by Gravett, has a chapter called "The Knightly Code of Honor" listing the rules of chivalry. It also has some crafts. *The Knight's Handbook* is out of print but you may be able to find it at your library or find a used copy on the Internet.

Bible 3. Make and memorize a Code of Conduct for becoming a modern day knight. Also, memorize the verses as directed below.

Robert Lewis, author of *Raising a Modern-Day Knight*, suggested the following code of conduct based on Scripture:

- *A will to obey*, God's will: True satisfaction in life is directly proportionate to one's obedience to God. Read and memorize Ecclesiastes 12:1.
- *A work to do*, according to his own unique design: Read and memorize I Peter 4:10.
- *A woman to love*: Read Genesis 2:18 and Ephesians 5:25–30. In the story of King Arthur when Percival left home his mother admonished him, "If you encounter, near or far, a lady in need of help, or any damsel in distress, be ready to aid her if she asks you to, for all honor lies in such deeds. When a man fails to honor ladies, his own honor must be dead."

Bible/ Art
4. These ten Biblical ideals are essential to following the Code of Conduct. Which ones did you see demonstrated in the character Peter?

1. Loyalty (Hosea 6:6)	7. Self-Discipline (I Timothy 4:7–8)
2. Servant-Leadership (Matthew 20:26–27)	8. Excellence (I Corinthians 9:24)
3. Kindness (Proverbs 19:22)	9. Integrity (Proverbs 10:9)
4. Humility (Philippians 2:3)	10. Perseverance (Galatians 6:9)
5. Purity (I Timothy 4:12)	—Robert Lewis, *Raising a Modern-Day Knight,*
6. Honesty (Ephesians 4:25)	Wheaton: Tyndale House Publishers, 69–70.

 Make a poster illustrating Peter displaying each Biblical ideal you think he demonstrated. This may extend several days. Color the whole poster, not leaving any bare paper. Be sure to label it, preferably with calligraphy or some other appropriate lettering.

5. Draw Peter, Susan, Edmund, and Lucy as kings and queens around the lamp-post.

Art

6. Review each of the children's reactions upon first hearing Aslan's name in Chapter 7. Relate them to what became of each child by the end of the story.

Writing

As an alternative, compare the changing moods of Aslan from his first appearance in Chapter 12 to the last in Chapter 17.

7. Discuss the following questions:

Critical Thinking

- Do you think it was by chance the White Stag came when it did and led the children to Lantern Waste?
- Why did the professor believe the children?
- Think back to Lucy's first meeting with Mr. Tumnus. How might the story have been different if he had turned Lucy over to the Witch? How does your answer differ from your answer to this question in Chapter 2?

8. Review the list of Seven Deadly Sins found in *Further Up and Further In*, Chapter 15 of *The Magician's Nephew*.

Literature/ Bible

Of the remaining six sins, which one was the cause of the problem in *The Lion, the Witch and the Wardrobe*? See answer in Answer Appendix.

9. Review vocabulary words by completing *The Lion, the Witch and the Wardrobe* Crossword Puzzle. The answers may be found in the Answer Appendix.

Vocabulary

>·•◇·•O·•◇·•·◁

Complete any unfinished assignments prior to going on to *The Horse and His Boy.*

THE LION, THE WITCH AND THE WARDROBE
CROSSWORD PUZZLE

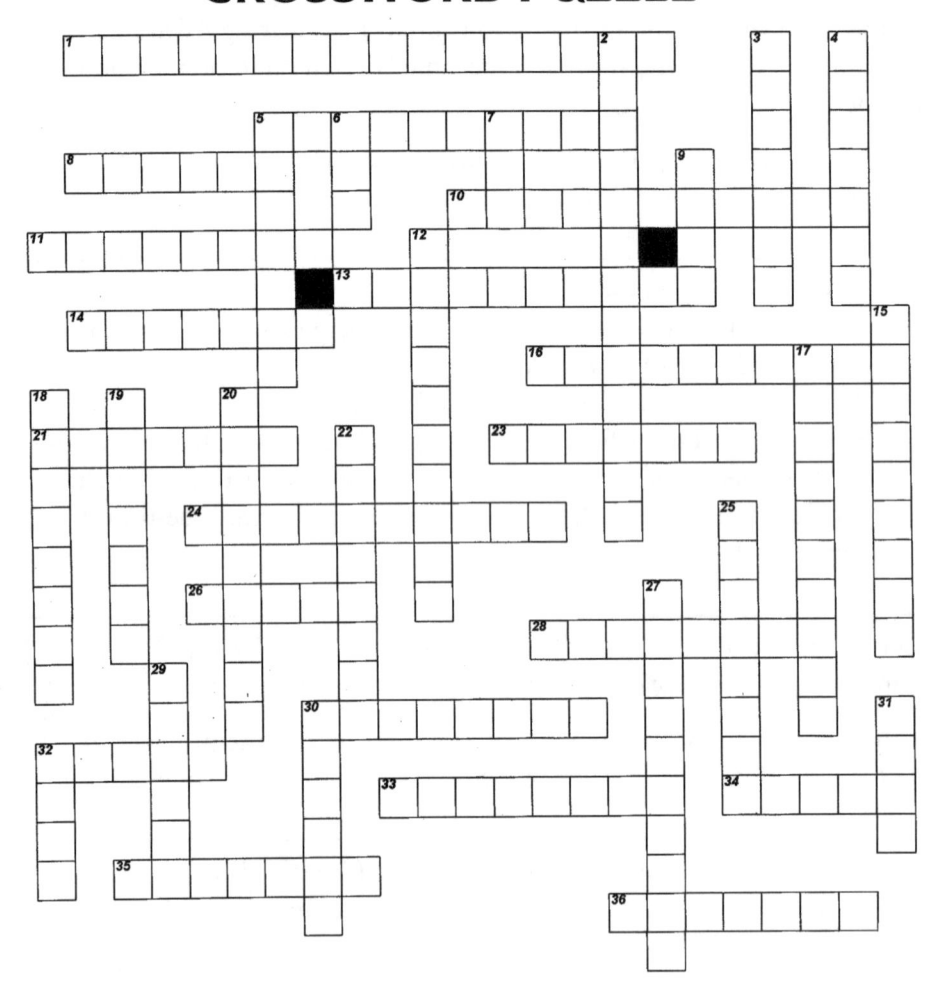

ACROSS

1 humanization of God

5 premonition

8 sleigh

10 prying

11 rescue

13 mingle

14 solid essential oil

16 mistress of an estate

21 Judas

23 brave

24 phenomenal

26 attack

28 ornamental building

30 excess in food or drink

32 gain a point

33 waterproof cloths

34 uncanny

35 snicker

36 feathers

DOWN

2 making meaningful

3 polite

4 waive

5 streamer

6 tiff

7 obnoxious noises

9 despicable

12 sickly sweet

15 sordid

17 leniency

18 normal

19 caves

20 flatterers

22 catty

25 crowd

27 discardable

29 pests

30 meaningless talk

31 sharpen by rubbing

32 brood

THE HORSE
AND HIS BOY

P. MARTIROSIAN

⧗ PLANNING GUIDE – CHAPTERS 1-4

Gather These Items:

1. *The Horse and His Boy* by C.S. Lewis.

2. Book of sea paintings or photographs, Chapter 2.

3. Biography of an artist noted for seascapes, such as Winslow Homer, Chapter 2.

4. A book about storytelling and/or recordings of good storytellers, Chapter 2.

5. *The Narnia Cookbook* or recipes and ingredients for:
   • Meat pasties, Chapter 2. See Activity Appendix.
   • Punch and sherbet, Chapter 4.

6. Cheese and dried figs, Chapter 2.

7. World map, Chapter 4.

8. Old magazines or seed catalogs with pictures of plants and flowers that can be cut out, Chapter 4.

9. *Hamlet* by William Shakespeare (original or children's version), Chapter 4.

Suggested Information to Gather:

Encyclopedia or books about:

1. Horses, Chapter 1 (Science).

   ....

2. Thatched roof, Chapter 1 (History).

   ....

3. Horses in war, Chapter 2 (History).

   ....

4. Women's rights in Muslim countries, Chapter 3 (Social Studies).

   ....

5. Seven Wonders of the Ancient World, Chapter 4 (History).
   • These and several other "Seven Wonders" lists are available at <www.wonderclub.com>. At the site, click on *World Wonders*.
   • *More True Tales from the Times of Ancient Civilizations and the Bible*, audiocassette by Diana Waring. See Resource Appendix.

   ....

6. Seven Natural Wonders, Chapter 4 (History).

   ....

7. Famous gardens, such as Claude Monet's garden in Giverny, France or the Royal Botanical Gardens in Ontario, Canada, Chapter 4 (Art).

....

Suggested Videos:

Suggested Field Trips:

1. Go horseback riding, Chapter 2. If you are an inexperienced rider, watch someone trot, canter, and jump a horse.

Suggested Memorization:

1. Your choice of Matthew 25:31–46; Romans 12:9–16; I Timothy 3:2; Titus 1:7–9; Hebrews 13:2–3; or I Peter 4:9, Chapter 1.

2. Parts of a horse, saddle, and bridle, Chapter 1.

Notes:

STUDY GUIDE – CHAPTERS 1-4

Vocabulary:

🔑 **Look up the words in a dictionary before you read the chapter and write them, along with a definition, in your vocabulary notebook.**

✏️ Using your vocabulary words, fill in the blanks. The answers may be found in the section entitled Answer Appendix.

☀️ *Extra assignment*: Find a picture of a thatched roof.

1. The _____ student frequently found herself in trouble.

2. The _____ lord had an audience with the King.

3. The _____ of the family living in the wet _____ touched the _____ hearts of the missionaries.

4. It is important not to use Christian _____ when talking to the unchurched.

5. The sunlight _____ the ground underneath the apple tree.

6. The Arab came after his foe with a _____ .

7. Don't let her _____ her way into your home.

8. The toddler kept her mother running _____ .

9. The _____ on the diabetic's feet went undetected.

10. The horse trotted around the perimeter of his _____ .

Vocabulary Words:

indigence

dappled

scimitar

wheedle

carbuncle

beneficent

hovel

august

loquacious

apace

jargon

paddock

Read Chapter 1 of *The Horse and His Boy*.

☀️ Assignments:

📓 1. The fisherman did not dare to refuse hospitality to the stranger. What is hospitality and what does the Bible say about it?

📖 Read Matthew 25:31–46; Romans 12:9–16; I Timothy 3:2; Titus 1:7–9; Hebrews 13:2–3; and I Peter 4:9.

🦁 Choose at least one of these passages to memorize.

Bible

English · 2. Copy the conversation between the Tarkaan and the fisherman, then rewrite the conversation in your own words. You may want to review the correct usage of quotation marks.

Art · 3. Reread the description of Arsheesh on page 4 and of the Tarkaan and his horse on page 5 and draw or paint the two meeting.

Science · 4. In an encyclopedia, find pictures of a horse with all the parts of the body labeled.

Learn the parts of the horse and the parts of the saddle and bridle.

English · 5. Shasta had been hearing the sound of the sea day and night for as long as he could remember, so he hardly noticed it anymore. Close you eyes and listen to the sounds of your house. What sounds do you hear that you do not normally notice because you hear them so often?

Jot down the sounds you hear in the English section of your notebook.

⊱━⟡━◯━⟡━┥

Chapter 2

Vocabulary Words:

copse

booty

spoil

downs

cob

Vocabulary:

Look up the words in a dictionary before you read the chapter and write them, along with a definition, in your vocabulary notebook.

Using your vocabulary words, fill in the blanks. The answers may be found in the section entitled Answer Appendix.

1. The hunter lost the rabbit in the _____ .

2. God instructed the Israelites not to take the _____ .

3. The only gained _____ was ammunition.

4. The _____ trotted over the _____ .

Melancholy comes from two Greek words, *melas*, meaning black, and *khole*, meaning bile. At one time it was believed black bile (a secretion of the liver) caused feelings of gloom and depression.

Read Chapter 2 of *The Horse and His Boy*.

☀ Assignments:

⚷	1. If you do not live near the ocean, look at books of seascape paintings or photographs to see the many different moods and colors of the sea.	Art
✋	Use watercolor paints and paint waves or a calm sea with objects reflected in it.	

✎	2. Write a report on an artist, such as Winslow Homer, who was known for seascapes.	Art/ English

📖	3. Read about the art of storytelling and listen to recordings of people telling stories. What makes a good storyteller? Practice telling stories in a way that others will want to listen.	English

⚷	4. Find a recipe for meat pasties and make some. A recipe may be found on page 18 in *The Narnia Cookbook* or see the Activity Appendix.	Cooking
✋	Also try dried figs and cheese. If possible, make a meal of these three things.	

⚷	5. Find out about the role of horses in war. The article about horses in your encyclopedia will probably have a section on horses in history. Alexander the Great had a horse named Bucephalus. Robert E. Lee's most famous horse was Traveler. Teddy Roosevelt rode Little Texas on his charge up San Juan Hill. Comanche was one of the survivors of the Battle of the Little Big Horn, and Chief was the last United States Cavalry horse.	History
✎	Pick one of these horses and write a one-page story about his exploits with his owner. Tell the story from the point of view of the horse.	

📇	6. Shasta and Bree discussed whether spending the Tarkaan's money would be stealing or not. Was it stealing? What would you have done?	Critical Thinking

✋	7. Go horseback riding. If you are an inexperienced rider, watch someone trot, canter, and jump a horse.	Life Skills

➤┼◇➤─○─◄┼◄

Vocabulary Words:

feign

inexorable

pith

inquisitive

dowry

rite

Vocabulary

🔑 **Look up the words in a dictionary before you read the chapter and write them, along with a definition, in your vocabulary notebook.**

✏️ Using your vocabulary words, fill in the blanks. The answers may be found in the section entitled Answer Appendix.

1. A 'possum will _____ death in order to save himself.

2. The _____ king refused to sign the Magna Carta.

3. A central _____ can be used to help identify a plant.

4. The wedding ceremony is a _____ of passage.

5. The father had no money for a _____ for his daughter.

6. The journalist became increasingly _____ as she investigated the town council.

The word **delusion** comes from a Latin word meaning to play. How do you think this word came to mean, "to cause to be deceived"?

Read Chapter 3 of *The Horse and His Boy*.

☀ Assignments:

Character	✏️	1. Throughout the story C.S. Lewis has included observations of human nature. Make an ongoing list of these observations. Hint: Look for one at the bottom of page 44 and another in the middle of page 45. Continue this throughout the story.
Bible	📓	2. Hwin said very little because she was shy. What was Aravis' reason for not speaking to Shasta unless she had to?
	📖	Read and discuss James 2:1–13.
Bible	📖	3. The servant said, "To hear is to obey." Read Luke 11:28. Do you think this passage inspired C.S. Lewis' statement?
Critical Thinking	📓	4. Discuss with your parent what you think about Aravis' deception of her father. Use Hosea 10:13 and II Corinthians 4:2 in your discussion.
Critical Thinking		5. In this chapter the Tarkheena told how she almost committed suicide. Suicide is the third leading cause of death among teens. Five times more

males than females end their life in this way. Depression often plays a factor in suicide. From the story, how do you know the Tarkheena had been depressed?

Read Isaiah 50:10. Did the Tarkheena feel as if she were walking in darkness without one ray of light? Suicide is NEVER the right choice because it is the final denial of our trust in God. What does the second half of Isaiah 50:10 say?

Discuss whether or not you think God would forgive someone who commits suicide.

Many of the symptoms of suicidal feelings are similar to those of depression. Parents should be aware of the following signs of adolescents who may try to kill themselves:
- change in eating and sleeping habits
- withdrawal from friends, family, and regular activities
- violent actions, rebellious behavior, or running away
- drug and alcohol use
- unusual neglect of personal appearance
- marked personality change
- persistent boredom, difficulty concentrating, or a decline in the quality of schoolwork
- frequent complaints about physical symptoms, often related to emotions, such as stomachaches, headaches, fatigue, etc.
- loss of interest in pleasurable activities
- not tolerating praise or rewards

A teenager who is planning to commit suicide may also:
- complain of being a bad person or feeling "rotten inside"
- give verbal hints with statements such as: "I won't be a problem for you much longer," "Nothing matters," "It's no use," and "I won't see you again"
- put his or her affairs in order, for example, give away favorite possessions, clean his or her room, throw away important belongings, etc.
- become suddenly cheerful after a period of depression (the Tarkheena did this)
- have signs of psychosis (hallucinations or bizarre thoughts)

Here are some ways to be helpful to someone who is threatening suicide:
- STAY: Do not leave the person alone unless you are in danger of harm. Studies show that most people will not harm themselves when they are with someone.
- LISTEN: What might seem trivial to you can be overwhelming and consuming to the person in pain.
- GET HELP: The person receiving the cry for help does not have to be a counselor. Be a link, be a lifeline . . . call for help.
- Youth: CALL your parents, their parents, another trusted adult, or 911!
- Adults: CALL their parents, other help, 911, or a suicide prevention or crisis center. In case of emergency, call 1-800-SUICIDE.

Suicide victims are not trying to end their life—they are trying to end the pain!

Social
Studies

☞🗝 6. Find out about women's rights in predominately Muslim countries.

➤-┼-◆➤-○-◄◆-┼-◄

Chapter 4

Vocabulary Words:

pinnacle

minarets

colonnades

brazen

arcades

truant

avouch

dazzle

treat

luxurious

scapegrace

refuse

Vocabulary:

☞🗝 **Look up the words in a dictionary before you read the chapter and write them, along with a definition, in your vocabulary notebook.**

✐ Using your vocabulary words, fill in the blanks. The answers may be found in the section entitled Answer Appendix.

1. The _____ motel was a memorable _____ for the family.

2. The _____ made travel between stores easy in the rain.

3. _____ marked the entryway to the university.

4. We climbed to the mountain's _____ .

5. In some British towns, the Friday noon prayer is permitted to be "called" from the _____ .

6. A _____ remark can stir up strife.

7. The _____ employee was fired.

8. The sunlight will _____ you after being in a cave.

9. Despite his innocence, no one could be found to _____ for him.

10. The _____ should never marry.

11. The front yard was tidy, but the back yard was piled with _____ .

Tash is probably from the Scottish *tash* or *tache* meaning blemish, stain, or fault.

Hastlitude is an archaic word for spear-play.

While Edmund and Susan were discussing how to leave Tashbaan, Edmund said, "There's the rub." This is a phrase borrowed from Shakespeare's *Hamlet*, which means, "There's the catch." Michael Macrone says in his book, *Brush Up Your Shakespeare*, "Rub is the sportsman's name for an obstacle which, in the game of bowls, diverts a ball from its true course." In Shakespeare's time bowling was played on lawns, not lanes.

Read Chapter 4 of *The Horse and His Boy*.

☀ Assignments:

---

1. Tashbaan was one of the wonders of the Narnian world. What were the Seven Wonders of the Ancient World? What are the Seven Natural Wonders? You may be able to find these listed in your encyclopedia. Try to find a book that has pictures of each one or use the Web site listed in the Planning Guide.

   For more information, listen to Diana Waring's, *More True Tales from the Times of Ancient Civilizations and the Bible*.

History

---

2. On a map, locate each of the Seven Wonders of the Ancient World and the Seven Natural Wonders. Make a symbol representing each of these, cut it out, cover with contact paper, and pin onto its location.

   Choose two wonders daily and write a paragraph about each.

Geography

---

3. Design the prettiest garden you can imagine. What kinds of plants would you plant? Cut out pictures from seed catalogs or magazines and make a picture of your garden. You may want to look at pictures of famous gardens from around the world such as Claude Monet's garden in Giverny, France or the Royal Botanical Gardens in Ontario, Canada. At <www.gardeningplaces.com> you can see photographs of many famous gardens around the world.

Art

---

4. Kathryn Lindskoog says, in *Journey Into Narnia*, that the sherbet mentioned in this chapter is what we would call fruit punch.

   Invent your own punch recipe.

   There are two recipes for sherbet in *The Narnia Cookbook* on pages 105 and 106.

   If you have never tasted what, in America, we call sherbet, try some.

Cooking

---

5. Read Hamlet's "To Be, or Not to Be" soliloquy to see the phrase, "there's the rub," used in context (*Hamlet*, Act III, Scene 1). This is in the Recommended Reading Appendix. Read it aloud.

   A **soliloquy** is a dramatic discourse in which a character speaks aloud to himself in order to let the audience know what he is thinking. In a soliloquy the actor does not address the audience. An **aside** is addressed directly to the audience but the other characters are not supposed to hear it. For an example see *Hamlet*, Act III, Scene 2, beginning with lines 188 or 211 in the Recommended Reading Appendix.

English

⧗ Planning Guide – Chapters 5-8

Gather These Items:

1. *The Narnia Cookbook* or see Activity Appendix for a recipe and the ingredients for gooseberry fool, Chapter 5.

Suggested Information to Gather:

Encyclopedia or books about:

1. Geographical areas: plains, mountains, etc., Chapter 6 (Geography).

Suggested Videos:

Suggested Field Trips:

Suggested Memorization:

1. I Corinthians 15:36–38, Chapter 6.

Notes:

THE HORSE AND HIS BOY CHAPTER 8
CROSSWORD PUZZLE

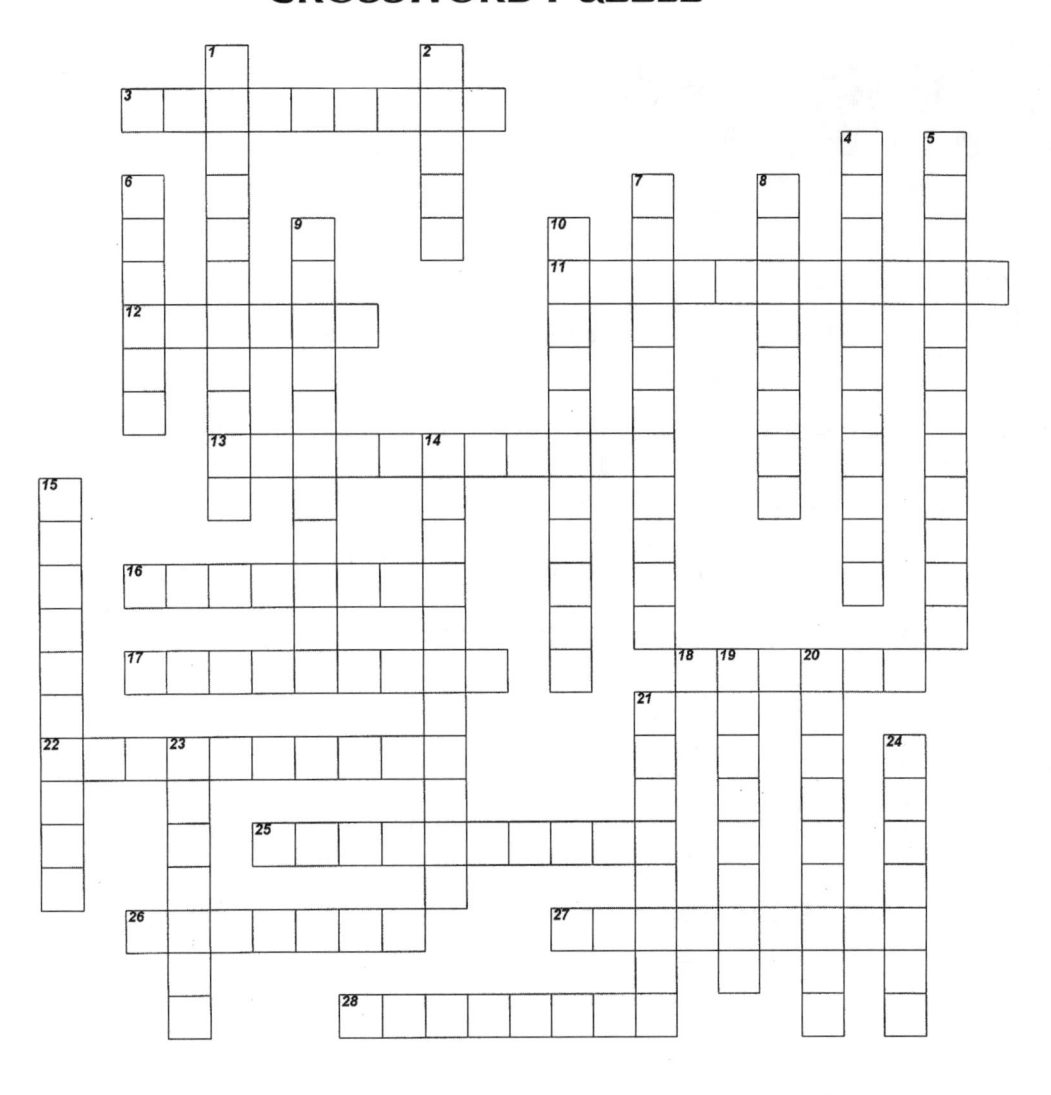

ACROSS

3 savage

11 illuminated

12 stop

13 prudent

16 discretion

17 compel

18 characteristic

22 unbeatable

25 faultless

26 solemnity

27 aged

28 serene

DOWN

1 foretelling

2 axiom

4 undeniable

5 endless

6 inhibit

7 uncopyable

8 fervid

9 insight

10 one who changes
opinion easily and often

14 evil

15 certain to succeed

19 healthful

20 respectable

21 fatherly

23 menace

24 having wisdom

STUDY GUIDE – CHAPTERS 5-8

Vocabulary Words:

chafed

oasis

bazaar

embark

flagon

stoup

tilt

closefisted

Vocabulary:

🗝 **Look up the words in a dictionary before you read the chapter and write them, along with a definition, in your vocabulary notebook.**

✏ Using your vocabulary words, fill in the blanks. The answers may be found in the section entitled Answer Appendix.

1. The _____ boss had trouble keeping employees.

2. The coarse material _____ against his skin.

3. After several hot, dusty days of travel they reached the _____ .

4. Wine dripped out of the crack in the _____ .

5. One may find fresh figs at the _____ .

6. After several days of preparation they were ready to _____ upon their journey.

7. The priest blessed the child with holy water from the _____ .

8. A _____ with a windmill was Don Quixote's preoccupation.

Joust—a combat with lances between two mounted knights. This word comes from the Latin word *juxta*, which means, close together. This is the same word from which we get the word *juxtapose* which means, to place side by side.

The English language has an interesting history and words from other languages are always being borrowed and added to it. **Oasis** originally came from an Egyptian word and **bazaar** is Persian.

Read Chapter 5 of *The Horse and His Boy*.

☀ Assignments:

✏	1. Write your own story that explains why Shasta and Corin look alike.	English
✋	2. Make a meal like the one the Faun served Shasta. Find a recipe for gooseberry fool (page 88 in *The Narnia Cookbook*) in a British cookbook. Serve this for dessert. A recipe for gooseberry fool can also be found in the Activity Appendix.	Cooking
▯	3. Discuss the difference between being impressive and being agreeable to look at. Think of something that is impressive but not agreeable to look at. Think of something that is agreeable to look at but not impressive.	Critical Thinking
▯	4. Reread the discussion among the Narnians about how to get out of Tashbaan. Explain what the Dwarf meant by, "Yes, just as the beggar's only difficulty about riding is that he has no horse." What did Edmund mean when he said, "his suit was likely to be cold"?	Critical Thinking

>·+·◊·•·O·•·◊·+·<

Chapter 6

Vocabulary Words:

queue

skulk

Vocabulary:

🗝 **Look up the words in a dictionary before you read the chapter and write them, along with a definition, in your vocabulary notebook.**

Queue—How do you think an Old French word meaning tail came to mean, a line of people or vehicles waiting individual turns?

The word **skulk** is of Scandinavian origin.

Read Chapter 6 of *The Horse and His Boy*.

✸ Assignments:

Bible		1. Shasta wondered if anything happens to people after they are dead. What do you believe happens to people after they are dead? Why do you believe this? What does Scripture say?
		Read I Corinthians 15; II Corinthians 4:16–5:10; and Revelation 2:7, 11, 17, 26–28; 3:5, 12, 21.
		Memorize I Corinthians 15:36–38.
English		2. Write about a day that seemed 100 hours long to you.
Geography		3. In what kind of geographical area do you live: desert, plains, mountains, coast? Do a report on one of these areas that you have never seen or where you think you would like to live.
Critical Thinking		4. Discuss where the cat came from. • What are you afraid of in the dark? • Do you cover your head or do you want to be able to see? • Do the tombs remind you of something similar in our world? Hint: *Pyramids*.

➤┼◆➤─O─◄┼◄

Vocabulary:

☞ **Look up the words in a dictionary before you read the chapter and write them, along with a definition, in your vocabulary notebook.**

🖉 Using your vocabulary words, fill in the blanks. The answers may be found in the section entitled Answer Appendix.

1. The sheik reclined on the _____ .

2. The superstitious man clasped his _____ for protection.

3. Tom Sawyer crossed the river with the neighbor's _____ .

4. It takes a _____ to get to the next village from here.

punt

talisman

divan

fortnight

Read Chapter 7 of *The Horse and His Boy*.

☀ Assignments:

✋	1. Illustrate the scene of Lasaraleen passing Aravis on the litter.	Art
🔖	2. Lasaraleen liked making people stare. Do you think this is an admirable trait? What are some names for this trait? See answer in Answer Appendix. How do you think Lasaraleen got her ideas about Narnia?	Critical Thinking
	3. Aravis and Lasaraleen ate a "meal" which was mainly of the whipped cream and jelly, fruit, and ice sort.	Science
🔖	Which food groups were represented in this meal? Which food groups were missing? What nutrients would be missing if all of one's meals only consisted of foods like these?	
🔖	4. Discuss how this meal reinforced the characterization of Lasaraleen?	Literature

Vocabulary:

☞ **Look up the words in a dictionary before you read the chapter and write them, along with a definition, in your vocabulary notebook.**

barbarian	subdue	estimable	aspect
venerable	salutary	gravity	maleficence
enlightened	prudence	decorum	irrefutable
tranquil	circumspect	interminable	sapient
invincible	weathercocks	infallible	constrain
desist	paternal	impeccable	vehement
illimitable	imperil	maxim	impetuous
discernment	apophthegms	prognostics	

Read Chapter 8 of *The Horse and His Boy*.

☀ Assignments:

English/ Vocabulary	🖉	1. Do *The Horse and His Boy* Chapter 8 Crossword Puzzle. It may be found after this unit's Planning Guide.
English	☞	2. Look up the prefix *mal* in a dictionary. Many, but not all, words that begin with mal have a bad **connotation** (a suggested meaning in addition to the literal meaning). Find some other mal words, besides maleficence, that have a bad meaning.
English		3. Different words that have the same meaning are called **synonyms**, but words that are synonyms do not always have the same connotation. You may find the words *curious* and *nosy* used synonymously in the dictionary but it is often considered acceptable to be curious but not nosy. Being silent may be admirable, but being laconic or taciturn may be considered rude. A **thesauraus** gives synonyms for words.
	☞	Find synonyms for three of your vocabulary words. Pick synonyms which have different connotations.
	🖉	Write one sentence for each of the three vocabulary words and for each of the synonyms you have chosen. If this is too challenging, pick three common words and their synonyms to use in sentences.

4. The Narnian's ship is called the *Splendor Hyaline*. Look up the two words in the name. What is the name meant to suggest about the ship?

English

5. Prince Rabadash believes the change in Narnia from a land of ice and snow to a wholesome and fruitful land was brought about by alteration of the stars and natural causes. Can you give any reasons why he might think this way?

Critical Thinking

⏳ PLANNING GUIDE – CHAPTERS 9-12

Gather These Items:

1. Old magazines or seed catalogs with pictures of plants and flowers that can be cut out, Chapter 9.

2. Chalk and stick, Chapter 9.

3. Cassette tape of bird songs, especially one which includes nightingales, Chapter 9. (Bird songs are also available online.)

4. Goats' milk, Chapter 10.

5. *The Narnia Cookbook* or recipes and ingredients for:
   • Porridge, Chapter 10.
   • Bacon, eggs, and mushrooms, Chapter 12.

6. *The Tale of Mrs. Tiggy-Winkle* by Beatrix Potter, Chapter 12.

7. A poem by Robert Browning, Emily Dickinson, or Robert Frost, in addition to the one studied in this unit, Chapter 12.

Suggested Information to Gather:

Encyclopedia or books about:

1. Desert, Chapter 9 (Science).

   ....

2. How a sundial works, Chapter 9 (Science).

   ....

3. Fallow deer, Chapter 10 (Science).

   ....

4. Heather, oaks, beeches, silver birches, rowans, and sweet chestnuts, Chapter 10 (Science).

   ....

5. Marathon, Chapter 11 (History).

   ....

6. Cliches, Chapter 12 (Vocabulary).

   ....

7. Hedgehogs, Chapter 12 (Science).

   ....

8. Dwarfs, Chapter 12 (Science).

....

9. Biographical information on either Robert Browning, Emily Dickinson, or Robert Frost, Chapter 12 (English).

....

Suggested Videos:

1. *The Three Godfathers* with John Wayne, Chapter 9.

Suggested Field Trips:

Suggested Memorization:

1. Memorize your favorite verse from this selection: Psalm 20:7; Psalm 40:3; Psalm 49:1–14; and Psalm 146:3–4, Chapter 9.

Notes:

HEDGEHOG WORKSHEET

FOR USE WITH CHAPTER 12

1) Description: _____

_____

_____

_____

2) Life Span: _____

3) Diet: _____

_____

_____

4) Enemies: _____

_____

5) Habitat: _____

_____

_____

6) Behavior: _____

_____

_____

Draw a Picture

Draw a Track

Favorite Fact: _____

_____

_____

_____

_____

_____

Words to Learn:

aestivate

insectivores

nocturnal

venom resistant

Kingdom > Phylum > Class > Order > Family > Genus > Species

Animalia > Chordata > Mamalia > Insectivora > Erinacedidae> Genus and Species Vary

STUDY GUIDE – CHAPTERS 9-12

Vocabulary:

🔑 **Look up the words in a dictionary before you read the chapter and write them, along with a definition, in your vocabulary notebook.**

✏ Using your vocabulary words, fill in the blanks. The answers may be found in the section entitled Answer Appendix.

1. The most challenging spot floating on the river was when we went over the _____ .

2. Queen Esther had to _____ in the presence of her husband.

3. Everyone took turns being the cook's _____ .

4. The Victorian manner of dress lent itself to being _____ .

5. It was a tiring walk up the _____ .

6. The 28th Massachusetts Volunteer Infantry Regiment was known as the _____ -a- ballagh regiment; this was a Gaelic war cry meaning "clear the way."

7. They were afraid, but they never _____ .

Vocabulary Words:

grovel

faugh

scullion

quailed

prim

hummocks

cataract

Read Chapter 9 of *The Horse and His Boy.*

✏ Before reading the chapter think back to Chapter 5 where Shasta heard the Raven telling how to cross the desert. Without rereading that section, write down as much as you can remember.

☀ Assignments:

1. Compare the directions you wrote before reading this chapter to those the Raven gave as well as the actual crossing. Would you have gone the right way?

Critical Thinking

2. Lasaraleen thought if the Tisroc was going to do it, it must be right. What does the Bible say about putting our trust in man?

Bible

📖 Read Proverbs 3:5. Is any man worthy of that much blind faith?

Read Psalm 20:7; Psalm 40:3; Psalm 49:1–14; and Psalm 146:3–4.

 Memorize your favorite verse from this selection of scriptures from Psalms.

Science 3. If you did not already study deserts while reading Chapter 6, find out about the fluctuation of temperature between day and night in the desert. What causes these extreme temperature differences?

Deserts cover about one fifth of the earth's surface. Find out how little rainfall an area can receive and be termed a desert. See answer in Answer Appendix.

How much rainfall does your community receive each year?

 Make a graph comparing the rainfall in your community with the rainfall of the Mojave desert, the Sonoran desert, and one other desert.

Learn what kinds of vegetation can survive in a desert. How did God specifically design the plants to survive in a desert?

Draw ten native desert plants in your plant notebook and identify each.

 Make a map of the world's deserts. Are deserts only hot places?

Science 4. Add a picture of a cypress tree and a picture of a nightingale to your notebooks.

Geography 5. Refer to the map in the book as Rabadash tells his father his plan. Then trace the route Shasta and his friends take.

Critical Thinking 6. Discuss the following questions:
- What is the purpose of the repetition in the paragraph on page 130 of *The Horse and His Boy* which begins, "On again"?
- If you were in Shasta's situation, what kind of games might you play to try to make the time pass?

Science 7. Look up how a sundial works.

Put a stick in your yard. Using chalk, hourly mark and measure the direction of the shadow as well as its length. How did the shadow change during the day?

Both artists and writers use observation to make their work more realistic.

 On page 131, how did C.S. Lewis describe the passing of the day?

 Read the poem by Robert Louis Stevenson, "My Shadow." See Recommended Reading Appendix.

Draw an object with a shadow as it would occur in the morning and again as it would be in the afternoon. Or, using what you have learned, write a descriptive paragraph using the sun to show the passage of time.

8. Listen to bird songs on a cassette tape or a Web site until you can identify at least five birds by their songs.   Science

Find pictures of the birds you can identify by their song. Is one of them a nightingale?

9. Did you find any of C.S. Lewis' observations of human relations in this chapter? If so, remember to add them to your list. See Chapter 3, Activity 1.   Critical Thinking

10. Watch *The Three Godfathers*.   Science/ Life Skills

What trials beset the group as they crossed the desert? Watch for references to the Bible.

Chapter 10

Vocabulary Words:	

Vocabulary:

turbulent

⚷ **Look up the words in a dictionary before you read the chapter and write them, along with a definition, in your vocabulary notebook.**

fetlock

✏ Skim the chapter for the word *turbulent*. Write at least one sentence from this chapter containing the word under its dictionary definition. Follow each sentence with a citation.

Read Chapter 10 of *The Horse and His Boy*.

✳ Assignments:

Bible

1. When Aravis was torn by the lion, Hwin wanted the Hermit to tell her if Aravis would live; but the Hermit said he did not even know who would be alive by sunset.

📖 Read Matthew 6:25–34 and James 4:13–15. Do these scriptures remind you of anything in the story?

Critical Thinking

2. The Hermit also said that in all his years he had never met such a thing as Luck. Do you believe in luck? Why or why not?

Cooking

3. Taste goats' milk.

Cook porridge with cream. In *The Narnia Cookbook*, the recipe for porridge is on page 2.

Art

4. Draw the inside of the enclosure as described on page 145. Include the Hermit as described on page 143.

Science

5. What is a fallow deer?
What does heather look like? Where does it grow?
Identify oaks, beeches, silver birches, rowans, and sweet chestnuts.

Critical Thinking

6. Discuss the following questions:
   • Do you think Bree heard Shasta tell him to go back?
   • What were the real causes of Bree's shame?
   • Discuss the idea that although the horses were doing all they thought they could, they might not have been doing all they actually could.

➤—◆—○—◆—◄

Vocabulary:

Vocabulary Word:

mettle

Look up this word in a dictionary before you read the chapter and write it, along with a definition, in your vocabulary notebook.

Skim the chapter for your vocabulary word. Write at least one sentence from this chapter which contains the word under its dictionary definition. Follow each sentence with a citation.

Read Chapter 11 of *The Horse and His Boy*.

☀ Assignments:

---

1. On a sidewalk or other level surface, measure a furlong. It is 220 yards or about 201 meters.

Science

---

2. Shasta was very tired and hungry which made him feel sorry for himself.

Read I Kings, Chapters 18 and 19.

Discuss the great things Elijah had done. What was Elijah's attitude? What was God's response? Compare Shasta with Elijah. Is there any truth in the statement, "first comes fear, then depression, then deception."

Bible

---

3. Reread the paragraph on page 165 where Aslan answered the question, "Who are you?"

Then read Exodus 3:13–15; I Kings 19:8–13; and John 8:58.

Discuss the similarities.

Bible

---

4. Find out how the word *marathon* came to mean a 26 mile race. Your dictionary may give you the history of the word, or you may have to look in your encyclopedia. What happened to the first person who ran the marathon?

History

---

5. Poetry is not written to be read in the same way prose is read.

Poetry is written to be read aloud. Poetry is the earliest and remains the most concentrated and intense form of communication among the arts of language. Its uses of words are finer, richer and more powerful than those of prose, and it has played a larger part in the whole literary tradition. —Elizabeth Drew

Literature

Read a poem carefully and read it more than once. Practice reading the poem aloud. Look up any unknown words. Decide what the poem is about. Who is the speaker? What do you know about him or her? To whom is the author speaking? What is the occasion of the poem? What is the central purpose of the poem?

What is the **tone**—the author's attitude toward the subject or audience? Is it humorous, satiric, sad, ironic, serious, light, sarcastic, bitter, or complimentary? How does this tone affect the meaning? What kinds of descriptive language are used to suggest mental images or ideas?

 Read Robert Browning's poem, "How They Brought the Good News from Ghent to Aix," and Robert Frost's poem, "The Road Not Taken." Both of these poems are in the Recommended Reading Appendix.

 Samuel Taylor Coleridge said poetry is "the best words in their best order." Tell what you think about this statement by Laurence Perrine in *Sound and Sense*: "Initially poetry might be defined as a kind of language that says more and says it more intensely than does ordinary language."

English   6. Use a dictionary or writer's handbook to help you define *alliteration*, *simile*, *metaphor*, and *imagery*. Find an example of each in the poems you have read. Answers may vary. See the Answer Appendix.

Literature   7. From the Recommended Reading Appendix, read Emily Dickinson's poem, "A Narrow Fellow in the Grass."

In this poem the subject is never named. Yet because of the excellent use of imagery, by the end of the poem we know the author is talking about a snake.

In his poem, "The Bells," Poe used words to suggest the tolling of bells. The rhythm of "How They Brought the Good News from Ghent to Aix" resembles the beat of galloping horses. Notice the rhythm of "A Narrow Fellow in the Grass." Is it regular or irregular? Does it create a particular feeling?

Geography   8. Look for a clue on page 157 to tell which direction everyone was riding then refer to the map and see where Shasta ended up.

Critical Thinking   9. No one ever saw anything more terrible and beautiful than the light that came from the Lion.

Discuss how something can be both terrible and beautiful? Have you ever seen anything that was like this?

➤┤◆┼◦┼◆├◄

Vocabulary:

Vocabulary Words:

lintels

extremity

valiant

lief

excruciating

☞ **Look up the words in a dictionary before you read the chapter and write them, along with a definition, in your vocabulary notebook.**

✎ Using your vocabulary words, fill in the blanks. The answers may be found in the section entitled Answer Appendix.

1. The _____ Shackleton charged across the glacier on Lake Wales Georgia.

2. _____ are designed to provide support over openings at the eaves.

3. Pluto is at the outermost _____ of our solar system.

4. The torture brought forth _____ pain.

5. I'd as _____ go as not.

☞ Find a book that explains where some of our cliches came from. Where do we get the phrase, *hammer and tongs*, and what does it mean?

Read Chapter 12 of *The Horse and His Boy*.

✳ Assignments:

---

1. After Aslan left Shasta, a spring came from a print of the Lion's front right paw.

   📖 Read Psalms 78:15–16 and 107:35; also John 4:10 and 7:37–38.

Bible

---

2. At the time Peter was ruling Narnia, the smaller woodland people were so safe and happy they had gotten a little careless. In America, we will not keep our freedom if we get careless and forget to watch. As Christians we will not be ready to resist the Devil and meet Jesus when he comes if we do not watch and pray.

   ☞ Use a concordance and read the references which contain the word *watch* in the New Testament.

   What does Jesus say about watching and being ready? What are we to watch for?

Bible

---

3. Animals who sleep during the day are called nocturnal. What are animals who sleep during the night called?

Science

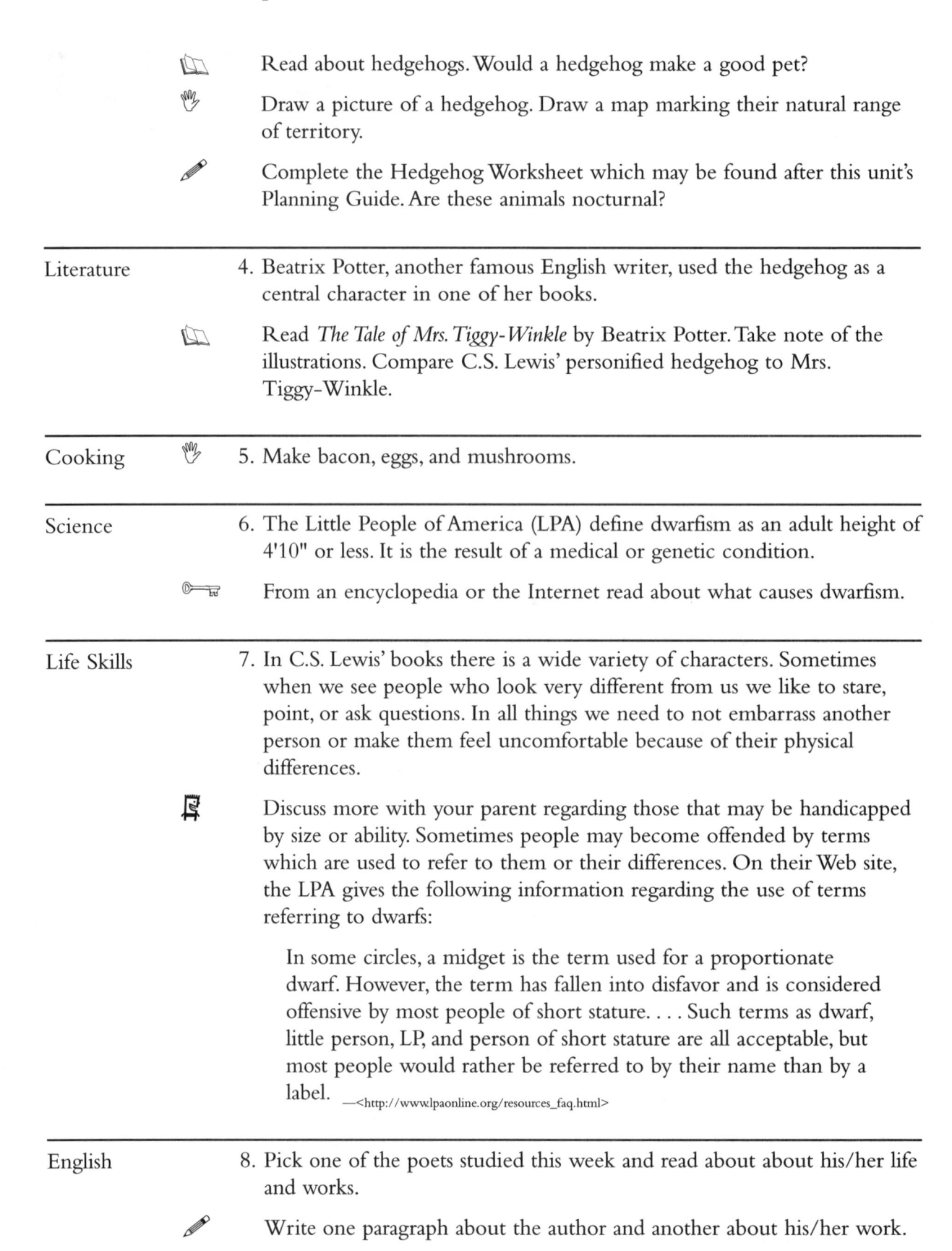

Read about hedgehogs. Would a hedgehog make a good pet?

Draw a picture of a hedgehog. Draw a map marking their natural range of territory.

Complete the Hedgehog Worksheet which may be found after this unit's Planning Guide. Are these animals nocturnal?

Literature   4. Beatrix Potter, another famous English writer, used the hedgehog as a central character in one of her books.

Read *The Tale of Mrs. Tiggy-Winkle* by Beatrix Potter. Take note of the illustrations. Compare C.S. Lewis' personified hedgehog to Mrs. Tiggy-Winkle.

Cooking   5. Make bacon, eggs, and mushrooms.

Science   6. The Little People of America (LPA) define dwarfism as an adult height of 4'10" or less. It is the result of a medical or genetic condition.

From an encyclopedia or the Internet read about what causes dwarfism.

Life Skills   7. In C.S. Lewis' books there is a wide variety of characters. Sometimes when we see people who look very different from us we like to stare, point, or ask questions. In all things we need to not embarrass another person or make them feel uncomfortable because of their physical differences.

Discuss more with your parent regarding those that may be handicapped by size or ability. Sometimes people may become offended by terms which are used to refer to them or their differences. On their Web site, the LPA gives the following information regarding the use of terms referring to dwarfs:

> In some circles, a midget is the term used for a proportionate dwarf. However, the term has fallen into disfavor and is considered offensive by most people of short stature. . . . Such terms as dwarf, little person, LP, and person of short stature are all acceptable, but most people would rather be referred to by their name than by a label. —<http://www.lpaonline.org/resources_faq.html>

English   8. Pick one of the poets studied this week and read about about his/her life and works.

Write one paragraph about the author and another about his/her work.

Find another poem by this author and share it with your family.

>-+-◇-○-◇-+-<

⏳ PLANNING GUIDE – CHAPTERS 13-15

Gather These Items:

1. *The Narnia Cookbook* or recipes and ingredients for meat pies, Chapter 15.

Suggested Information to Gather:

Encyclopedia or books about:

1. Eagles, Chapter 13 (Science).

....

2. Energy, Chapter 13 (Science).

....

3. Heraldry, Chapter 14 (History).

....

Suggested Videos:

1. Richard "Little Bear" Wheeler's, *The Kit Carson Story: Lessons in Atonement.* Borrow from a friend or see Resource Appendix for a supplier, Chapter 13.

Suggested Field Trips:

1. Go to an archery range and shoot a bow and arrow, Chapter 13.

Suggested Memorization:

1. A historical poem, Chapter 15.

Notes:

EAGLE WORKSHEET

FOR USE WITH CHAPTER 13

1) Description: _____

_____

_____

_____

2) Life Span: _____

3) Diet: _____

_____

_____

4) Enemies: _____

_____

5) Habitat: _____

_____

_____

6) Behavior: _____

_____

_____

Draw a Picture

Draw a Track

Favorite Fact: _____

_____

_____

_____

_____

_____

Words to Learn:

carnivore

rodent

depth perception

Kingdom > Phylum > Class > Order > Family > Genus

Animalia > Chordata > Vertebrata > Aves > Strigiformes > Accipitridae

STUDY GUIDE – CHAPTERS 13-15

Vocabulary:

**Vocabulary
Words:**

sortie

portcullis

defiance

🗝 **Look up the words in a dictionary before you read the chapter and write them, along with a definition, in your vocabulary notebook.**

✏ Using your vocabulary words, fill in the blanks. The answers may be found in the section entitled Answer Appendix.

1. The lord dropped the _____ when he saw the army advance.

2. The King stopped the _____ of his lords by giving their lands away.

3. On the somewhat dubious theory that the weather would probably get worse before it would get better, he decided to make a quick return _____ to the northernmost point in Scotland, and then to Inverness and proceed along the southern route.

The Latin word **portare** means to carry; **porta**, also Latin, means gate. It can sometimes be difficult to guess the meaning of words beginning with **port**. Something that is **portable** may be carried. A **portal** is a doorway. A **porter** may open a door for you or carry your luggage.

Read Chapter 13 of *The Horse and His Boy*.

☀ Assignments:

1. Discuss the following questions:
   • What can we learn from Shasta's realization Aslan had been between him and the edge all the time?
   • Why had everyone always taken Rabadash seriously in Tashbaan?
   • What is different in Narnia?
   • What could Rabadash have learned here if he had wanted to?

Critical
Thinking

2. Discuss the decision of Corin and Shasta to disobey and go into battle. How might things have come out differently for them or for others if they had not disobeyed?

Bible

God places people in authority over us. Bill Gothard has said, "The essence of submission is not getting under the domination of authority, but rather getting under the protection of authority." (See Ephesians 6:1–3; Proverbs 6:20–21; and Proverbs 15:5.) Discuss with your child the principle of being under parental authority. It is similar to being under an umbrella: it only protects if the person remains under the umbrella.

 For further study on obedience, view Richard "Little Bear" Wheeler's *The Kit Carson Story: Lessons in Atonement.*

Science

3. Study eagles. Do eagles eat dead things?

 Fill in the Eagle Worksheet which may be found after this unit's Planning Guide.

History

4. Archery is one of the oldest arts still practiced. The earliest people known to have used the bow and arrow were the ancient Egyptians who adopted it at least 5000 years ago for purposes of hunting and warfare. In 1200 B.C. the Hittites used the bow in light, fast chariots and became dreaded opponents in Middle Eastern battles. Their neighbors, the Assyrians, used archery extensively. They built bows from several different types of material: tendon, horn, and wood. They also gave the bow a new, recurved shape that was far more powerful and, as it was shorter, it was more easily handled by an archer on horseback.

In the Greco-Roman period, the bow was used more for personal exploits or hunting, rather than warfare. Archers are frequently seen on pottery from that time. The Romans were said to have been second-rate archers until the sixth century when they began drawing the arrow to the face instead of the chest, giving the shot far more accuracy. Their opponents often had far better skills. The Parthians, for instance, were horsemen who developed the skill of swiveling around in the saddle and could shoot backwards at full gallop.

Middle Eastern superiority in archery equipment and technique continued for centuries. With bows like those of the Assyrians and Parthians, Attila the Hun and his Mongols conquered much of Europe and Asia and Turkish archers threw back the Crusaders.

For Native Americans, the bow was both a means of subsistence and existence before and during the days of English and later American colonization. This has been the case, and still is, in some countries on the African continent.

The popularity of archery is reflected in the many ballads and folklore about archers, such as Robin Hood, to name the most famous one. In Greek mythology, reference is often made to archers.

English literature honors the longbow for famous victories in the battles of Crecy, Agincourt, and Poitiers. The first known organized competition in archery was held at Finsbury, England in 1583 and included 3000 participants! By the time of the Thirty Years War (1618–1648), it was clear the bow as weapon belonged to the past, due to the introduction of gun powder. Since then, archery has developed as a recreational sport. (<http://www.archery.org/what_is_archery/history.htm>).

 Tell your instructor one new interesting fact you learned from reading this information.

---

5. Archery is a perfect example of potential and kinetic energy. Potential energy is the energy stored in elastic materials as the result of their stretching or compressing. Elastic potential energy can be stored in rubber bands, bungee chords, trampolines, springs, an arrow drawn into a bow, etc. The amount of elastic potential energy stored in such a device is related to the amount of stretch of the device—the more stretch, the more stored energy. Kinetic energy is the energy of movement. Let the bow snap back into its normal position, and the potential energy is changed to kinetic energy.   Science

 Energy is the ability to do work. Read about energy in the encyclopedia.

 In your vocabulary notebook, define *energy, power, force, potential energy,* and *kinetic energy.*

---

6. See potential and kinetic energy in action; go to an archery range and shoot a bow and arrow.   Field Trip

Chapter 14

Vocabulary Words:

halberd

cambric

embezzling

heraldry

brick

Vocabulary:

☞ **Look up the words in a dictionary before you read the chapter and write them, along with a definition, in your vocabulary notebook.**

✎ Using your vocabulary words, fill in the blanks. The answers may be found in the section entitled Answer Appendix.

1. The _____ took the practical joke well.

2. The _____ sheets were luxurious.

3. The chief executive officer was caught _____ the corporation's funds.

4. While Americans are usually fascinated by the beauty of _____ , they are rarely familiar with its meaning and traditions and, therefore, often misunderstand and even abuse this rich cultural heritage.

5. The _____ enabled a foot soldier to successfully fight with an armored man on horseback; the pike head was used to keep the horseman at a distance, and the ax blade could strike a heavy cleaving blow to finish the opponent.

Read Chapter 14 of *The Horse and His Boy*.

☀ Assignments

Bible	📜	1. Compare Aslan's command to Bree to touch him and smell him and see that he was a true beast to John 20:24–29. Do you think Lewis may have had these verses in mind when he wrote this? How are the circumstances the same/different? How do Bree's and Thomas' unbelief differ?
Critical Thinking	📜	2. Discuss Shasta's idea that Aslan seemed to be at the back of all the stories. Have you ever felt as Bree did in the last sentence of this chapter?
History/ Art	☞	3. Find out more about heraldry. The emergence of heraldry is due to the evolution of military equipment from the latter part of the 11th century to the middle of the 12th century, when fighters were unrecognizable under their helmets. (There is a nice illustration from the 11th century Bayeux tapestry showing William lifting his helmet so as to be recognized by his troops in battle.) This led fighters to paint emblems on their shields.

What ideals are important to your family? To manhood? What would be your family motto? Discuss this with your parent. How could this be symbolized on a family crest?

Design a family crest.

><+>+0+<+><

Chapter 15

Vocabulary:

Vocabulary Words:

Look up the words in a dictionary before you read the chapter and write them, along with a definition, in your vocabulary notebook.

Skim the chapter for the words *pajock* and *lay*. Write at least one sentence from this chapter containing these words under their dictionary definitions. Follow each sentence with a citation.

boudoir

gentilesse

pajock

Pajock means peacock and is used as a contemptuous name. King Lune used it in reference to Rabadash because Rabadash was being proud and foolish. Hamlet called his uncle, King Claudius, a pajock:

lapsed

lay

> A whole one, I.
> For thou dost know, O Damon dear,
> This realm dismantled was
> Of Jove himself; and now reigns here
> A very, very pajock.

cheer

phantasm

> —William Shakespeare, *Hamlet*, Act III, Scene 2

Lay is used on page 221 referring to a ballad, as in Scott's, "The Lay of the Last Minstrel."

Using your vocabulary words, fill in the blanks. The answers may be found in the section entitled Answer Appendix.

1. Her _____ was decorated Victorian style.

2. The book _____ out of print.

3. Dickens used _____ to make his point in *The Christmas Carol.*

4. His _____ calmed the situation.

5. We bid you good _____ .

6. The king called the noble a _____ because of his proud behavior.

7. The minstrel's _____ was exquisite.

Read Chapter 15 of *The Horse and His Boy*.

☀ Assignments:

English	🖊	1. Write as many adjectives as you can think of describing Rabadash.

Bible	📖	2. Can you think of any Bible character who ate grass like a donkey might? Hint: *Read Daniel 4.*

Bible		3. King Lune and Aslan both tried to reason with Rabadash but he would not even stop talking long enough to listen.
	📖	Read Proverbs 8:33; 12:1; 13:1, 18; 15:5, 32; 16:22; and 19:20. What one word from these verses describes Rabadash?

Cooking	✋	4. Make a meat pie and eat it with bread and cheese. *The Narnia Cookbook* has a recipe for pigeon pie on page 15.

History/ Literature		5. For thousands of years history was passed down by word of mouth. Often a minstrel was responsible for making songs that would help people remember specific events. Most people could not read or write and a story that rhymes or is set to music is easier to remember and repeat than a story simply told in everyday words.
	📖	Find examples of poems that relate historical events such as, "The Midnight Ride of Paul Revere" by Henry Wadsworth Longfellow or "The Charge of the Light Brigade" by Alfred, Lord Tennyson. These two poems may be found in the Recommended Reading Appendix. Many historical poems are about battles, perhaps because of the tradition of kings having their own minstrels who followed them around and made up poems about their heroic feats.
	🦁	Find one poem that interests you, learn the background of the poem, and memorize it. If memorizing is difficult for you, try singing the poem.

Critical Thinking	🖊	6. Recall Aravis' attitude toward Shasta and others in the beginning of the story. Write about the ways in which she has changed.
	📖	Discuss the following questions: • Cor's father told his story so many times that, although Cor had wanted it told at first, he began to wish it had never happened. Have you ever felt this way about anything? • What might we say rather than, "Maybe apes will grow honest"? Think of other sayings that are synonymous with unlikely happenings. Answers may vary. See Answer Appendix for some examples.

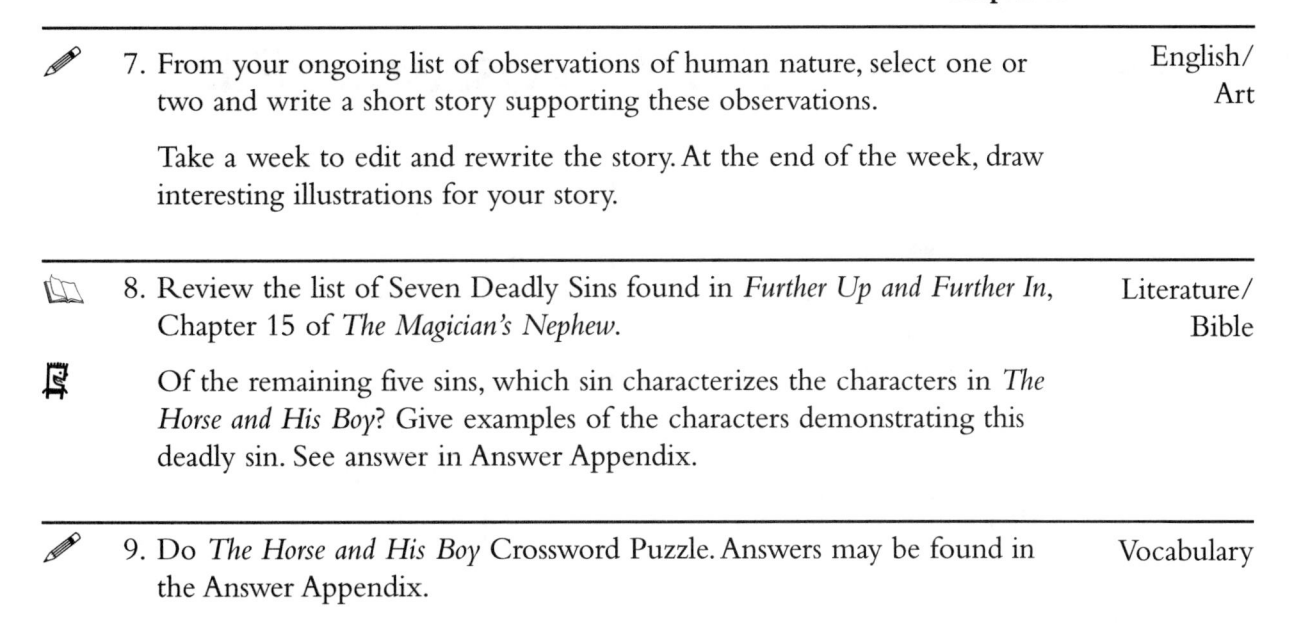

7. From your ongoing list of observations of human nature, select one or two and write a short story supporting these observations.

   Take a week to edit and rewrite the story. At the end of the week, draw interesting illustrations for your story.

   English/
   Art

8. Review the list of Seven Deadly Sins found in *Further Up and Further In*, Chapter 15 of *The Magician's Nephew*.

   Of the remaining five sins, which sin characterizes the characters in *The Horse and His Boy*? Give examples of the characters demonstrating this deadly sin. See answer in Answer Appendix.

   Literature/
   Bible

9. Do *The Horse and His Boy* Crossword Puzzle. Answers may be found in the Answer Appendix.

   Vocabulary

Complete any unfinished assignments prior to going on to *Prince Caspian*.

THE HORSE AND HIS BOY CROSSWORD PUZZLE

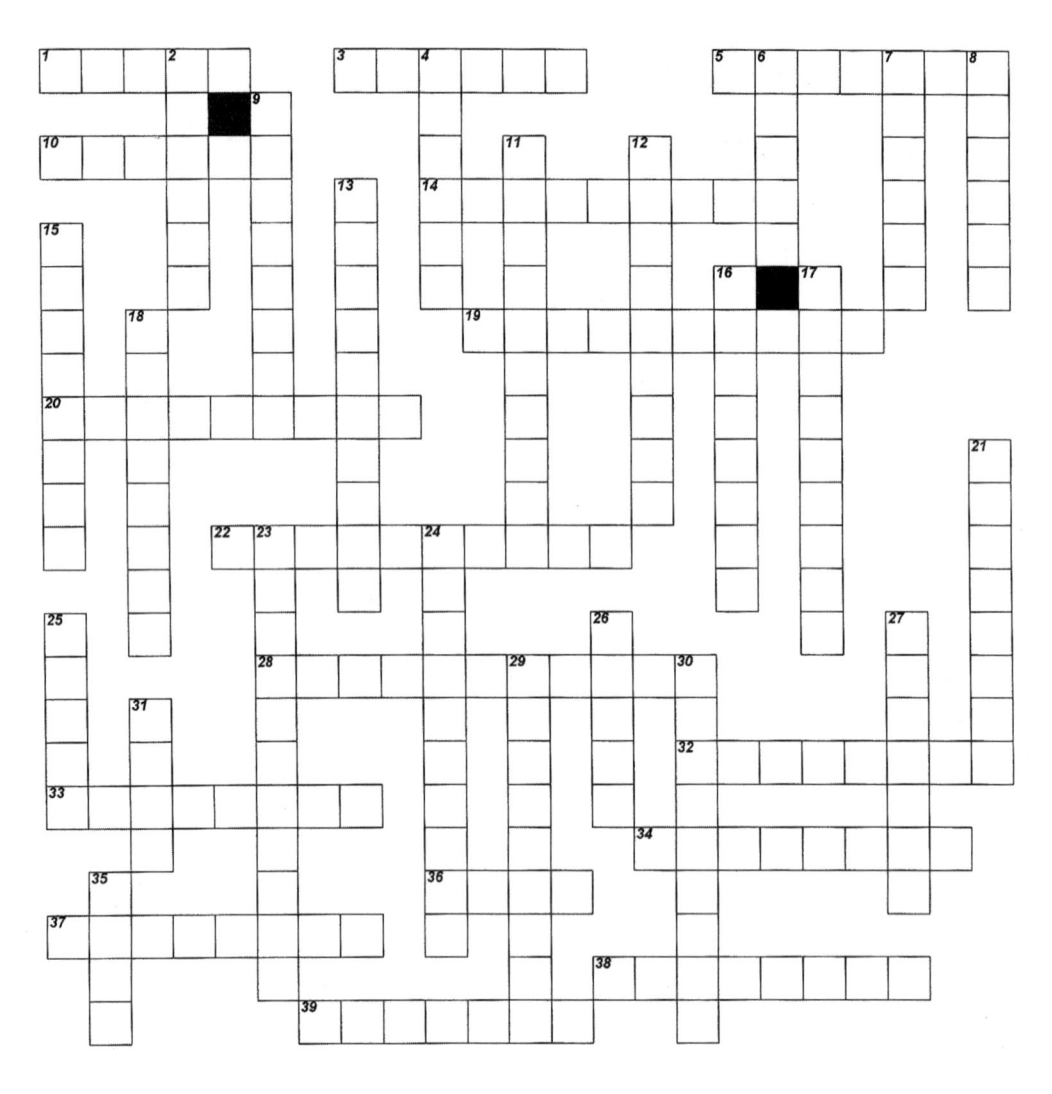

ACROSS

1 rub

3 stately

5 cajole

10 marketplace

14 aged

19 talkative

20 choppy

22 charitable

28 questioning

32 amulet

33 saber

34 insolent boldness

36 dear

37 turrets on
a mosque

38 waterfall

39 spotted

DOWN

2 bottle

4 beg

6 hut

7 overpower with
light

8 begin a journey

9 mild

11 unrelenting

12 savage

13 inflamed ulcers

15 apparition

16 highest point

17 deluxe

18 science of
recording
genealogies

21 a menial

23 informed

24 unconquerable

25 fertile desert area

26 backless couch

27 mound

29 penury

30 limb

31 reserved

35 center

PRINCE CASPIAN

⧗ PLANNING GUIDE – CHAPTERS 1-4

Gather These Items:

1. *Prince Caspian* by C.S. Lewis.

2. A world map, Chapter 1.

3. Colored seeds and beans or fish tank gravel and colored sand, Chapter 1.

4. *My Side of the Mountain* by Jean Craighead George or *Hatchet* by Gary Paulsen, Chapter 1.

5. Recipes and ingredients for cooking apples, Chapter 3.

6. Recipes and ingredients for cooking fish, Chapter 3.

7. Items and directions to make a small chain-mail piece, Chapter 3.

Suggested Information to Gather:

Encyclopedia or books about:

1. Seaweed, anemones, tide pools, Chapter 1 (Science).

   ....

2. Water cycle, Chapter 1 (Science).

   ....

3. Land features: peninsula, isthmus, etc., Chapter 2 (Geography).

   ....

4. Gems, Chapter 2 (Science).

   ....

5. Pomona, Chapter 2 (Mythology).

   ....

6. Wars of the Roses, Chapter 3 (History).

   ....

7. Dwarfs in mythology, Chapter 4 (Mythology).

   ....

Suggested Videos:

Suggested Field Trips:

1. If the time of year is right, pick apples, Chapter 1.

2. Visit a jewelry store, Chapter 2.

3. Go to a Renaissance Fair and see chain-mail up close, Chapter 3.

Suggested Memorization:

1. Memorize the five oceans of the world, Chapter 1.

Notes:

STUDY GUIDE – CHAPTERS 1-4

Vocabulary:

🔑 **Look up the words in a dictionary before you read the chapter and write them, along with a definition, in your vocabulary notebook.**

✏️ Using your vocabulary words, fill in the blanks. The answers may be found in the section entitled Answer Appendix.

1. There was no obvious evidence that the island was

   _____ .

2. Being sent away to _____ at such a young age would be difficult.

3. Don Quixote considered himself a knight _____ .

4. We knew that once we sailed around the _____ we would be out of sight of the pirate ship.

5. They were supposed to meet him at the _____ of the two highways.

Vocabulary Words:

junction

boarding school

inhabited

promontory

errant

Read Chapter 1 of *Prince Caspian.*

✳ Assignments:

🏛 1. Answer the following questions orally:
   • Who was the one grown-up the children had told about their previous adventure in Narnia?
   • How long had it been since the children came back to our world at the end of *The Lion, the Witch and the Wardrobe*?
   • Why was the wardrobe magic?
   • Which of the children seems to be the practical one?
   • What made them realize the island had been inhabited?

Reading Comprehension

---

2. Seawater is not good to drink. It contains about 3.5% salts. Drinking seawater increases thirst and may make a person ill. Why would the water from the stream be better to drink farther away from the beach?

Science

🔑 Look in your encyclopedia or a book about the ocean to find out more about seaweed, anemones, and tide pools.

Science		3. Peter said any streams there might be were bound to come down to the sea.
	🔑	Study the water cycle.
	✋	Make a poster demonstrating the water cycle.

Geography		4. What is the difference between an ocean and a sea? In the past, explorers talked about the "Seven Seas." The "Seven Seas" are now called the five oceans. The five oceans are the Pacific, Atlantic, Indian, Arctic, and Antarctic Oceans. Presently we use the term **sea** for a body of saltwater smaller than an ocean.
	🦁	Locate and memorize the five oceans of the world.
	🔑	On a map, locate at least 10 different seas. Be sure to find the Caspian Sea.

| Art | ✋ | 5. Using descriptions from the chapter, draw an aerial view of the island where the children entered Narnia. Label north, south, east, and west on your picture. You could make your map using different colored seeds and beans glued on paper in a mosaic pattern. Or use sand and colored fish tank gravel. Use your imagination and think of other things that could represent sand, water, trees, grass, and ruins. |

| English | ✏️ | 6. Write a sequential paragraph about the mood changes of the children from the beginning of this chapter to the end. Example: When the children were at the train station, they felt _____ because _____ . Then when they found themselves on a beach _____ . |

| Literature | 📖 | 7. *My Side of the Mountain* by Jean Craighead George and *Hatchet* by Gary Paulsen are both fictional stories about young people surviving in the wilderness alone. One of these may be of interest to you. |

| Life Skills | ✋ | 8. If the time of year is right, pick apples. |

| Critical Thinking | 📜 | 9. What did the children think about going back to school? The ancient Spartans sent their boys to boarding school. It was there the boys were challenged physically as well as academically. They were "protected" from the softening effect of their mothers and became dutiful to the state. (*Theras and His Town* is a novel about the boarding schools of Sparta.) Later in history, knights were sent away to be trained. At the age of seven or eight an aspiring knight was sent to another household to be a page. He endured long and arduous discipline. At the age of 12 or 14 he became a squire to the lord of the manor. He was trained in warfare and was a personal servant to the master. Parents continue the tradition of sending children to boarding school for training and education |

today. Why do you think it has been important for cultures throughout history to send their children away for training? What schooling method is opposite to the boarding school one? Compare and contrast the advantages and disadvantages of these schooling methods.

Chapter 2

Vocabulary:

🗝️ **Look up the words in a dictionary before you read the chapter and write them, along with a definition, in your vocabulary notebook.**

✏️ Using your vocabulary words, fill in the blanks. The answers may be found in the section entitled Answer Appendix.

1. He would have preferred giving his speech from the floor instead of standing on the _____ .

2. That _____ is far too gaudy for me to wear.

3. The _____ which had been worn by King Fred was on display in the museum.

4. We will certainly _____ if we are not rescued soon.

Vocabulary Words:

dais

brooch

coronet

perish

Read Chapter 2 of *Prince Caspian.*

✳️ Assignments:

🔖 1. Answer the following questions orally:
   • At what point did you realize where the children were?
   • Did you figure it out before they did?
   • What do you remember about where the gifts came from?
   • At first Susan could hardly remember being a queen in Narnia, then by that same night she could hardly remember the name of the place where they had lived in our world. Why do you think this happened?

Reading Comprehension

🗝️ 2. Use a dictionary or encyclopedia to find out about these land features:

Geography

    peninsula   *mesa*   *bay*   *plain*
    plateau   *ishthmus*   *island*   *steppe*

✋ Now draw a map of an imaginary island country. Include at least one river, a lake, a bay, a peninsula, mountains, and a desert.

Use different colors to show each type of land feature on your map, i.e. use one color for deserts, one for other types of land, and one for water. Mountains may be shown with upside down V's. If you need more help or ideas, your encyclopedia should have an article on maps.

Science 3. Look up *gems* in your encyclopedia. What do *diamonds*, *rubies*, *carbuncles*, *emeralds*, *topaz*, and *amethysts* look like? How is each created?

 Add these gems and a brief description of each to your vocabulary notebook.

 Visit a jewelry store. See how many of the gems you have studied you can identify. Which one is your favorite?

Literature   4. Find the mention of Pomona in this chapter. What did she do? Historically she was a wood nymph and was sometimes elevated to a goddess. No one excelled her in love of the garden or the culture of fruit. She cared for and loved the cultivated country and the trees that bear delicious apples.

Read more about this mythological goddess.

Critical Thinking   5. Sherlock Holmes maintained that when trying to solve a mystery you must eliminate the impossibilities and whatever is left, no matter how improbable, must be the truth. Edmund thought it was impossible the place they were in could be Cair Paravel because everything was so old and it had only been a year since they had last been in Narnia. Even though Peter could not explain the apparent passage of decades or centuries, he proved his assertion they were indeed at Cair Paravel by using the physical evidence.

 What were the four points in Peter's argument? See answer in Answer Appendix.

What were the last two pieces of evidence that proved to all of them it really was Cair Paravel? See answer in Answer Appendix.

In the treasure chamber, what was missing from among the gifts Peter, Susan, and Lucy had received from Father Christmas? Try to guess where it is.

⊱┄✦┄○┄✦┄⊰

Vocabulary:

☞ **Look up this word in a dictionary before you read the chapter and write it, along with a definition, in your vocabulary notebook. Look up the etymology of this word as well as the present meaning.**

Vocabulary Word:

gist

Read Chapter 3 of *Prince Caspian*.

☀ Assignments:

📜	1. Why did both soldiers in the boat swim away instead of fighting?	Reading Comprehension
📖 ✏️	2. In an encyclopedia, read a short explanation of the Wars of the Roses. Write one paragraph explaining the Wars of the Roses. Write another paragraph about any similarities between the Wars of the Roses and the struggles in Narnia.	History
✋	3. Sleep outside for one night with no tent or mattress.	Life Skills
✋	4. Find at least five different recipes for cooking apples. Try to find at least one you could make with only a campfire.	Cooking
✋	5. Have fish and apples for breakfast.	Cooking
✋	6. Make a small chain-mail article.	Life Skills
✋	7. Go to a Renaissance Festival. See chain-mail up close. This was the predominant armor of knights for many years.	History

➤━◆━○━◆━┥

Chapter 4

Vocabulary Words:

tutor

buskins

turrets

battlements

leads

Vocabulary:

🔑 **Look up the words in a dictionary before you read the chapter and write them, along with a definition, in your vocabulary notebook.**

✏️ Using your vocabulary words, fill in the blanks. The answers may be found in the section entitled Answer Appendix.

1. I would have been able to stand completely inside the giant's _____ .

2. The archers stationed themselves along the _____ in preparation for defending the castle.

3. There is only one stairway leading to the top of the _____ and the door is guarded by two fierce dogs.

4. I have taught you everything I know about math. We will have to hire a _____ to teach you algebra.

5. The northern _____ allowed us access to the other side of the mountain.

Read Chapter 4 of *Prince Caspian.*

✸ Assignments:

Bible	1. Dr. Cornelius told Caspian what he could do as king to help bring back Old Narnia.
	📖 Read about the things King Josiah did when he rediscovered the Law in II Kings 22:1–23:30.

Bible	2. Cornelius is a Biblical name. What did the Biblical Cornelius do?
	📖 If you cannot remember, read Acts, Chapter 10.
	📝 Discuss any similarities you see between the two characters.

Bible	3. Caspian did not realize he should not talk of Aslan. The lack of his discretion endangered his nurse.
	🔑 Look up *discretion* in a dictionary.
	📖 Read Proverbs 1:4, 2:11, and 19:11.
	📝 Discuss ways you need to show discretion.

4. This chapter is written as a flashback. A **flashback** is a literary device in which an earlier event is inserted into the normal chronological order of the story.

   What are the advantages of telling the story this way? Disadvantages? Why do you think Lewis chose this way to tell the story?

   English

5. Dr. Cornelius and Caspian had a short discussion about the usage of *who* and *whom*. Find the conversation between the two. **Who** does something; it is a subject like the pronoun *he*. **Whom** has something done to it; it is an object like the pronoun *him*. Ask yourself, "Who is doing what to whom?" Simplify the sentence. What is the subject of the sentence? The verb? The object? Who was correct, the student or the teacher?

   English

6. Draw Dr. Cornelius.

   Art

7. Discuss the following questions:
   - What impression does the name Prunaprismia give you of Caspian's aunt?
   - Do you think Lewis meant for us to think she was a nice person?
   - Compare Caspian's feeling about becoming king to those of Frank the Cabby in *The Magician's Nephew* and the four children in *The Lion, the Witch and the Wardrobe*.
   - Can you think of something we believe from history to be true but for which we now have no physical evidence? Answers may vary. See Answer Appendix.
   - Can you think of something we believe to be myth which was once believed to be true? Answers may vary. See Answer Appendix.

   Critical Thinking

8. During the study of *The Horse and His Boy* we studied about human dwarfs. Mythological dwarfs are related to fairies and elves. The fairy tradition in literature begins in the 1380's with Chaucer and Gower. Scandinavian influence is certainly present in the names which refer to dwarfs.

   Mythology

    Read about mythological dwarfs.

⧖ PLANNING GUIDE – CHAPTERS 5-8

Gather These Items:

1. *Carry On, Mr. Bowditch* by Jean Lee Latham, ISBN 0-590-45577-X, Chapter 5.

2. Recorder (musical instrument), Chapter 5. Check your local school supply or music store or see the Resource Appendix.

3. Modeling clay or ingredients to make clay, Chapter 7. See Activity Appendix for a recipe.

4. *Arabian Nights*, Chapter 8.

Suggested Information to Gather:

Encyclopedia or books about:

1. Navigation, Chapter 5 (History).

   ....

2. Biographies of famous explorers such as Christopher Columbus, Ferdinand Magellan, and James Cook, Chapter 5 (History).

   ....

3. Badgers, Chapter 5 (Science).

   ....

4. Manners, Chapter 6 (Life Skills).

   ....

5. Squirrels, Chapter 6 (Science).

   ....

6. Armor, Chapter 6 (History).

   ....

7. Blacksmithing, Chapter 6 (History).

   ....

8. Last names, Chapter 6 (History).

   ....

9. Chronometer, Chapter 6 (Science).

   ....

10. History of lamps, Chapter 7 (History).

    ....

Suggested Videos:

Suggested Field Trips:

1. Visit a modern day blacksmith, Chapter 6.

2. Learn how to use a bow and arrow and go to an archery range, Chapter 8. Your local 4-H, YMCA, or recreation center may have an archery club and/or information. Also you can contact your local sporting goods store.

Suggested Memorization:

Notes:

BADGER WORKSHEET

FOR USE WITH CHAPTER 5

1) Description: _____

_____

_____

_____

2) Life Span: _____

3) Diet: _____

_____

_____

Draw a Picture

4) Enemies: _____

_____

5) Habitat: _____

_____

_____

6) Behavior: _____

_____

_____

_____

Draw a Track

Favorite Fact: _____

_____

_____

_____

_____

_____

Words to Learn:

burrowing

nocturnal

setts

Kingdom > Phylum > Class > Order > Family > Genus
Animalia > Chordata > Mamalia > Carnivoia > Mustelidae > Taxidea

Squirrel Worksheet

For use with Chapter 6

1) Description: _____

_____

_____

_____

2) Life Span: _____

3) Diet: _____

_____

_____

4) Enemies: _____

_____

5) Habitat: _____

_____

_____

6) Behavior: _____

_____

_____

_____

Draw a Picture

Draw a Track

Favorite Fact: _____

_____

_____

_____

_____

_____

_____

Words to Learn:

lichen

fungi

predator

Kingdom > Phylum > Class > Order > Family > Genus

Animalia > Chordata > Mammalia > Rodentia > Sciuridae > Genus and Species Vary

Chapter 5

Vocabulary Words:

usurp

theorbo

pother

treason

truffle

Vocabulary:

🗝 **Look up the words in a dictionary before you read the chapter and write them, along with a definition, in your vocabulary notebook.**

✏ Using your vocabulary words, fill in the blanks. The answers may be found in the section entitled Answer Appendix.

1. The pigs were extremely good at finding the _____ .

2. A _____ is much too complicated an instrument for me to learn to play.

3. The regent's attempt to _____ the throne was thwarted by the prince's supporters.

4. The supporters of the regent were then tried for _____ .

5. We didn't find out what all the _____ was about.

🗝 What would you study if you were learning *Cosmography*, *Rhetoric*, *Heraldry*, *Versification*, *Alchemy*, *Physic*, and *Astronomy*?

✏ Add these words to your vocabulary notebook.

Destrier is Old French for *war-horse*.

Read Chapter 5 of *Prince Caspian*.

✴ Assignments:

Reading Comprehension	1. Answer the following questions orally: • What subject did Caspian not study? Why not? • Why was the country of Narnia unhappy? • What event put Caspian's life in danger? • What two gifts did Cornelius give Caspian? • Where was Caspian to go? Why was he to go alone? • What made Caspian believe even more in Aslan? • Caspian knew his captors disliked the king. Was it wise to tell his captors the king wanted to kill him?
History	2. Read about the history of sea navigation. Your encyclopedia should give some general information. How is navigating different now from how it was in the time of Columbus or Magellan?

Digging Deeper: If you are interested in some of the discoveries and innovations of navigation, you could read *Carry On, Mr. Bowditch* by Jean Lee Latham. It is a true story written for young people. You could also read the biographies of famous explorers such as Christopher Columbus, Ferdinand Magellan, and James Cook.

---

3. Learn to play the musical instrument called a recorder.

Music

---

4. Draw a picture of Caspian as he wakes up surrounded by the Badger and the two Dwarfs.

Art

---

5. In *The Magician's Nephew* when Aslan made some of the animals in the newly created Narnia able to talk, he gave them a warning. What warning from Aslan had not been heeded by the beasts that were now no different from the poor dumb, witless creatures you would find in any other country?

Critical Thinking

---

6. Use your concordance to look up what the Bible says about flatterers and flattery.

Bible

---

7. How did the Badger describe characteristics of humans and dwarfs? Contrast these characteristics with those of God.

Bible

---

8. Read about badgers.

Science

What personality characteristics does a badger have? Fill out the Badger Worksheet. It may be found after this unit's Planning Guide.

Vocabulary:

☞ **Look up the words in a dictionary before you read the chapter and write them, along with a definition, in your vocabulary notebook.**

smithy	descendant	gorge
glade	hedgerow	glen
rabble	rooks	rapier
foxglove	contempt	subterranean
ravine	martial	tongs
bellows	anvil	

✎ Using your vocabulary words, fill in the blanks. The answers may befound in the section entitled Answer Appendix.

1. I do not want to cross this _____ on that flimsy rope bridge.

2. The musketeer drew his _____ and prepared to defend his honor.

3. The deer watched and sniffed for danger before entering the _____ to graze.

4. The king surrounded himself with his bodyguards before confronting the unruly _____ .

5. He was careful to conceal his _____ for them.

6. A tiny stream ran through the bottom of the _____ .

7. An annual celebration of the anniversary of the pioneer's arrival in Oregon was still a tradition among his _____ generations after his death.

8. _____ comes from two Latin words meaning "under" and "earth."

9. The _____ music helped boost the morale of the troops.

10. She had always wondered what the yard on the other side of the _____ looked like.

11. Every year the _____ return to nest in the trees in the city park.

12. A picturesque waterfall plummets down the _____ .

13. Digitalis is made from _____ .

14. The boys loved to go to the _____ and watch the blacksmith work.

15. My father needed his _____ to turn the meat on the grill.

16. Sparks flew as the blacksmith hit his iron on the _____ .

17. The _____ fanned the flame.

A **wold** is an unforested rolling plain but it comes from an Old English word, *weald*, that means forest.

Look up *subterranean* in your dictionary. What are the two Latin words from which subterranean is formed? See Answer Appendix.

Read Chapter 6 of *Prince Caspian*.

☀ Assignments:

---

1. Answer the following questions orally: Reading
   • In order to be polite, what did Caspian do? What did it cost him?   Comprehension
   • How did Caspian know seeing the Fauns was not a dream?

---

2. Caspian unknowingly was discourteous toward the squirrel. Trufflehunter   Bible
   was kind enough to softly rebuke Caspian. Proverbs 9:7–9 reads:

   He that reproveth a scorner getteth to himself shame: and he that
   rebuketh a wicked man getteth himself a blot. Reprove not a
   scorner, lest he hate thee: rebuke a wise man, and he will love thee.
   Give instruction to a wise man, and he will be yet wiser: teach a just
   man, and he will increase in learning.

   Trufflehunter must have already sensed Caspian was not a scorner.

   How would you know a scorner?

   Proverbs 27:5–6 says, "Open rebuke is better than secret love. Faithful are
   the wounds of a friend; but the kisses of an enemy are deceitful." Also
   read Proverbs 28:23. Proverbs 13:18–20 reads:

   Poverty and shame shall be to him that refuseth instruction: but he
   that regardeth reproof shall be honoured. The desire accomplished is
   sweet to the soul: but it is abomination to fools to depart from evil.
   He that walketh with wise men shall be wise: but a companion of
   fools shall be destroyed.

   Thank someone for caring enough to rebuke you.

---

3. Would it be bad manners to look where someone kept their money or   Bible
   jewelry? I Thessalonians 5:22–23 says:

   Abstain from all appearance of evil. And the very God of peace
   sanctify you wholly; and I pray God your whole spirit and soul and

body be preserved blameless unto the coming of our Lord Jesus Christ.

How could watching where someone kept their money or jewelry appear evil?

Life Skills		4. Each day until the end of this unit, read and discuss a book which will improve your manners.

Science		5. Read about squirrels.
		Write about what you have read and complete the Squirrel Worksheet which may be found after this unit's Planning Guide.

History/ English		6. Learn about armor.
		Write the definitions of *greaves*, *gauntlet*, *solleret*, *cuirass*, and *hauberk* in your vocabulary notebook.

Literature/ Bible		7. Read "The Village Blacksmith" by Henry Wadsworth Longfellow in the Recommended Reading Appendix.
		Define *sinew*, *brawny*, *sexton*, *repose*, and *wrought*. Add the definitions to your vocabulary notebook.
		What did Longfellow mean by our fortunes being wrought in a forge and our deeds and thoughts shaped on an anvil?
		Read I Corinthians 3:13–15; I Peter 1:7; and Revelation 3:18.

In the King James translation of the Bible, John 3:21 says, "But he who practices the truth comes to the light, that his deeds may be manifested as having been wrought in God." The word that is translated **wrought** here is from a word meaning, to toil. We should not think that doing what God wants us to do is going to be easy.

History		8. Read about the art and history of blacksmithing.
		Visit a modern-day blacksmith. What types of projects does he work on? What does he view as the hardest part of his work? What does he enjoy the most?

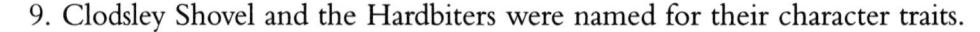

History		9. Clodsley Shovel and the Hardbiters were named for their character traits.
		Your encyclopedia should have an article on names. Where did your last name come from? When did last names come into use and what were some of their sources?
		Look in your telephone book. Try to find some last names that are colors, occupations, or character traits.

10. The mole's name, Clodsley Shovel, was a play on Admiral Sir Cloudsley Shovel's name. He was a British naval hero. The critical importance of determining longitude was tragically brought to focus in 1707 when a fleet commanded by Shovel ran into the Scilly Islands. Four ships and 2,000 men, including Sir Cloudsley, were lost. The British Crown responded by offering £20,000 (about 2 million dollars in today's money) for a chronometer good enough to determine longitude with an accuracy of 30 miles.

History/
Science

What is a chronometer and how does it work?

11. Discuss the following questions:
   • From what you know of the history of Narnia, why would Nikabrik say the White Witch was not an enemy of the dwarfs?
   • Trumpkin and Trufflehunter seem to be on the side of good and Nikabrik leans toward the bad. Discuss some things that might have been different if it had been two against one the other way.
   • Nikabrik wanted to get rid of the Telmarines. He did not care whether this was accomplished by the White Witch or Aslan. Name some Bible characters who decided not to follow God in order to have their own way. What were some of the consequences? Did the end justify the means? See Answer Appendix. Answers may vary.

Critical
Thinking

Chapter 7

Vocabulary:

Look up the words in a dictionary before you read the chapter and write them, along with a definition, in your vocabulary notebook.

Using your vocabulary words, fill in the blanks. The answers may be found in the section entitled Answer Appendix.

1. The opposing army sent a _____ to parley.

2. A wise person doesn't venture into a lion's _____ .

3. The watchmen are on alert because they expect a _____ from the people in the besieged city tonight.

4. We will _____ here until daylight.

Consort comes from two Latin words that mean together and fate. If you are someone's consort (noun) or consort (verb) with someone, your fates are likely to be the same.

**Vocabulary
Words:**

contingent

lair

sortie

bivouac

Read Chapter 7 of *Prince Caspian*.

Assignments:

Reading Comprehension	🗝	1. Answer the following questions orally: • What is Aslan's How? • From what three places did Cornelius think help might arrive? • Who did they think would come to help them?
Art/ History	🗝 ✋	2. Find out about the different ways people have made lamps over the years. With clay, make a lamp such as Caspian might have used in Aslan's How. See Activity Appendix for a recipe for making clay.
Critical Thinking	🗝	3. Discuss the following questions: • What do you think Aslan's How was originally? What do you think the writing is about? • Trumpkin knew the difference between giving advice and taking orders. What is the difference?

>─┼─◆>─○─<◆─┼─<

Vocabulary Words:

scanty

seneschal

Jinn

offense

jibe

grueling

pelt

pompous

Vocabulary:

🗝 **Look up the words in a dictionary before you read the chapter and write them, along with a definition, in your vocabulary notebook.**

 Using your vocabulary words, fill in the blanks. The answers may be found in the section entitled Answer Appendix.

1. The Lord entrusted all of the details of the running of his household to his _____ .

2. The superstitious people would not go into the desert for fear of the _____ that they imagined lived there.

3. I did not mean to cause _____ by that thoughtless comment.

4. It will be a long time before she will forget that nasty _____ .

5. They _____ the beaver with large stones hoping to kill him and take his _____ .

6. His _____ attitude repelled everyone with whom he came in contact.

7. No one could imagine how he had survived the _____ journey.

8. My _____ breakfast left me ravenous before lunchtime.

Read Chapter 8 of *Prince Caspian.*

☀ Assignments:

1.	Discuss the following questions: • Why did Susan not relish the idea of hitting the apple? • For what does D.L.F. stand?	Reading Comprehension
2.	If you have never tried archery, find a place where you can take a lesson, perhaps at your local 4-H, YMCA, or recreation center.	Field Trip
3.	Read some of the stories from *Arabian Nights.* What is a Jinn?	Literature
4.	Now that you know how the children ended up in Narnia again, explain why their entry was different from before—painful with a sense of being pulled.	Critical Thinking
5.	Trumpkin did not believe the four children could be of much help. What four things did the children do which convinced him? Name some people in the Bible who needed to be convinced. What did God do to convince them? See Answer Appendix.	Bible

>─◆─○─◆─<

⧗ Planning Guide – Chapters 9-12

Gather These Items:

1. Picture book of trees, Chapter 9.

2. Compass, Chapter 9.

3. Bear meat, Chapter 10.

Suggested Information to Gather:

Encyclopedia or books about:

1. Trees, Chapter 9 (Science/Art).

....

2. Rowing, Chapter 9 (Life Skills).

....

3. Use of a compass, Chapter 9 (Life Skills).

....

4. Bears, Chapter 9 (Science and Health/Safety).

....

5. Elements of giving a demonstration speech, Chapter 9 (Life Skills).

....

6. Eye, optical illusions, Chapter 10 (Science).

....

Suggested Videos:

1. *Grand Canyon Catastrophe: New Evidence of the Genesis Flood*, Chapter 9. Borrow from a friend, church library, or see Resource Appendix.

Suggested Field Trips:

1. Rowing, Chapter 9.

Suggested Memorization:

1. Joshua 24:15, Chapter 10.

2. Psalm 121, Chapter 11.

3. Psalm 40:1, Chapter 11.

Notes:

BEAR WORKSHEET

FOR USE WITH CHAPTER 9

1) Description: _____

_____

_____

_____

2) Life Span: _____

3) Diet: _____

_____

_____

_____

Draw a Picture

4) Enemies: _____

_____

5) Habitat: _____

_____

_____

6) Behavior: _____

_____

_____

_____

Draw a Track

Favorite Fact: _____

_____

_____

Words to Learn:

omnivore

hibernate

cub

sow

_____

_____

Kingdom > Phylum > Class > Order > Family

Animalia > Chordata > Mamalia > Omnivoia > Ursidae

Study Guide – Chapters 9-12

Chapter 9

Vocabulary Words:

twilight

rueful

bracken

precipice

Vocabulary:

Look up the words in a dictionary before you read the chapter and write them, along with a definition, in yourvocabulary notebook.

Using your vocabulary words, fill in the blanks. The answers may befound in the section entitled Answer Appendix.

1. Walking in the woods was made difficult by the thick growth of _____ .

2. As _____ fell, we began to hurry because we had to be home before dark.

3. I could tell by his _____ expression he would still be trying to forgive himself long after I had forgotten the incident.

4. If you get too near the _____ , we may not be able to keep you from falling.

Read Chapter 9 of *Prince Caspian*.

☀ Assignments:

Reading Comprehension		1. Answer the following questions orally: • As the children tired from rowing, what did they wonder? • How did Lucy attempt to sleep? • Why did Lucy know the stars in Narnia better than the ones in England? • What is "pardonable sharpness"? • What did Edmund think was the worst of girls? • Why did Edmund want to go up the hill? Why did Susan want to go down?
Science/ Art		2. Find a good picture book of trees. Look at pictures of silver birch, oak, mountain ash, willow, beech, elm, holly, and rowan trees.
		Choose at least two of these types of trees and draw them as you think they would look as tree people.

3. Find out something about the sport of rowing.

   Try to find a place where you can learn to canoe or row.

Life Skills

4. Find out about land navigation and try some exercises in finding your way by compass.

Life Skills

5. Trumpkin asserted the landmarks could have changed in the last several hundred years. Watch *Grand Canyon Catastrophe: New Evidence of the Genesis Flood*. Recorded on location, this video explores the "breached dam" theory that catastrophic drainage of vast post-floodlakes may have carved the Grand Canyon rapidly and recently. Proof that similar canyons were formed rapidly at Mount Saint Helens and Grand Coulee challenges conventional geology. Also, vivid images bring alive Native American legends of catastrophic floods. Borrow the video from a friend or your church library. See the Resource Appendix if you are interested in purchasing it.

Science

6. In this chapter, the children encountered a wild bear. Read about what you should do if you encounter a bear. See Recommended Reading Appendix.

Health/
Safety

7. Give a speech or demonstration on Bear Safety to a younger sibling or friend.

Life Skills

8. Learn more about bears.

   Fill in the Bear Worksheet. It may be found after this unit's Planning Guide.

Science

Chapter 10

Vocabulary Word:	**Vocabulary:**
tremulous	⚷ **Look up this word in a dictionary before you read the chapter and write it, along with a definition, in your vocabulary notebook.**
	✎ Skim the chapter for *tremulous*. Write at least one sentence from this chapter containing the word under its dictionary definition. Follow each sentence with a citation.

Read Chapter 10 of *Prince Caspian*.

☀ Assignments:

Science	📖	1. Study the human eye, then read about optical illusions and what causes them.
Cooking	✋	2. Try cooking meat over an open fire. If possible, try bear meat.
Critical Thinking	🚩	3. Discuss the following questions: • What did Aslan mean when he said Lucy would find him bigger every year that she grew? • Why did Aslan not wake up all the children himself and tell them to follow him? • Why do you think Lucy is the one who keeps seeing Aslan before anyone else can?
Bible	🚩	4. How did Lucy come to realize she had been wrong not to follow Aslan? Did he accuse her?
	🦁	Read and memorize Joshua 24:15.

✦◦○◦◦✦

Vocabulary:

Vocabulary Words:

grousing

rum

blown (adj.)

tinker

vixen

grape (shot)

☞🔑 **Look up the words in a dictionary before you read the chapter and write them, along with a definition, in your vocabulary notebook.**

✐ Using your vocabulary words, fill in the blanks. The answers may be found in the section entitled Answer Appendix.

1. Carrying a chicken in her mouth, the _____ hurried home to her kits.

2. Please take this pan to the _____ to see if he can mend it.

3. Stop _____ and start doing your share of the work.

4. By the time we got to the top of the hill I was completely

   _____ .

5. Injuries were many and severe when the soldiers fired the _____ into the crowd.

6. We would have been successful if it hadn't been for the _____ turn of events.

Read Chapter 11 of *Prince Caspian*.

☀ Assignments:

1. When Lucy fixed her eyes on Aslan, she forgot all the things she would have liked to say to Susan. Compare this to the statement in *The Magician's Nephew* on page 110 that, when you saw the Singer, you forgot everything else.

   📖 Read these verses about keeping our eyes fixed on Jesus: Hebrews 12:1–2; Psalm 25:15; Psalm 121; and Psalm 141:8.

   🦁 Memorize Psalm 121.

   Bible

2. Aslan told Susan she had listened to her fears. What happens when we listen to our fears instead of keeping our eyes on Jesus?

   📖 Read Matthew 14:22–33, 25:14–30, and 26:69–75. What has God said about fear? See II Timothy 1:7 and I John 4:18.

   Bible

Critical Thinking		3. Discuss the following questions:

3. Discuss the following questions:
- Edmund fully intended to back Lucy up, but he was annoyed at being awakened and decided to do everything as sulkily as possible. Have you ever behaved like this? Did it make you feel better? How did it make others feel? Despite Edmund's poor attitude, what did Aslan tell him?
- What do you think the reasons were for the order in which Aslan became visible to each of the children?
- At the end of the chapter nothing has yet been done to defeat the enemy. Why is everyone celebrating?

Games

4. Play *Tig*, *Blind Man's Bluff*, and *Hunt the Slipper*. See Activity Appendix for directions.

English

5. How did C.S. Lewis describe a good grape? Describe a different piece of fruit.

Bible

6. It was exciting when Trumpkin heard the voice of Aslan. Many have been converted to Christianity as a result of Lewis' writings. Lewis claimed the "the salvation of a single soul is more important than the production or preservation of all the epics and tragedies in the world" (quoted in *The Essential C.S. Lewis* edited by Lyle W. Dorsett, New York: Macmillan Publishing, 1988, 8). "To him, Christianity is more than true, it explains all truth" (Dorsett 17).

Tell about a time someone you know came to know the Lord.

Memorize Psalm 40:1.

Vocabulary:

Look up the words in a dictionary before you read the chapter and write them, along with a definition, in your vocabulary notebook.

Write sentences using each of your vocabulary words.

Read Chapter 12 of *Prince Caspian*.

☀ Assignments:

Vocabulary Words:

dotard

rheumatics

cantrips

practical

1. Go back to page 79 of *The Magician's Nephew* where Lewis said witches are terribly practical. What did he mean? Did he mean it was a good thing?

   Look up the meaning of *practical*. Nikabrik said a Witch who ruled one hundred years was something practical. In the case to which Nikabrik was referring, was it a good thing? In what ways is being practical a good thing?

Critical Thinking

2. How does God feel about witches?

   Read Leviticus 19:31, 20:6, 27; Deuteronomy 18:14; I Samuel 28; and I Chronicles 10:13–14.

Bible

3. Nikabrik said Aslan just fades out of the stories and there is no proof he came back to life after the Witch killed him. Why did Aslan fade out of the stories?

   Read in the Gospels about the things Jesus did after His resurrection: Matthew 28; Mark 16; Luke 24; John 20; and Acts 1:1–11. Why did He go away? Read John 16:7–11.

Bible

4. Nikabrik had gone sour inside from long suffering and hating. Where did his hate come from? What is suffering supposed to do for us?

   To find out, read James 1:3, 5:10–11, and II Peter 1:5–7.

Bible

Critical
Thinking   5. Nikabrik said no one really knew the truth about the ancient days in Narnia. Why did no one know the truth? Who was responsible for their ignorance? How did ancient cultures pass on history to their children?

What did Nikabrik mean when he said, "When your sword breaks, you draw your dagger"?

>-I-◆>-0-◆-I-<

⧗ PLANNING GUIDE – CHAPTERS 13-15

Gather These Items:

1. *Perelandra* by C.S. Lewis, Chapter 13. Older students only.

2. *Till We Have Faces* by C.S. Lewis, ISBN 0-15-690436-5, Chapter 13. Older students only.

3. *The Odyssey* by Homer or *Tanglewood Tales* by Nathaniel Hawthorne or any book that has the story of "Circe's Palace," Chapter 14. These are available online. See Resource Appendix.

4. Pictures of fruit, Chapter 15.

5. *The Narnia Cookbook* or Activity Apendix for recipes and ingredients for oatcakes, Chapter 15.

6. Other food items: Your choice of peaches, pomegranates, nectarines, pears, grapes, strawberries, and raspberries, Chapter 15.

7. Butcher paper or shoeboxes, Chapter 15.

8. Feast fare for the tree people, Chapter 15.

Suggested Information to Gather:

Encyclopedia or books about:

1. Fencing, Chapter 13 (Life Skills).

   ....

2. Soil, Chapter 15 (Science).
   • See <http://school.discovery.com/schooladventures/soil/name_soil.html>.

   ....

3. Edible flowers, Chapter 15 (Cooking).

   ....

Suggested Videos:

1. Favorite movie with a fencing duel, Chapter 13.

Suggested Field Trips:

1. Collect different soil types, Chapter 15.

Suggested Memorization:

Notes:

Vocabulary:

🔑 **Look up the words in a dictionary before you read the chapter and write them, along with a definition, in your vocabulary notebook.**

✏️ Using your vocabulary words, fill in the blanks. The answers may be found in the section entitled Answer Appendix.

1. The prince spent his life attempting to _____ the death of his father.

2. Hoping to _____ , the besieged settlers waved the white flag.

3. The _____ Roman legions were feared throughout the world.

4. I will not allow you children to _____ to me.

5. I would never allow that _____ to accompany us on our expedition.

6. How could you have the _____ to ask that rude question?

7. The _____ was sent ahead to _____ the return of the scouting party.

8. The water was _____ by the shadows of the overhanging branches.

9. The king knew it would be a mistake to _____ war against his powerful neighbors to the north.

10. Peter said he had been made High King by the _____ of Aslan.

Vocabulary Words:

herald

dictate

effrontery

avenge

prescription

levy

parley

fell

dappled

dastard

Figuring out the meaning of a word by looking at how the word is used and from the other words around it is learning from the **context**. By looking at the context, what do you think *monomachy* and *effusion* (page 177) mean?

Read Chapter 13 of *Prince Caspian*.

☀ Assignments:

Reading Comprehension	1. Answer the following questions orally: • What is a scholar never without? • What two reasons made Peter choose the giant to carry the message to Miraz? What does this tell you about Peter's character? • What did Miraz do (or not do) which encouraged Glozelle and Sopespian to be unfaithful? • Who were to be the marshals of the lists? What is their responsibility? • Why did no one ever laugh at a Centaur? • Why did Glozelle and Sopespian urge Miraz not to fight Peter?

Bible

2. What did Peter mean by "single combat"?

 Read the story of David and Goliath, I Samuel 17. Then read Romans 5:12–21. Jesus is our champion in single combat.

Two books by C.S. Lewis which also have single combat are *Perelandra*, Chapter 12, and *Till We Have Faces*, Part I, Chapter 19. How do these compare with Peter's combat?

English

3. Copy Peter's letter to Miraz.

Write a letter to a friend or relative using an introduction and greeting as Peter did.

English

4. Write a paragraph describing Centaurs.

Life Skills

5. Learn what you can about fencing and the terms used in the sport.

Watch a fencing match or your favorite movie with a fencing duel.

>—+—◆—O—◆—+—<

Vocabulary:

Vocabulary Word:

☞ **Look up this word in a dictionary before you read the chapter and write it, along with a definition, in your vocabulary notebook.**

tussock

✎ Skim the chapter for *tussock*. Write at least one sentence from this chapter containing the word under its dictionary definition. Follow each sentence with a citation.

Read Chapter 14 of *Prince Caspian*.

☀ Assignments:

1. Answer the following questions orally:
   - What happened to the bridge?
   - What type of history was taught in Narnia during Miraz's rule?
   - Lewis compared the waiting before the duel to the moment before the pistol goes off at an important race. Have you experienced an event that helped you understand this feeling? Describe it.

Reading Comprehension

2. Draw a picture of the revelers as they looked when they met Miraz's army at the river.

Art

3. Look up the meaning of the words *horrible* and *magnificent*.

How can something be both horrible and magnificent? Can you think of other examples?

English

4. In this chapter a group of boys who were very much like pigs are said to have turned into pigs. The story of "Circe's Palace" is another instance in literature in which men turned into pigs because of the way they behaved.

Read "Circe's Palace" in Nathaniel Hawthorn's *Tanglewood Tales* or in Homer's *Odyssey*, Book X.

English

5. Why do you think Lewis told the story of the duel through the eyes of the other characters?

In literature **point of view** refers to the way a story is presented. A story told in the **first person** is written as though the narrator is a character in the story and can only tell what he sees, hears, and thinks.

English

In **third person limited**, the narrator tells the story from the point of view of a single character. In **third person omniscient**, the narrator knows what each character is thinking and feeling.

Retell the story of the duel aloud, then rewrite it in third person omniscient.

Critical
Thinking

6. All of the girls in the Narnian school were dressed in uncomfortable clothing and had their hair done tightly. After Gwendolen met Aslan, the first thing the Maenads did was to help her take off some of her uncomfortable and unnecessary clothes.

Do you think this might represent something besides merely undressing?

>—+‹›—0—‹›+‹

Vocabulary:

**Look up the words in a dictionary before you read the chapter and write them, along with a definition, in your vocabulary notebook.**

✎ Using your vocabulary words, fill in the blanks. The answers may be found in the section entitled Answer Appendix.

1. At the critical moment in the battle, the poltroon fled from the

    _____ .

2. The _____ cherubs were too ornate for my taste.

3. The jester was mistaken when he thought he could play a trick on the
    _____ serving maid.

4. The dwarf had trouble drinking from the _____ .

5. How could I help feeling sorry for the _____ little boy?

6. The fertile _____ was an excellent soil in which to plant flowers.

Vocabulary Words:

woebegone

mazer

canny

gilt

fray

loam

Read Chapter 15 of *Prince Caspian*.

☀ Assignments:

1. Answer the following questions orally:
   • What were the new conditions under which anyone who chose might stay in Narnia?
   • Were they really new?
   • Why do you think Lewis added the last line, which was spoken by Edmund?

Reading Comprehension

2. Aslan's mane outshone them all.

   Read these verses about the brightness of Jesus: Mark 9:3 (also recorded in Matthew 17:2 and Luke 9:29); Revelation 1:16 and 21:23.

Bible

3. Reread the first sentence of Chapter 15. What will everyone do when Jesus returns? Read Philippians 2:5–11.

Bible

Cooking/ Art		4. Read the list of fruits on page 211. Try any you have never tasted.
		Draw what you think cataracts of fruit would look like or cut pictures of fruit out of magazines and make a "cataract of fruit" collage.
		In *The Narnia Cookbook* on page 34 there is a recipe for the oatcakes that were served with the fruit. Use this recipe or one of the ones in the Activity Appendix to make oatcakes.

Critical Thinking		5. Can you explain why being descended from Adam and Eve is both honor and shame?
		Why would not having believed in lions make the Telmarines' fear greater?

Science		6. What is the difference between soil and dirt? Name some of the plants and animals that live in soil and their purpose in soil. What is silt? Clay? Sand? Loam? What breaks down bedrock?

This activity reinforces the order in which soil is formed. Students will demonstrate knowledge of what constitutes a soil profile by creating either a mural on butcher paper or stacked dioramas depicting the levels of soil. You will need five different colored strips of butcher paper or five shoeboxes if you are going to construct dioramas and cards with the names of the animals written on them. Students will need access to "The Dirt on Soil." See <http://school.discovery.com/schooladventures/soil/name_soil.html>.

Provide students with some time to read "The Dirt on Soil." Divide the learning area with butcher paper—one color for each level. Label each level: ground level, topsoil, subsoil, weathered parent material, and bedrock. Review that first came the bedrock, then parent material, and so on.

You might want to build your display by showing the bedrock layer, then attaching the parent material layer next, etc. Discuss key terms: *soil profile, decomposers, humus, organic matter,* and *parent material.* Have the students describe what a soil profile is and then direct them that they will recreate the soil profile they just studied in poster (or diorama) form. Keep your mural (or diorama) on display. It will be used to review later.

Have students review their notes and plan what needs to go into each layer. Once they have a plan, allow them to swing into action building or drawing their replica. Check that everyone has the correct information.

Investigate Soil in your Backyard:

Contact your local U.S. Geological Survey office (<http://search.usgs.gov/query.html>) to determine where in your area you can find roadside cutouts that expose loamy, sandy, and clay soils. Take a family outing to take pictures of soil or get samples.

As they read through "Name That Soil," require the students to write in their own words descriptions of the three types of soil described.

Name That Soil:

Gravel: larger than 2 mm; feels coarse

Sand: 2 to 0.05 mm; feels gritty

Silt: 0.05 to 0.002 mm; feels like flour

Clay: smaller than 0.002 mm; feels sticky when wet

Every soil type is a mixture of sand, silt, clay, and organic matter.

Samples are compared with the notes from "Name That Soil." Challenge the students to order the samples to match the layers in the cutout's soil profile. Have the students compare the samples with the soil in their neighborhood or nearby parks.

At the next session, discuss the findings. Place on the map where the soil was loamy, sandy, or clay. If you do not have a map, try to draw a schematic of the area that your school draws from. Discuss if the soil samples were similar or different. Could there be a reason for this (sandy soil means that sandstone was the bedrock that created the soil, etc.)? The local U.S.G.S. might be able to provide more interpretation to the findings.

---

7. Pretend you are tree people. Make loam, somerset, chalky soil, finest gravels, and silver sand. Decorate with edible flowers. See Activity Appendix for recipes.

Cooking

---

8. Review the list of Seven Deadly Sins found in *Further Up and Further In*, Chapter 15 of *The Magician's Nephew*.

Literature/ Bible

Of the remaining four sins, which sin did Miraz display in *Prince Caspian*? Give examples of Miraz demonstrating this deadly sin. See answer in the Answer Appendix.

---

9. Complete the crossword puzzle for *Prince Caspian*. Answers may be found in the Answer Appendix.

Vocabulary

>─◆─○─◆─<

Complete any unfinished assignments prior to going on to *The Voyage of the* Dawn Treader.

Prince Caspian Crossword Puzzle

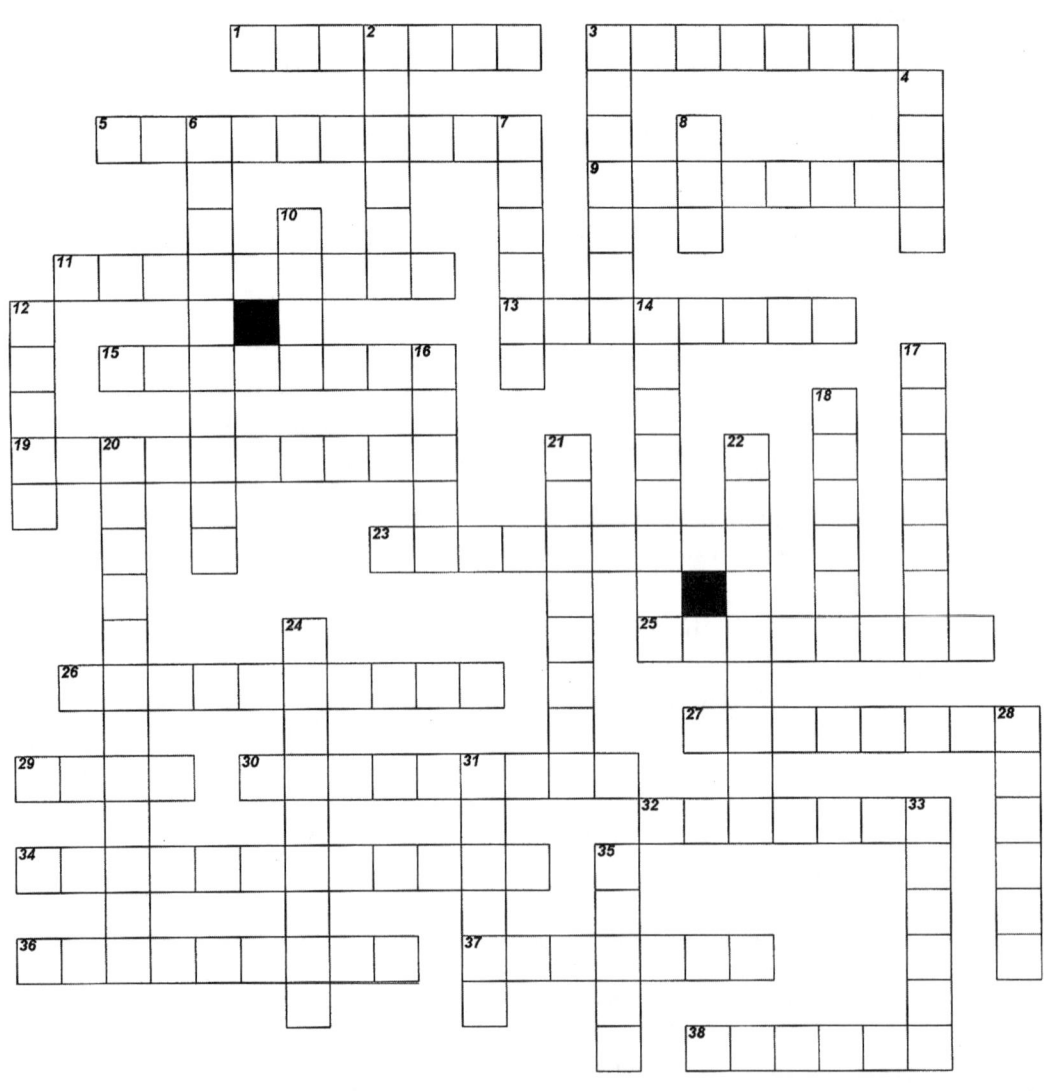

ACROSS

1 turgid

3 decree

5 pains caused
by arthritis

9 fungal delicacies
hunted with pigs

11 royal flatterers

13 line of shrubs

15 scorn

19 offspring

23 cliff

25 hard

26 headland

27 source of the
drug digitalis

29 affray

30 rain barrel

32 resembles laced
half-boots

34 medical recipe

36 dependent

37 wreath

38 discuss the
terms of

DOWN

2 agitate

3 coward

4 essence

6 shameless
boldness

7 blacksmith's
workshop

8 liquor

10 fit

12 forest clearing

14 grumbling

16 instructor

17 coarse fern

18 repentant

20 under the earth

21 dusk

22 shaking

24 dwelt

28 untrue

31 clasp

33 scarce

35 burst

THE VOYAGE OF THE DAWN TREADER

P. Martirosian
1·2002

⌛ PLANNING GUIDE – CHAPTERS 1-4

Gather These Items:

1. *The Voyage of the Dawn Treader* by C.S. Lewis.

2. *Surprised by Joy: The Shape of My Early Life* by C.S. Lewis, Chapter 1.

3. Paint and paper, Chapter 1.

Suggested Information to Gather:

Encyclopedia or books about:

1. Limericks, Chapter 1 (English).

   ....

2. Isle of Wight, Chapter 1 (Geography).

   ....

3. Ships, Chapter 1 (History).
   - *Ship* by David MacAuley, Houghton Mifflin, ISBN 0395524393 (Reading level: ages 9–12).
   - *Eyewitness: Boat* by Eric Kentley, James Stevenson (Illustrator), Tina Chambers (Illustrator), Jim Stevenson (Photographer), D.K. Publishing, ISBN 078945758X.
   - *Boats, Ships, Submarines, and Other Floating Machines (How Things Work)* by Ian S. Graham, Kingfisher Books, 1993, ISBN 1856978672 (Reading level: ages 9–12).

   ....

4. Water safety, Chapter 1 (Health/Safety).

   ....

5. The *Queen Mary*, Chapter 2 (History).

   ....

6. Slavery, Chapter 4 (History).

   ....

Suggested Videos:

    1. Watch a movie depicting the slave trade, Chapter 4.

Suggested Field Trips:

    1. Visit the *Queen Mary* or other large ship, Chapter 2.

Suggested Memorization:

    1. Memorize the parts of a ship, Chapter 1.

Notes:

🐾 LIMERICK WORKSHEET/CHAPTER 1

Try this:

Write down the names of five or six places, perhaps places you have lived
or faraway places you know a little about. Choose one that seems easiest to
rhyme. Do a little experimenting. There are not many words that rhyme with
Narnia, which is what made it difficult for Eustace. For example, it would be
easier to think of words that rhyme with New York (cork, fork, pork, stork)
or Montana (banana, bandana).

_____

_____

_____

Now try filling in the blanks:

There once was a _____ from _____ ,

Who couldn't learn how to _____ .

_____ jumped in a _____ ,

quickly realized _____ ,

That silly _____ from _____ .

Next try writing a limerick about one of your pets or an animal you have
known:

There once was a _____named _____ ,

Who always _____ .

When s/he _____ ,

S/he _____ ,

That _____ named _____ .

Read your limericks aloud. Are the rhyme pattern and meter correct?

🐾 WORKSHEET/CHAPTER 2

What Became of the Seven Lost Lords

Lord Revilian	
Lord Bern	
Lord Argoz	
Lord Mavramorn	
Lord Octesian	
Lord Restimar	
Lord Rhoop	

STUDY GUIDE – CHAPTERS 1-4

Vocabulary:

Vocabulary Words:

🗝 **Look up the words in a dictionary before you read the chapter and write them, along with a definition, in your vocabulary notebook.**

✏ Using your vocabulary words, fill in the blanks. The answers may be found in the section entitled Answer Appendix.

1. I thought it was merely flattery when she said my haircut was _____ .

2. His _____ reply seemed rude.

3. The goldfish couldn't live in the _____ water.

4. Aunt Betty was a strict _____ .

5. Many people considered the man old-fashioned, but I appreciated his _____ manner.

6. Some poets use _____ rather than strict rhyme.

7. She refused to read anything that contained any hint of _____ .

8. Some of our slang is considered _____ only because it originated with the common people.

9. He loved to stand in the _____ of the boat and feel the spray of the waves on his face.

10. During the rain the sailor went into the _____ .

11. One must know left and right to know the _____ and _____ of a ship.

teetotaler

assonance

briny

vulgar

curt

courtly

prow

sentiment

exquisite

port

starboard

poop

Read Chapter 1 of *The Voyage of the* Dawn Treader.

☀ **Assignments:**

Critical Thinking	🔖	1. Why would C.S. Lewis want King Arthur to come back to Britain?

English		2. C.S. Lewis was tutored as a young man, just as Peter was tutored by Professor Kirke. Lewis' tutor was Mr. Kirkpatrick, sometimes called, "Kirk" or "The Great Knock."
	📖	You may read about him in *Surprised by Joy: The Shape of My Early Life*, Chapter 9.

Art	✋	3. Paint the picture Edmund and Lucy were looking at when they fell into Narnia.

English	🗝	4. Why did Lucy object to Eustace's limerick? A **limerick** is a short, humorous poem that conforms to a prescribed structure. A proper limerick consists of five lines. The first two lines contain three beats, that is, three stressed syllables; there are two unstressed syllables between each. This is the **anapestic** meter. The next two lines contain two beats, and the last line has three. The rhyme pattern is **a–a–b–b–a**. Lines one and two rhyme, lines three and four rhyme, and the last line rhymes with the first two. *(Lucy objected to Eustace's limerick because the second line did not rhyme with the first.)*
	📖	Limericks are meant to be read aloud. Part of what makes limericks funny is their rhyme pattern and meter. A limerick has a sing-song rhythm and the last line is the punch line of the joke. See the limericks in the Recommended Reading Appendix and read them aloud. Do the Limerick Worksheet found after this unit's Planning Guide.

English	✏	5. Write a description of Eustace from what you know of him from the first chapter. Add to it as you read through the book. Record further information and changes. Lewis says Eustace was a puny little person. Do you think he means only his physical size?

Geography	🗝	6. Find the Isle of Wight on a map. How far is it from Cambridge?

History	🗝	7. Find a simple book on ships and learn the parts of a ship or go further and learn about different types of ships and the history of ship building.
	🦁	Memorize the parts of a ship.

8. What did Lucy do right in order to survive in the water?

Drowning is the SECOND leading cause of accidental deaths for persons 15–44 years of age. What is really surprising is that two-thirds of the people who drown never had any intention of being in the water!

Read about water safety. The four major causes of drowning are:
- Not wearing a life preserver
- Abuse of alcohol
- Lack of sufficient swimming skills
- Hypothermia

Your life may depend on a better understanding of cold water. Many suspected drowning victims actually die from cold exposure or hypothermia. This is a condition in which the body loses heat faster than it can produce it. Violent shivering develops which may give way to confusion and a loss of body movement.

If you fall in the water, in any season, hypothermia may occur. Many of our nation's open waters are mountain-fed and water temperatures, even in late summer, can run low enough to bring on hypothermia under certain conditions.

It is important to remember:

- Do not discard clothing. Clothing layers provide some warmth that may actually assist you in fighting hypothermia. This includes shoes and hats.
- Wear your life jacket! This helps hold heat into the core areas of your body and enables you to easily put yourself into the HELP (Heat Escape Lessening Posture) position. You get into the HELP position by drawing your limbs into your body; keep your armpits and groin areas protected from unnecessary exposure—a lot of heat can be lost from those areas, as well as the head.
- Other tips: Dress warmly with wool clothing.

Make a poster illustrating an important aspect of water safety.

Chapter 2

Vocabulary Words:

tribute

regent

galley

disposition

boatswain

cog

galleon

poltroon

supple

dromond

carrack

Vocabulary:

🗝 **Look up the words in a dictionary before you read the chapter and write them, along with a definition, in your vocabulary notebook.**

✏ Using your vocabulary words, fill in the blanks. The answers may be found in the section entitled Answer Appendix.

1. The conquered people were forced to pay _____ to their conquerors.

2. The Spanish _____ sank in a fierce storm and the treasure on board was lost forever.

3. As the young prince approached the age when he would be allowed to rule for himself, the _____ began to plot ways to get rid of him once and for all.

4. The young sailor had to quickly learn the names for every rope and sail on the _____ to which he had been assigned.

5. Eustace wanted to lodge a _____ against everyone on board the *Dawn Treader* because he couldn't have his own way.

6. These shoes are so stiff they hurt my feet. How can I make the leather more _____ ?

7. When the sailor didn't learn the ropes quickly enough to suit the _____ , the punishment was severe.

8. The huge three-masted _____ was impressive even from the great distance at which it first came into sight.

9. What is the difference between a galleon and a _____ ?

10. Of course, he had no choice but to fight the duel; the officer had called him a _____ .

11. In this chapter the word *galley* is used twice; once meaning a ship propelled by _____ , and once meaning a ship's _____ .

Read Chapter 2 of *The Voyage of the* Dawn Treader.

✳ Assignments:

Reading Comprehension	✏	1. Using the chart found after this unit's Planning Guide, record what happened to each of the seven lost lords as you read this book.
	📖	Where did the cordial Lucy used on Eustace come from?
Bible	🗝	2. Use a concordance to find Bible references to the East. Do you think C.S. Lewis had a reason for making Aslan's country to the East?

3. How big is the *Queen Mary*? Where is she today? You may be able to find pictures in an encyclopedia or on the Internet. — History

Visit the *Queen Mary* or another large ship.

4. From the description given in this chapter, draw a cross section of the *Dawn Treader*. If you are really interested in ships and are very ambitious, make a model. — Art

5. In 1942, Edmund, Lucy, and Eustace began their voyage. In 2306 Narnian time, Caspian began his voyage. Start a time line beginning with what Caspian told about the voyage up to the time Edmund, Lucy, and Eustace joined the ship. Add details as you read and are given more information about how long the *Dawn Treader* spent in each place and how long it took to get from one place to the next. — History

6. Lucy felt quite sure they were in for a lovely time. What do you think? Write down some predictions and read them again at the end of the book. — Critical Thinking

7. Do you know some Bible stories in which prophecies were made about a character while he or she was a baby? — Bible

Read Luke 2:25–35. The Bible is not only the inspired Word of God, but it is also great literature which has inspired many other pieces of literature. Can you think of some fairy tales in which prophecies were made about a character?

Chapter 3

Vocabulary

Look up the words in a dictionary before you read the chapter and write them, along with a definition, in your vocabulary notebook.

Using your vocabulary words, fill in the blanks. The answers may be found in the section entitled Answer Appendix.

1. Enough of this _____ , let's get down to business.

2. How long do you think we will have to _____ in this dungeon before we are rescued?

3. We would not want to eat any animal that lives on _____ .

Vocabulary Words:

consul

carrion

rigmarole

liege

languish

fief

4. I could never betray you, my _____ .

5. We will have to take this matter up with the _____ who represents your country.

6. He was granted a large _____ by the lord.

Read Chapter 3 of *The Voyage of the* Dawn Treader.

☀ Assignments:

English	🖉	1. Write a story about why the Lone Islands belong to Narnia.

Critical Thinking	📑	2. Governor Gumpas was called His Sufficiency. What is the usual title of respect for a ruler?
		Drinian and Lord Bern came up with a plan to trick Gumpas into thinking Caspian had more than just one ship. In what other story did we read about a similar plan to escape? See answer in Answer Appendix.

⊱—◦—⊰

Chapter 4

Vocabulary Words:

postern

languid

vagabond

bilious

slovenly

victuals

galling

dossier

Vocabulary:

🔑 **Look up the words in a dictionary before you read the chapter and write them, along with a definition, in your vocabulary notebook.**

🖉 Using your vocabulary words, fill in the blanks. The answers may be found in the section entitled Answer Appendix.

1. Eventually the romance of his _____ lifestyle faded and he began to wish he had a home.

2. It was _____ to see her win the prize when I had worked so hard in an effort to win it.

3. You are usually so energetic. Why are you so _____ today?

4. The starving seamen hoped the king of the island would provide them with enough _____ to feed them on their voyage home.

5. Be waiting for me at the _____ tonight at midnight and I will tell you the secret password.

6. It would be a mistake to go to your job interview in such _____ attire.

7. Whenever he had that _____ look about him, everyone stayed out of his way.

8. It gave me a very uncomfortable feeling to know they were keeping a _____ on me.

Read Chapter 4 of *The Voyage of the* Dawn Treader.

☀ Assignments:

---

1. Jesus drove the money changers from the temple on two occasions; the first instance is recorded in John 2:13–16. You can read about the second instance in Matthew 21:12–13; Mark 11:15–19; or Luke 19:45–47.

   How is the evil here the same? If you do not understand why Jesus was so angry with these people, you may need to do a little research using a Bible dictionary or a study Bible.

Bible

---

2. According to your encyclopedia, when, how, and why did slavery begin? Does slavery continue today?

History

---

3. Watch a movie depicting the slave trade.

History

---

4. Use your concordance to find out what the Bible says about slavery.

   Do you think slavery is right or wrong? Can you defend your answer with Scripture?

Bible

---

5. Gumpas said their present burst of prosperity depended on the slave trade. How does this compare to the situation in our Southern states before the Civil War?

History

⧗ Planning Guide – Chapters 5-8

Gather These Items:

1. A chess game, Chapter 5.

2. "The Golden Touch" in, *A Wonder Book for Girls and Boys* by Nathaniel Hawthorne, or in any book with the story of King Midas, Chapter 8. Hawthorne's book is available online. See Resource Appendix.

Suggested Information to Gather:

Encyclopedia or books about:

1. Perspiration, heatstroke, Chapter 5 (Health/Safety).

   ....

2. Liquid measures, Chapter 5 (Math).

   ....

3. Playing chess, Chapter 5 (Life Skills).

   ....

4. Snakes, Chapter 7 (Science).

   ....

5. Land measurements, Chapter 8 (Math).

   ....

6. The game of cricket, Chapter 8 (Games).

   ....

Suggested Videos:

Suggested Field Trips:

Suggested Memorization:

Notes:

SNAKE WORKSHEET

FOR USE WITH CHAPTER 7

1) Description: _____

_____

_____

_____

2) Life Span: _____

3) Diet: _____

_____

_____

4) Enemies: _____

_____

5) Habitat: _____

_____

_____

6) Behavior: _____

_____

_____

_____

Draw a Picture

Draw a Track

Favorite Fact: _____

_____

_____

_____

_____

Words to Learn:

fang

venom

molt

cold-blooded

Kingdom > Phylum > Class > Order > Family

Animalia > Chordata > Reptile > Squamata > Colubridae

Study Guide – Chapters 5-8

Chapter 5

Vocabulary Words:

scree

appalling

fiend

fathom

jerkin

Vocabulary:

🗝 **Look up the words in a dictionary before you read the chapter and write them, along with a definition, in your vocabulary notebook.**

✏ Using your vocabulary words, fill in the blanks. The answers may be found in the section entitled Answer Appendix.

1. Those who knew her best did not believe her to be the _____ that some people supposed.

2. That was certainly the most _____ accident I had ever witnessed.

3. It had taken years for the _____ at the bottom of the hill to build up to such a depth.

4. The ancient leather _____ was shrunken and cracked from years of hard wear.

5. 20,000 leagues under the sea would be more than fifty-two million _____ under water.

Read Chapter 5 of *The Voyage of the* Dawn Treader.

☀ Assignments:

Bible	🗝	1. In Eustace's diary, he said, "it was hardly my business to get them out of their scrape." Are they not all literally in the same boat? He sounds a little like Cain in Genesis 4:9, who said, "Am I my brother's keeper?" Are you your brother's keeper? What does the Bible say about this? Use a concordance to find verses that tell us how we are to treat others. Try looking under words such as *kind* and *care*. Who is your brother? What does Luke 10:25–37 say?
Bible	📖	2. Read II Thessalonians 3:10.
	🗒	Discuss how this verse applies to Eustace.
English	✏	3. Rewrite Eustace's journal, making it truthful.

4. What is the purpose of perspiration? What is heatstroke? How much of the human body is water? In most individuals, approximately 60% of the total weight is water. This percentage varies between 50% and 70%, with the exact value primarily dependent on a person's fat content. Since fat has very low water content, individuals with more fat will have a lower overall percentage of body weight as water.

Health/
Safety

5. How much is a pint? How many pints are in a gallon? How many pints are in a quart? How many quarts are in a gallon? How many cups are in a gallon? See Answer Appendix.

Math

How deep in feet was the water in the bay where the *Dawn Treader* dropped anchor on September 11?

6. Learn to play chess.

Life Skills

7. Make a costume to look like the character you like best. You may want to save this costume for an end of the year Narnia party.

Art

Chapter 6

Vocabulary:

Look up the words in a dictionary before you read the chapter and write them, along with a definition, in your vocabulary notebook.

Using your vocabulary words, fill in the blanks. The answers may be found in the section entitled Answer Appendix.

1. The thieves hadn't taken the weight of the gold _____ into account when they planned the theft.

2. There are very strict rules that must be observed if someone is going to _____ plants or animals into the United States.

3. We thought the opossum was dead but he was only _____ .

4. The _____ from the peak was treacherous.

5. It takes years of practice for a ballerina to achieve such _____ movements.

6. The climbers carried oxygen with them on their _____ because the air would become thinner as they neared the peak.

7. Lumber is an important _____ for the Pacific Northwest states.

Vocabulary Words:

lithe

ascent

descent

export

import

ingot

shamming

Read Chapter 6 of *The Voyage of the* Dawn Treader.

☀ Assignments:

Reading Comprehension		1. Answer the following questions orally: • We are slowly given clues as to what is happening to Eustace as Lewis describes how Eustace felt. When did you realize what had happened? • Using transitional words such as first, next, then, and last, list the chain of circumstances that brought Eustace into the cave. • What character traits helped Eustace get into trouble?
Art		2. Draw Eustace the Dragon crying by the pool.
Critical Thinking		3. Discuss the following questions with your instructor: • Have you ever been badly frightened? Describe the circumstances and how you felt. • What books have you read that gave you clues as to what might be in a dragon's lair and how dragons behave? • When they were about to confront the dragon, why did everyone feel fonder of everyone else than at ordinary times?
English		4. Read Aesop's Fable, "Androcles and the Lion." This is included in the Recommended Reading Appendix. How does this fable apply to the story?
English		5. In your notebook, keep a record of when, and in what form, Aslan appears throughout this story.

>─◄◆─○─◆►─◄

Vocabulary:

🔑 **Look up the words in a dictionary before you read the chapter and write them, along with a definition, in your vocabulary notebook.**

🖊 Using your vocabulary words, fill in the blanks. The answers may be found in the section entitled Answer Appendix.

1. I would not recommend that you read that _____ story.

2. The Pilgrims gave God the credit for their _____ .

3. They were not very good at playing _____ but they had a good time.

4. The _____ pain wore him down and made recovery difficult.

5. The _____ of the sailors were not fit to be printed.

prosperity

unmitigated

ghastly

quoits

ejaculation
(p. 100)

Read Chapter 7 of *The Voyage of the* Dawn Treader.

☀ Assignments:

📖 1. Answer the following questions orally:
   • Eustace said he had hated the name of Aslan. In other books, who has hated the name?
   • Why was Eustace afraid of the lion even though Eustace, himself, was a dragon?
   • Why do you think that Reepicheep was Eustace's most constant comforter?

Reading Comprehension

🖊 2. Write out Eustace's story as he might have had he been able to write it in the sand.

English

📖 3. Using an encyclopedia or a book about snakes, find out why and how snakes cast their skins.

Science

🖊 Also complete the Snake Worksheet found after this unit's Planning Guide.

📖 4. Eustace's telling of how the lion undressed him is a word picture of what Jesus does for us when we give our lives to Him. Reread this story and discuss it in relation to your own life. C.S. Lewis would not say from that time on Eustace was a different boy, but that "he began to be a different

Critical Thinking

boy." What is the difference? Would it have been believable if he had said Eustace never had a relapse?

Discuss Edmund's answer when Eustace asked if he knew Aslan, "Well—he knows me."

Chapter 8

Vocabulary Words:

vermilion

valor

Vocabulary:

Look up the words in a dictionary before you read the chapter and write them, along with a definition, in your vocabulary notebook.

Skim the chapter for today's vocabulary words. For each vocabulary word, write at least one sentence from this chapter which contains the word under its dictionary definition. Follow each sentence with a citation.

Read Chapter 8 of *The Voyage of the* Dawn Treader.

Assignments:

Math		1. Use a dictionary to find out how big an acre is. How big was Death Water Island? To what can you compare the size of the island in order to get an idea of its size?
Math		2. Near the pool where one of the missing Lords was found, some Narnian coins were also found: real Narnian "Lions" and "Trees." Draw some designs for Narnian coins and make up a money system for Narnia. What is the basic unit? How many different coins are there and what is each worth? Does it have paper money?
Literature		3. Read the story of King Midas. You can read Nathaniel Hawthorne's version in *A Wonder Book for Girls and Boys*, Chapter 2, "The Golden Touch."
Games		4. Find out something about how the game of cricket is played. What would be the length of a pitch?

⧗ PLANNING GUIDE – CHAPTERS 9-13

Gather These Items:

1. "A Midsummer Night's Dream" in *Tales from Shakespeare* by Charles and Mary Lamb, Chapters 9, 10 and 11. The text may be found online.

2. *The Adventures of Tom Sawyer* by Mark Twain, Chapters 9, 10 and 11.

3. Lemon juice and a candle, Chapters 9, 10 and 11.

4. *The Narnia Cookbook* or recipes and ingredients for:
   • Ice cream, Chapters 9, 10 and 11.
   • Curds, Chapters 9, 10 and 11.
   • Mead, Chapters 9, 10 and 11.

5. "The Rime of the Ancient Mariner" by Samuel Taylor Coleridge, Chapter 12. The text may be found online or at your public library.

Suggested Information to Gather:

Encyclopedia or books about:

1. A book about illuminations (hand drawn illustrations), Chapters 9, 10 and 11. On the Internet, search under "Medieval Illustrations."

   ....

2. Old maps, Chapters 9, 10 and 11 (Art/History).

   ....

3. Albatross, Chapter 12 (History).

   ....

4. Constellations, Chapter 13 (Science).

   ....

Suggested Videos:

1. *A Midsummer Night's Dream*, Chapters 9, 10 and 11.

Suggested Field Trips:

Suggested Memorization:

1. James 3:5–6, Chapters 9, 10 and 11.

2. Proverbs 29:25; Psalm 118:6; or Hebews 13:6, Chapters 9, 10 and 11.

Notes:

STUDY GUIDE – CHAPTERS 9-13

Chapters 9, 10 & 11

Vocabulary Words:

flagged

conspicuous

courtyard

crestfallen

monopod

astrolabe

orreries

infallible

chronoscope

enmity

inaudible

grimace

mead

theodolind
(see theodolite)

Vocabulary:

🔑 **Look up the words in a dictionary before you read the chapter and write them, along with a definition, in your vocabulary notebook.**

Eavesdropping—The **eavesdrop** of a building is the space of ground where water falls from the eaves. An **eavesdropper** was originally someone who stood in the eavesdrop in order to overhear private conversations taking place inside.

Poesimeter—an imaginary instrument for measuring the meter of poems.

Choriambus—an imaginary device for measuring choriambs, metrical feet consisting of four syllables: long, short, short, long.

✏ Match each of the words in the first column to the phrase in the second column that tells what each item measures or represents. The answers may be found in the Answer Appendix.

1. astrolabe   a. solar system

2. orrery   b. time

3. chronoscope   c. altitude of celestial bodies

4. theodolinds   d. horizontal or vertical angles

✏ Using your vocabulary words, fill in the blanks. The answers may be found in the section entitled Answer Appendix.

5. The strong _____ between the neighbors eventually resulted in a bloody feud.

6. His only reaction to the pain of the bee sting was a fleeting _____ .

7. She was the only one who believed she was _____ ; we all knew that she had made many mistakes.

8. They picked their way carefully over the uneven _____ walkway.

9. The captain's commands were _____ amidst the sounds of the howling storm.

10. Try not to make yourself _____ as we pass through the hotel lobby.

11. For refreshment they offered us cakes and _____ .

12. They looked so _____ after losing the baseball game that I didn't have the heart to criticize their performance.

13. All of the people assembled in the _____ to greet the new queen.

14. Those sleeping storks look like _____ .

Read Chapters 9, 10 & 11 of *The Voyage of the* **Dawn Treader**.

☀ Assignments:

---

1. After Lucy listened in on her friends' conversation she did not think she would ever be able to forget what she heard. Aslan assured her she would not. Words spoken can never be taken back and they can be a trap for you.

   Read Psalm 64; Proverbs 6:2, 10:19, 12:6, 12:18, 15:1, 18:6–7; and James 3:2–12.

   Memorize James 3:5–6.

Bible

---

2. Have you ever said something you did not mean because you were afraid of what someone else would think? Have you ever not said something you should have said for the same reason?

   Choose one of the following verses to memorize:

   "The fear of man bringeth a snare: but whoso putteth his trust in the Lord shall be safe." Proverbs 29:25

   "The Lord is on my side; I will not fear: what can man do unto me?" Psalm 118:6

   "So that we may boldly say, the Lord is my helper, and I will not fear what man shall do unto me." Hebrews 13:6

Bible

---

3. Illustrate a Dufflepud boating.

Art

---

4. Research the history and technique of **illumination**, the illustration of handwritten books.

   Copy a poem or scripture by hand onto one plain sheet of paper and make your own illuminations.

Art

Geography		5. Find pictures of old hand-drawn maps.
		Make a map of your state in the old style.

English 6. "Least said, soonest mended" is an **adage** or **maxim**; a short and sweet way of expressing a principle or truth. How would you rephrase this maxim to explain what it means? See Answer Appendix.

When Caspian realized they were going to have to deal with invisible enemies, he said, "This is an ugly furrow to plow." Judging from the context, what do you think he meant? (A more common way of saying this might be, "a tough row to hoe.") Put this saying into your own words. See Answer Appendix.

The Chief Voice said the island had belonged to the magician "time out of mind." What do you think the phrase, "time out of mind" means? Another way to put this is "since time immemorial." Put this saying into your own words. See Answer Appendix.

English 7. If you do not know who Bottom is, read "A Midsummer Night's Dream" from *Tales from Shakespeare* by Charles and Mary Lamb.

Then watch a video or read sections of the original Shakespeare play.

English 8. A **simile** is a figure of speech in which two unlike things are compared in a phrase using *like* or *as*. An example from these chapters is the Monopods "bouncing like footballs."

Look for other similes in these chapters and make up some of your own.

English 9. One of the spells in the book Lucy had to read was a cure for warts. In Mark Twain's *The Adventures of Tom Sawyer*, you can read about another cure for warts in the chapter titled "Tom Meets Becky."

Science 10. Lemon juice can be used as invisible ink. Dip a toothpick or small brush in lemon juice and write a message on a plain sheet of paper. You will be able to read the message if you carefully hold the paper to a candle flame or other source of heat that will heat, but not burn the paper. Why does this work? See Answer Appendix.

Cooking 11. What is mead? In *The Narnia Cookbook*, there are two recipes for mead substitutes on page 103. What are curds used for? In *The Narnia Cookbook*, there is a recipe for curds on page 96.

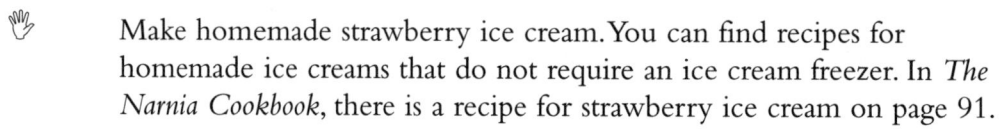

Make homemade strawberry ice cream. You can find recipes for homemade ice creams that do not require an ice cream freezer. In *The Narnia Cookbook*, there is a recipe for strawberry ice cream on page 91.

12. Discuss the following questions and comments with your instructor:

- What did you imagine might be causing the noise Lucy heard when she stopped to take a stone out of her shoe?
- Why were the spears of the Dufflepuds invisible until they left their hands, but the dishes were not?
- To Aslan all times are soon. Like God, Aslan is not bound by time, and someday we will not be either. C.S. Lewis believed we are always surprised by time. For example the statement, "Can you believe that so much time has passed?" is proof we were not made to live perpetually bound by time. Fish do not complain about being wet and other animals do not rebel against their natural habitats, but humans sometimes find their circumstances baffling because they were originally created for something else. What do you think?
- While looking through the Magician's Book, Lucy reads the spell for the refreshment of the spirit and she thinks it is the loveliest story she has ever read. Afterward, however, she can never quite remember what it was about, except that it told about a cup, a sword, a tree, and a green hill. In her book, *Journey Into Narnia*, Katherine Lindskoog says the spell may be the story of redemption. She speculates the cup could be the cup Jesus used at the Last Supper; the sword may be Peter's sword with which he cut off the ear of the servant of the High Priest or the sword used to pierce Jesus' side; and the tree may be the cross. The hill could be Calvary, the Mount of Olives, or the hill from which Jesus ascended into heaven after His resurrection. What do you think?

Chapter 12

Vocabulary Words:

impeachment

lurid

compose

poltroonery

extremity
(of terror)

Vocabulary:

🗝 **Look up the words in a dictionary before you read the chapter and write them, along with a definition, in your vocabulary notebook.**

✏ Using your vocabulary words, fill in the blanks. The answers may be found in the section entitled Answer Appendix.

1. Because his integrity was so well known, the attempted _____ of his character by his enemies was an utter failure.

2. Call out to God in your _____ , and He will hear you.

3. After such a display of _____ , no one wanted him in their hunting party.

4. I felt that the _____ headlines were shameful, but they increased newspaper sales last week.

5. You will have to _____ yourself before you go on stage.

Read Chapter 12 of *The Voyage of the* Dawn Treader.

✸ Assignments:

Bible		1. When Lucy remembered to call on Aslan for help, he sent the albatross.
	📖	Read these Psalms about calling on God: Psalm 4; Psalm 18:3; Psalm 55:16; Psalm 86; and Psalm 145:18–20. Will God hear you when you call? Will He help?
Art	✋	2. Draw and color a picture of the *Dawn Treader* heading into the Darkness as described on page 178.
Literature	📖	3. "Discretion is the better part of valor" is a quote from Act V, Scene 4, of Shakespeare's *The First Part of Henry the Fourth*. To understand the context of the quote, read this scene in the Recommended Reading Appendix.
	🗝	Look up *discretion* in a concordance. What does Proverbs have to say about it?

4. What is an albatross? What was the sailors' superstition about them? "The Rime of the Ancient Mariner," by Samuel Taylor Coleridge, is a ballad about a sailor who kills an albatross and the consequences of this action. This poem may be found online or at your public library. See the online information in the Resource Appendix.

History/ Literature

5. As the *Dawn Treader* headed toward the Dark Island, why was Rynelf ready to take soundings? How was this done?

Science

Look in your encyclopedia under *fathom, fathometer,* and *sonar.* These should tell you how soundings were done in the old days and how depth is measured now.

In the vocabulary section of your notebook, define each of the above italicized words.

6. What would have been your first thought when you understood what the rescued man meant by a place where dreams come true?

Critical Thinking

As the *Dawn Treader* was rushing back toward the light, why was everyone hearing something different?

What do you think about the statement that everybody realized there was nothing to be afraid of and never had been?

>-I-<>-O-<>-I-<

Chapter 13

Vocabulary:

Look up the words in a dictionary before you read the chapter and write them, along with a definition, in your vocabulary notebook.

Using your vocabulary words, fill in the blanks. The answers may be found in the section entitled Answer Appendix.

1. I don't believe that _____ grows in this area.

2. The _____ on our coat of arms signifies courage.

3. Although the moon appears _____ , it is actually reflecting the light of the sun.

4. It seemed a shame to walk on the soft green _____ .

5. She had never studied _____ , but she loved plants of all kinds and knew many of their names and habitats.

Vocabulary Words:

luminous

botany

turf

heather

device

Read Chapter 13 of *The Voyage of the* Dawn Treader.

☀ Assignments:

Art

1. On black paper with white crayon or chalk, draw what you think the Ship and Leopard constellations might look like.

Science

2. As the *Dawn Treader* sailed further east, new constellations became visible.

Someone at the same latitude will see the same constellations as you more or less. Someone directly opposite you in the other hemisphere will see stars you may never see, and not see stars that you might see any clear night.

What are some of the constellations that appear in the hemisphere opposite the one in which you live?

Use star stickers to make a constellation found only in the Southern Hemisphere.

⊱┈◈┈○┈◈┈⊰

⧗ PLANNING GUIDE – CHAPTERS 14-16

Gather These Items:

1. *The Odyssey* by Homer or a children's version of "Ulysses and the Sirens," Chapter 16.

2. *Le Morte d'Arthur* by Sir Thomas Malory (hardest); *Le Morte d'Arthur, A Rendition in Modern Idiom* by Keith Baines (easier); or *The Boy's King Arthur* by Sir Thomas Malory, edited by Sidney Lanier (easiest), Chapter 16.

Suggested Information to Gather:

Encyclopedia or books about:

1. Wind patterns, trade winds, Chapter 14 (Science/History).

   ....

2. Stars, Chapter 14 (Science).

   ....

3. Sea horses, Chapter 15 (Science).

   ....

4. Effect of ultraviolet light on the eyes, Chapter 15 (Health/Safety).

   ....

5. Water lilies, Chapter 16 (Science).

   ....

Suggested Videos:

Suggested Field Trips:

1. Visit an aquarium, Chapter 15.

Suggested Memorization:

Notes:

Chapter 14

Vocabulary Words:

stint

quay

oblivion

Vocabulary:

 Look up the words in a dictionary before you read the chapter and write them, along with a definition, in your vocabulary notebook.

Read Chapter 14 of *The Voyage of the* Dawn Treader.

☀ Assignments:

Critical Thinking		1. Discuss these questions with your instructor: • What is the difference between what we are and what we made of? • Why did Caspian not take Pittencream with him even after Pittencream decided to go? • What was Caspian's ploy to get the crew to go the rest of the way with him? • Why could Pittencream not bear mice?
Bible		2. Lewis may have been thinking of Isaiah 6:6–7 when he wrote about the fire-berries the birds brought to Ramandu.
	📖	Read the entire chapter of Isaiah 6.
		What do you think?
Science/ History		3. The sailors were worried about getting home because of the direction of the wind. Are there wind patterns on earth? How have they affected exploration and trade routes in the past? You should be able to find this information in your encyclopedia. Look under *weather* and *trade winds*. What is a *prevailing westerly*? The *horse latitudes*? The *doldrums*? Add the italicized words with their definitions to your vocabulary notebook.
Science		4. Eustace said stars are huge balls of flaming gas. What are stars made of? How much do some of them weigh? How do we know?

➤┤◆├○┤◆├◄

Vocabulary:

**Vocabulary
Words:**

🔑 **Look up the words in a dictionary before you read the chapter and write them, along with a definition, in your vocabulary notebook.**

kraken

✏️ Using your vocabulary words, fill in the blanks. The answers may be found in the section entitled Answer Appendix.

abdicate

falconing

1. The king was willing to _____ if it would help his country.

coronation

2. On the day of the _____ security was extremely tight around the cathedral.

keelhaul

maroon

3. _____ was the prince's favorite sport.

4. The captain threatened to _____ the guilty party when he discovered who had been stealing from the ship's stores.

5. It was a toss-up whether the sailor was more afraid of being keelhauled or thrown to the _____ .

6. His enemies plotted to _____ him on a deserted island.

Read Chapter 15 of *The Voyage of the* **Dawn Treader**.

✳️ Assignments:

🚩 1. In this chapter we find out the world in which Narnia exists is flat. Imagine a flat world. From what you have learned so far about our universe, speculate about what would be different in Narnia from our world? What would hold the oceans in place? Why would the sun look bigger and brighter as the *Dawn Treader* got closer to the east? How might weather patterns be different? What about the movement of the stars?

Critical
Thinking

Discuss the differences in the way we think about our mountains and valleys compared to how they would seem to people living under the sea?

🖐️ 2. Draw a picture of a sea horse.

Science

📖 Read about sea horses. Write one or two important findings at the bottom of your drawing.

🖐️ 3. Visit an aquarium.

Field Trip

| Health/ Safety | ⚷ | 4. What effect does the sun have on our eyes? What should we do to prevent damage from ultraviolet light? |

⊱ ⊰⊱ ⊰⊙⊱ ⊰⊱ ⊰

Chapter 16

Read Chapter 16 of *The Voyage of the* Dawn Treader.

✳ Assignments:

Reading Comprehension	📜	1. Did you account for all of the seven lost lords? What happened to each of them?
		How many times did Aslan appear in *The Voyage of the Dawn Treader*? Did he always appear as a lion?
		Review the predictions you made in Activity 6, Chapter 2, about the kind of "time" the children would have. How accurate were they?
Bible	📖	2. The Lamb on shore invited the children to come and have breakfast. Can you think of a time Jesus did this? Read John 21:1–14.
Critical Thinking	📜	3. What is the way into Aslan's country from our world?
Science	⚷	4. Learn about how water lilies grow. Add them to your plant notebook.
English	📖	5. The Sirens were referenced twice in this chapter. Read the story "Ulysses and the Sirens" in Homer's *The Odyssey*, Book XII, or read a simpler children's version.
Art	✋	6. Draw the fish-herdess.
English	📜	7. Compare the departure of Reepicheep to Chapter V of Book XXI in *Le Morte d'Arthur* by Sir Thomas Malory. (The text of this classic may be found online by doing a search for: "Le Morte D'Arthur" + text.) *Le Morte d'Arthur, A Rendition in Modern Idiom* by Keith Baines, is easier to understand. Or read Book VII, "Of the Death of King Arthur," in *The Boy's King Arthur* edited by Sidney Lanier.

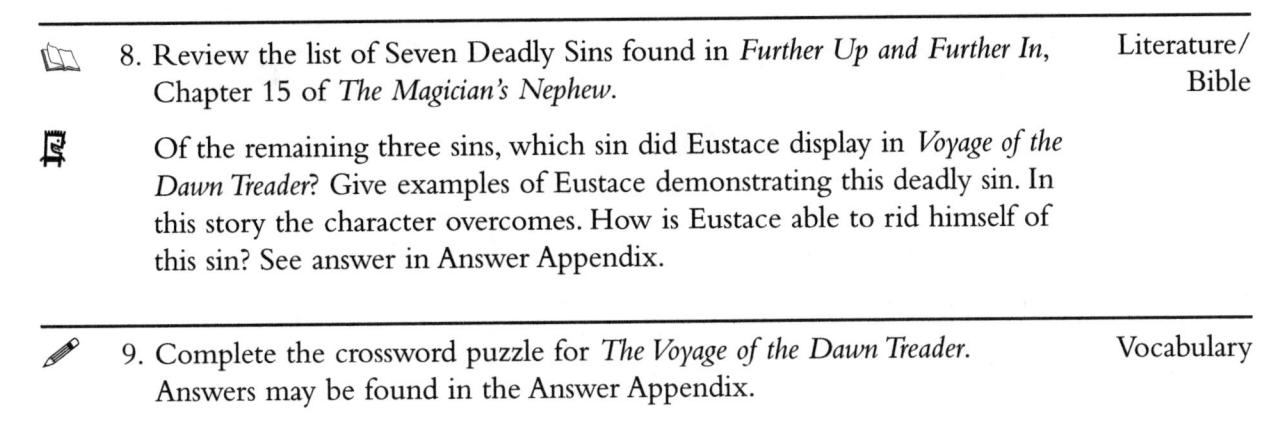

8. Review the list of Seven Deadly Sins found in *Further Up and Further In,* Chapter 15 of *The Magician's Nephew.*

   Of the remaining three sins, which sin did Eustace display in *Voyage of the Dawn Treader*? Give examples of Eustace demonstrating this deadly sin. In this story the character overcomes. How is Eustace able to rid himself of this sin? See answer in Answer Appendix.

Literature/
Bible

9. Complete the crossword puzzle for *The Voyage of the Dawn Treader.* Answers may be found in the Answer Appendix.

Vocabulary

Complete any unfinished assignments prior to going on to *The Silver Chair.*

THE VOYAGE OF THE DAWN TREADER
CROSSWORD PUZZLE

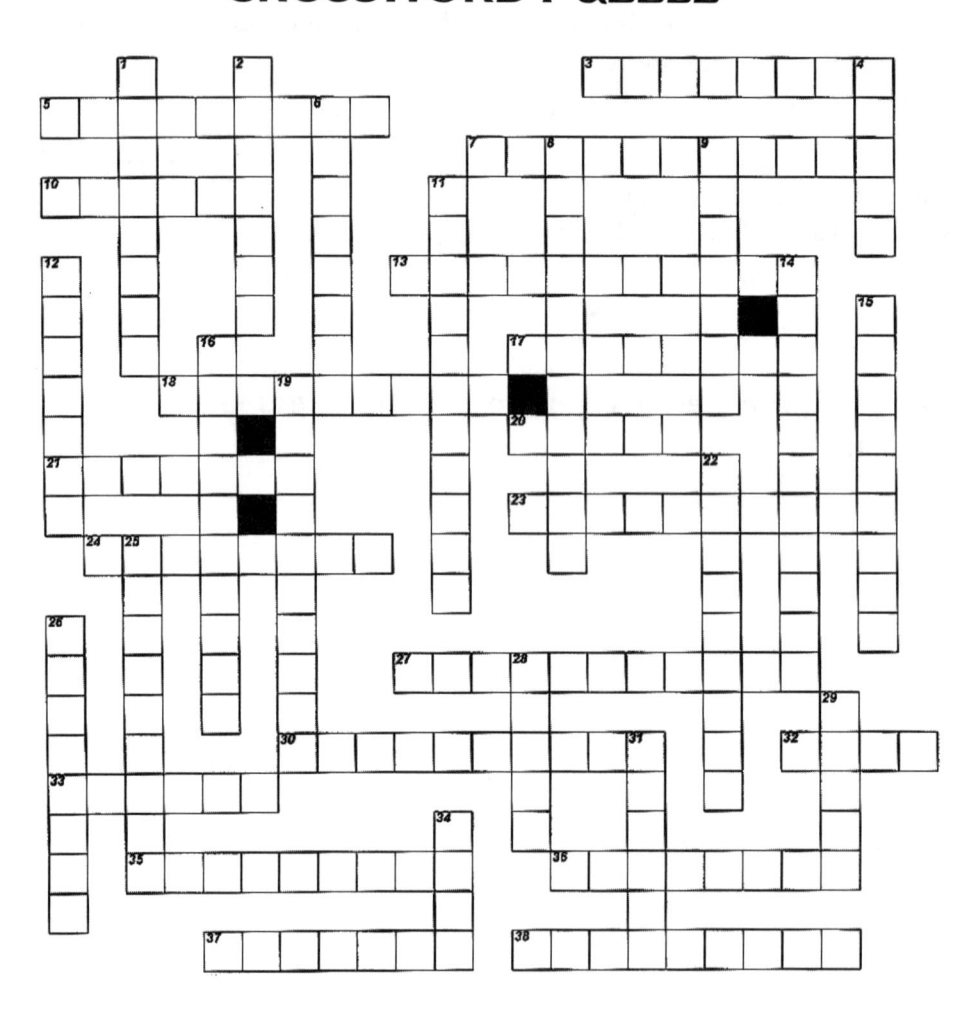

ACROSS

3 to rebuke severely

5 indistinct

7 charge with a crime

10 sovereign's substitute

13 unrelieved

17 briefs

18 in charge of boat's hull

20 block of metal

21 make

23 abundance

24 wanderer

27 dejected

30 complex and ritualisic procedure

32 front

33 ambassador

35 lovely

36 blowzy

37 marked

38 opinion

DOWN

1 long

2 food

4 graceful

6 aglow

8 cowardice

9 low growing shrub

11 obvious

12 large galleon

14 natural temper

15 patio

16 crowning

19 abstains from alcohol

22 red-orange

25 repetitive vowel sounds

26 to formally relinquish power

28 loose rock

29 saline

31 sell abroad

34 brew

⧗ PLANNING GUIDE – CHAPTERS 1-4

Gather These Items:

1. *The Silver Chair* by C.S. Lewis.

2. *The Narnia Cookbook* or recipes and ingredients for:
   • Pie, Chapter 3.
   • Soup, Chapter 3.

3. *Poems* by C.S. Lewis, Chapter 4.

4. Black paper, a white or yellow crayon or chalk or scratchboard, Chapter 4. (You may make your own scratchboard. See the Activity Appendix for a list of items needed and directions.)

5. Owl pellets, Chapter 4. See Resource Appendix.

Suggested Information to Gather:

Encyclopedia or books about:

1. Highest mountain peak, Chapter 1 (Geography/Science).

   ....

2. Laurels, Chapter 1 (Science).

   ....

3. Trafalgar Square, Chapter 2 (History).

   ....

4. Lord Nelson, Chapter 2 (History).

   ....

5. Homer, Chapter 3 (Literature).

   ....

6. Ear and hearing, Chapter 3 (Health/Safety).

   ....

7. Causes of deafness, Chapter 3 (Health/Safety).

   ....

8. Aids for the deaf, Chapter 3 (Health/Safety).

   ....

9. Owls, Chapter 4 (Science).

   ....

10. First aid book, snakebites and burns, Chapter 4 (Health/Safety).

    ....

Suggested Videos:

Suggested Field Trips:

1. Go for a ride in a hot air balloon, Chapter 2. (This may not be practical for most families due to lack of opportunity or funds.)

2. Visit a school for the deaf, Chapter 3.

3. Have your hearing tested, Chapter 3. (Frequently a university with an audiology department will perform this service for free in order to give their students practice.)

4. Visit a hospital and watch a newborn hearing screening, Chapter 3.

Suggested Memorization:

1. Psalm 119:9–16, Chapter 2.

Notes:

OWL WORKSHEET

FOR USE WITH CHAPTER 4

1) Description: _____

_____

_____

_____

2) Life Span: _____

3) Diet: _____

_____

_____

4) Enemies: _____

_____

5) Habitat: _____

_____

_____

6) Behavior: _____

_____

_____

_____

Draw a Picture

Draw a Track

Favorite Fact: _____

_____

_____

_____

_____

Words to Learn:

carnivore

rodent

depth perception

pellet

Kingdom > Phylum > Class > Order > Family > Genus
Animalia > Chordata > Vertebrata > Aves > Strigiformes > Strigidae

STUDY GUIDE – CHAPTERS 1-4

Chapter 1

Vocabulary Words:

moor

expel

psychology

despise

Vocabulary:

🔑 **Look up the words in a dictionary before you read the chapter and write them, along with a definition, in your vocabulary notebook.**

✏️ Using your vocabulary words, fill in the blanks. The answers may be found in the section entitled Answer Appendix.

1. A study of the _____ of other cultures will give you a better understanding of the people than will a superficial study of their dress and architecture.

2. Do not _____ the teaching of your parents.

3. It was a dark, misty night on the English _____ .

4. That is an offense for which the school should _____ them.

Read Chapter 1 of *The Silver Chair*.

☀ Assignments:

Reading Comprehension	📖	1. Discuss the following questions with your instructor: • At the beginning of the story, why was Jill crying? • What did Eustace do to comfort Jill? What worked? What did not? • What was said about Edith Jackle? What is the difference between being one of Them and what she was? • How did Jill meet the lion?
Bible	🔑	2. Eustace said he swore "by everything." Use a concordance to find out what the Bible says about swearing.
Art	✋	3. Some Narnian birds are different from birds in our world. Draw what you imagine some of the Narnian birds might look like.
English	✏️	4. Divide a sheet of paper into two columns. On one side list as many adjectives as you can find which were used to describe the surroundings and the kind of day it was at the school when Eustace and Jill met. On the other side list as many adjectives as you can find which describe the

place Eustace and Jill saw when they went through the doorway in the wall. In which place would you rather be?

5.	What is the highest point on earth? If you were at the top, would you be able to look down through the clouds? Is there snow on the top of this mountain year round? The article on geography in your encyclopedia may be a good place to start looking for the answer.	Geography/Science

6.	Why was Eustace acting so differently this term? In Acts 4:13, the priests and Sadducees recognized Peter and John as having been with Jesus.	Critical Thinking

Can others tell by your words and actions that you have been with Jesus?

7.	Look up information about laurels. Add a picture and information to your plant notebook.	Science

Chapter 2

Read Chapter 2 of *The Silver Chair*.

☀ Assignments:

1.	The lion Jill saw invited her to come and drink if she was thirsty. Can you think of a Bible story that is similar?	Bible

Read John 4:13–15, 6:35, and 7:37–38.

2.	Aslan told Jill she needed to know the signs by heart because down in Narnia things would not be so clear. The thicker air might confuse her and the signs would not look as she might expect them to look.	Bible

What kinds of things can confuse our minds here on earth and make us forget what Jesus said? Read and discuss: Deuteronomy 4:9; Proverbs 31:5; and Matthew 13:1–23.

Read and memorize Psalm 119:9–16.

What "signs" do you need to remember? Read II Timothy 2:8; Jude 17–18; Luke 17:31–33; John 15:20–21; Hebrews 13: 2–4; and Revelation 3:2.

From the scriptures above, make a list of those things the Lord wants you to remember. Each day for the remainder of this unit read this list.

English	3. Write about a dream you have had in which you tried to wake up and could not.

History	4. Where in England is Trafalgar Square? Find a picture of the lions. How big are they? You may look in your encyclopedia or a picture book of Britain or London. Trafalgar Square was laid out in the 1840's. In the center is the tall Nelson's Column paid for by the Nelson Memorial Committee. Lord Nelson was the admiral of the British fleet and Trafalgar was his greatest battle. What did Lord Nelson do?

Critical Thinking	5. When Jill realized the lion was speaking, she became frightened in a different way than she had been before. What do you think caused the change? In what way was she frightened then?

Field Trip	6. Ride in a hot air balloon. (This may not be practical due to finances or opportunity.)

Geography	7. Show your instructor which direction is east.

Vocabulary:

☞ **Look up the words in a dictionary before you read the chapter and write them, along with a definition, in your vocabulary notebook.**

ear-trumpet

🖑 1. Draw a picture of an ear-trumpet below its definition.

kettledrum

🖑 2. Draw a picture of a kettledrum below its definition.

hale

✎ 3. Skim the chapter for the word *hale*. Write at least one sentence from this chapter containing the word under its dictionary definition. Follow each sentence with a citation.

Read Chapter 3 of *The Silver Chair*.

☀ Assignments:

📕 1. Answer the following questions orally:
- Why had Jill and Eustace not heard of the terms "son of Adam" and "daughter of Eve"?
- What kind of person was it who was called to look after Jill?
- Why could Trumpkin not have been the person Aslan meant in the first sign?
- Why did Eustace not know of the glory and courtesy of Narnia?

Reading
Comprehension

📕 2. Discuss these questions with your instructor:
- What do you think C.S. Lewis thought of the current secular education of England?
- Although God forgives our sins and works things out to accomplish His will, we still have to suffer the consequences of our actions. What things would have been different if Jill and Eustace had stayed together and had both been told the signs?

Critical
Thinking

☞ 3. At the end of this chapter, a blind poet told the story of *The Horse and His Boy*. Lewis may have been thinking of Homer, who is believed to have been a blind poet who lived hundreds of years ago. In your encyclopedia, find out what you can about Homer and what he wrote.

Literature

🖑 4. Look at the list of foods served at the castle. Does it sound like they would make a good meal to you? Lewis made up the fish called a pavender and you probably will not be able to cook a peacock, but you could bake a pie and make some soup. Make a dinner and serve it in courses. Announce each course with a trumpeting noise or drumming.

Cooking

Health/
Safety

5. Diagram a sound coming to the ear canal and follow its path all the way to the brain.

Other than birth defects, name some causes of deafness. Can any of these be prevented?

Noise-induced hearing loss is preventable. All individuals should understand the hazards of noise and how to practice good auditory health in everyday life. Noise above 75 decibels has the potential to damage hearing.
  • Wear earplugs or other hearing protective devices when involved in a loud activity. (Special earplugs and ear muffs are available at hardware stores and sporting good stores.)
  • Be alert to hazardous noise in the environment.
  • Protect children who are too young to protect themselves.

Make a bar graph using these common noises as the run and the decibels emitted as the rise.
Ambulance siren.................120
Hand drill 98
Tractor 96
Chain saw 110
Hair dryer 90
Rock concert 120

What types of jobs can lead to hearing impairment from continuous exposure to toxic noise? Talk to people in these professions. What type of hearing protection do they wear? Have they experienced hearing loss or do they know of others who have?

What was the purpose of Trumpkin's silver ear-trumpet? What type of aids are made for the hearing impaired and deaf? There are devices that use flashing lights and vibrations to alert the hearing impaired to door knocks, bells, telephones, burglar alarms, smoke and fire alarms, baby cries, etc. In addition to devices, there are certified hearing dogs that are trained to respond to sounds and alert the hearing impaired to them.

Individuals with hearing impairment must stop, look, and listen in order to hear and understand speech. What should you do to communicate more effectively with a hearing impaired friend or family member?

Field Trip

6. Visit a school for the deaf. See what training is provided for living successfully in a hearing world.

Field Trip

7. Have your hearing tested by an audiologist or visit a hospital and watch a newborn hearing screening.

Vocabulary:

🔑 **Look up the words in a dictionary before you read the chapter and write them, along with a definition, in your vocabulary notebook.**

fusty

parliament

🖊 Using your vocabulary words, fill in the blanks. The answers may be found in the section entitled Answer Appendix.

physic

distraught

1. After the fire, the mother was _____ until her son was found playing happily across the street.

2. She did not enjoy the task of cleaning out the _____ old attic.

3. The small country's _____ voted to oust their king.

4. He dreaded the _____ his mother would administer if he admitted that he didn't feel well.

Read Chapter 4 of *The Silver Chair*.

✳ Assignments:

📜 1. Answer the following questions orally:
   • Who was Rilian's mother?
   • How long had the Prince been missing? Retell the touching story of Drinian telling King Caspian what he knew about his son's whereabouts.
   • Why do you think the owls would not go to the ruins?
   • Glimfeather said Trumpkin was as true as steel and would stick to the rules. Go back to *Prince Caspian* and read the end of Chapter 7. Is Trumpkin still the same?

Reading
Comprehension

---

2. It was thought the serpent that killed Rilian's mother and the woman Rilian visited before his disappearance were the same person.

📖 Read what the Bible says about Satan's craftiness and his ability to appear as something beautiful: II Corinthians 11:13–14; Ephesians 6:11; II Corinthians 2:11; and II Thessalonians 2:8–10.

Bible

✋ 3. On a black piece of paper with white or yellow crayon or chalk, draw Jill's view from the back of the owl. You could also try drawing the scene on scratchboard. Scratchboard is available at some art supply stores. Or you could try making your own. See Activity Appendix.

Art

| Science | 4. Dissect owl pellets. What had your owl eaten? In the story, what did the owl eat? |
| | Complete the Owl Worksheet found after this unit's Planning Guide. |

| Health/ Safety | 5. What is the proper treatment for snakebites? |

| Critical Thinking | 6. Discuss the following question with your instructor:
• Drinian felt the woman was something evil, but he did not want to be a tale-bearer. When is it good to speak out? |

⧗ PLANNING GUIDE – CHAPTERS 5-8

Gather These Items:

1. Recipes and ingredients to make the following:
   - Eel pie, Chapter 5. See Activity Appendix.
   - Either cookies or English biscuits with caraway, Chapter 7. See Activity Appendix.
   - Cock-a-leekie soup, Chapter 8. See Activity Appendix.
   - Posset, Chapter 8. See Activity Appendix.

2. Comfits, Chapter 8. See Resource Appendix.

Suggested Information to Gather:

Encyclopedia or books about:

1. Marshlands and the birds that live in them, Chapter 5 (Science).

   ....

2. Signs of early winter, Chapter 5 (Science).
   - *Farmer's Almanac.*

   ....

3. Eels, Chapter 5 (Science).

   ....

4. Saint Paul's Cathedral, Chapter 6 (Architecture).

   ....

5. Stonehenge, Chapter 6 (Architecture).

   ....

6. Frostbite, Chapter 7 (Health/Safety).

   ....

Suggested Videos:

Suggested Field Trips:

Suggested Memorization:

Notes:

STUDY GUIDE – CHAPTERS 5-8

Chapter 5

glum

reed

rushes

wigwam

bastion

sparring

belfry

funk

fricassee

tinderbox

cockshy

Vocabulary:

🗝 **Look up the words in a dictionary before you read the chapter and write them, along with a definition, in your vocabulary notebook.**

✏ Using your vocabulary words, fill in the blanks. The answers may be found in the section entitled Answer Appendix.

1. The _____ had been built near the stream where the Indians could conveniently fish and draw water for cooking.

2. Do not go into the _____ while the bells are being rung.

3. They retreated to the cliffs, their last _____ against the giants.

4. Everyone tried to avoid him when he was in a _____ .

5. You always look so _____ when you are on your way to school.

6. Do you know how to make whistles out of the _____ and _____ in the swamp?

7. Keep your _____ dry or you won't be able to start a fire tonight.

8. She could stretch the small amount of meat to feed more people by making a _____ .

9. Your continual _____ is beginning to irritate me.

10. His throw hit the ground two feet short of the _____ .

Read Chapter 5 of *The Silver Chair*.

☀ **Assignments:**

Reading Comprehension

📏   1. Discuss the following questions with your instructor:
   • Why did Eustace have more endurance and energy than Jill?
   • What did Jill think about sleeping in clothes? Eustace?
   • Why did Puddleglum think Jill and Eustace were well-raised?
   • What do we call a person whose attitude is like Puddleglum's?
   • Why did the children have trouble sleeping before they left on their adventure?

2. Draw Puddleglum. — Art

3. Write a report on marshlands and the birds that live in them, especially duck, snipe, bittern, and heron. — Science

4. What are some signs of an early winter? Try looking in a *Farmer's Almanac*. — Science

5. Read about eels, then tell your instructor what you have learned. Do they live in saltwater or freshwater? — Science

6. Make eel pie. See Activity Appendix for recipe. — Cooking

7. Pretend you are about to go on the trip with Puddleglum, Eustace, and Jill. What would you take with you? Remember that you will have to carry it. Make a list or assemble the items. — Critical Thinking

Chapter 6

Vocabulary:

Look up the words in a dictionary before you read the chapter and write them, along with a definition, in your vocabulary notebook.

Using your vocabulary words, fill in the blanks. The answers may be found in the section entitled Answer Appendix.

1. No one knows why the ancient inhabitants of this country built the _____ .

2. The staircase would be treacherous without the _____ .

3. Thank you! Dessert was _____ .

4. The lady's richly embroidered _____ signified her high station.

Vocabulary Words:

balustrade

cairn

scrumptious

kirtle

Read Chapter 6 of *The Silver Chair*.

Assignments:

Reading Comprehension		1. Answer these questions orally: • Why did they not travel in the gorge? • Did C.S. Lewis describe the first group of giants as being sharp intellectually?

Architecture

2. You should be able to find the answers to the following questions in your encyclopedia by looking up *Saint Paul's*, *arch*, and *Stonehenge*.
   • How high does the dome of Saint Paul's rise above the street?
   • When was the arch invented and who invented it?
   • Make a scale drawing of the arch bridge.
   • How would it look if its crown were as high above the cliff tops as Saint Paul's is above the street?
   • Each single stone was as big as those at Stonehenge. How big are the stones at Stonehenge?

Critical Thinking

3. Discuss these questions with your instructor.
   • Can you estimate about how long it has been since the giants were driven back to the North?
   • Was Puddleglum right not to trust the lady? Who do you think she is?
   • After Eustace's experiences on the *Dawn Treader*, do you think he should have been more careful?
   • Why do you think girls were not taught to curtsey at Experiment House? What does this show they were teaching?

Chapter 7

Vocabulary Words:

guffaw

cornice

loiter

crag

eddy

caraway

wet blanket

Vocabulary:

Look up the words in a dictionary before you read the chapter and write them, along with a definition, in your vocabulary notebook.

 Using your vocabulary words, fill in the blanks. The answers may be found in the section entitled Answer Appendix.

1. We were fascinated as we watched the water _____ and swirl around the rocks.

2. The librarian doesn't want you to _____ near the doorways.

3. It was dizzying to look up at the steep, rocky _____ .

4. Everyone in the room was startled by his loud _____ .

5. You can always count on her to be the _____ whenever an activity is suggested.

6. There were yards and yards of intricately carved _____ in the castle.

7. The smell of the _____ used to season the stew reminded me of my grandmother's kitchen.

Puttee is from the Hindi language. Many of the Hindi words that are familiar to us were absorbed into our language as a result of the British presence in India. India was ruled by Great Britain for almost 200 years and did not win complete independence until 1947. This is why, in *The Magician's Nephew*, Digory's father was in India.

✳ *Extra assignment*: If you have caraway in your spice cupboard, taste it. Describe caraway's appearance. Make biscuits or some other food item using caraway. See Activity Appendix.

Read Chapter 7 of *The Silver Chair*.

✳ Assignments:

1. Discuss the following question with your instructor: • What do you think will happen during the Autumn Feast?	Reading Comprehension
2. Draw Puddleglum, Eustace, and Jill at the castle door.	Art
3. Have you ever been cold enough to understand how Jill and Eustace felt? Write a short story about it. Older children: Read Jack London's short story, "To Build a Fire," in the Recommended Reading Appendix.	English
4. In this chapter it mentions that Jill's face was blue. Frostbite most commonly affects the toes, fingers, earlobes, chin, cheeks, and nose—body parts that are often left uncovered in cold temperatures. Frostbite can occur gradually or rapidly. The speed with which the process progresses depends upon how cold or windy the conditions are and the duration of exposure to those conditions.	Health/ Safety

What are the different stages of frostbite?

How can the risk of frostbite be reduced?
• Seek emergency care if any of the following occur: skin swelling (edema), loss of limb function and absence of pain, marked skin color changes, blisters, slurred speech, or memory loss.

If the patient cannot be transported to a hospital immediately, the following re-warming techniques may help until reaching a hospital.
- Bring patient indoors as soon as possible.
- Apply warm towels or immerse the area in circulating lukewarm water for twenty minutes. Hot water should not be used and the area should not be rubbed in any way.
- If blisters are present, leave them intact.
- Do not hold the affected area near fire since the area may be burned due to the reduced feeling in the area.
- Offer the patient warm coffee or tea, if alert, but never alcohol.
- Keep the affected area raised.

After re-warming, a superficial frostbite will redden and become painful as circulation resumes in the area. Blisters are likely to form within 24 hours. A deep frostbite injury will remain hard, cool to the touch, and may turn blue. Blisters may form and the area can turn black. Skin surrounding the affected area may become swollen and remain swollen for over a month. If gangrene develops, amputation may become necessary.

Did the children in the story handle the frostbite correctly?

Chapter 8

Vocabulary Words:

posset

comfits

poppet

Vocabulary:

🔑 **Look up the words in a dictionary before you read the chapter and write them, along with a definition, in your vocabulary notebook.**

✏️ Using your vocabulary words, fill in the blanks. The answers may be found in the section entitled Answer Appendix.

1. Whenever Aunt Lou called me her little _____ , I knew she was going to ask me to do something for her.

2. A _____ was originally a drink made of sweetened milk curdled with treacle, ale or wine, etc. and was given to anyone who had a cold.

3. The medieval feast customarily ended with spiced wine, sweet wafers, and _____ , spicy morsels such as crystallized ginger and sugared nuts.

Read Chapter 8 of *The Silver Chair*.

☀ Assignments:

✋ 1. Make Cock-a-leekie soup. A recipe may be found in the Activity Appendix.

Cooking

The medieval feast customarily ended with spiced wine, sweet wafers, and comfits—spicy morsels such as crystallized ginger and sugared nuts. Such sweetmeats were also the usual snacks on amorous or other festive occasions. Comfits seem to be tedious to make, but you might want to purchase some sugared fennel seeds. These little comfits offer the sweet licorice flavor of fennel complemented by a coating of multicolored sugar. They are the closest equivalent currently available for the "red anise in comfit" often called for as a garnish in medieval recipes. Many comfits originated in India, an English colony.

Serve comfits for dessert. See the Resource Appendix for a place where comfits may be purchased.

📜 2. Discuss the following questions with your instructor:
  • For what was Eustace never going to forgive Jill? Do you think he did?
  • Discuss Puddleglum's statement, "I'd no call to be trying. I ought to have done it."

Critical Thinking

📖 3. Read Numbers 13–14. Did it work for the Israelites to change their mind and go back? Do you think it will work for the children and Puddleglum?

Bible

✋ 4. Make posset, substituting sparkling grape juice for sherry. See Activity Appendix for a recipe.

Cooking

➤⊷◆⊶○⊷◆⊶◁

⧗ PLANNING GUIDE – CHAPTERS 9-12

Gather These Items:

1. "Hamlet" and "The Comedy of Errors" in *Tales from Shakespeare* by Charles and Mary Lamb, Chapter 10. (This book is also available online.)

2. Items to make a banner with the names of Jesus, Chapter 12.

3. Poster board, Chapter 12.

Suggested Information:

Encyclopedia or books about:

1. Speleology and spelunking, Chapter 9 (Science).

   ....

2. Carlsbad Caverns and other famous caves, Chapter 9 (Science).

   ....

3. Lithosphere, inner and outer core of the earth, Chapter 9 (Science).

   ....

4. Geothermal gradient, Chapter 9 (Science).

   ....

5. The world's deepest mines and the technological problems they face in going deeper, Chapter 9 (Science).

   ....

6. World War II, rationing, Chapter 12 (History).

   ....

7. World War II posters, Chapter 12 (History).

   ....

Suggested Videos:

1. *Hamlet* by Shakespeare, Chapter 10. (The movie starring Mel Gibson is an excellent version.)

Suggested Field Trips:

1. Visit a cave such as the famous Carlsbad Caverns, Chapter 9.

2. Go spelunking with an adult who is knowledgeable and practices proper safety procedures, Chapter 9.

Suggested Memorization:

1. Colossians 3:12–17, Chapter 10.

2. Matthew 1:23 or Isaiah 9:6, Chapter 12.

3. A Psalm of praise, Chapter 12.

Notes:

STUDY GUIDE – CHAPTERS 9-13

Chapter 9

Vocabulary Words:

prattle

biped

mantle

scullery

delicacy

shingle (p. 138)

Vocabulary:

🔑 **Look up the words in a dictionary before you read the chapter and write them, along with a definition, in your vocabulary notebook.**

✏️ Using your vocabulary words, fill in the blanks. The answers may be found in the section entitled Answer Appendix.

1. Walking through the _____ on the beach was difficult and painful to his bare feet.

2. I would never eat that, even though you may consider it a _____ .

3. Let me borrow your _____ while I go out to bring some more fire wood.

4. Once you have finished in the _____ you may go upstairs and make the beds.

5. Birds as well as humans are _____ .

6. Will your silly _____ never cease?

Read Chapter 9 of *The Silver Chair.*

✳ Assignments:

Reading Comprehension	📓	1. Answer this question orally: • What does it mean that Jill got hot all over when she remembered it afterward?
Science	📖	2. What is speleology? Read about caves in your encyclopedia and find out about some famous caves such as Carlsbad Caverns.
Field Trip	✋	3. Visit one of these caves.
	✋	What is spelunking? Have a knowledgable adult take you to a safe cave and go spelunking. What type of equipment will you need? What types of dangers are present in a cave?

4. Discuss these questions with your instructor:
   - Have you ever been in complete darkness where it made no difference whether your eyes were open or shut?
   - As the three ran into the crevice at the bottom of the stairs, Puddleglum was first in line and Jill was last. Where would you have wanted to be in line?

Critical Thinking

5. Caves are normally cool, but C.S. Lewis stated they knew they were deep in the earth because it was warm. Why would this be correct? (Instructor, please explain the following answer to your student.)

Science

If the sun were the only source of heat, the farther you went down in the earth, the colder it would get. We can tell the interior of the earth is hot by observing molten lava erupting from volcanoes, as well as by feeling increasing heat as we go down into a mine. Copper mines in Butte, Montana, are more than a mile deep and the temperature at their deepest levels will be anywhere from 75 to 204.8°F. The walls of the deepest diamond mine in South Africa are 284°F.

What is the geothermal gradient? (The average is for the temperature to increase 25°C for each kilometer increase in depth.)

Study about the inner layers of the earth. Use the information below as a starting place for your study. The information you find may vary. No one has ever been to the center of the earth and taken the temperature. The data I found for the temperature of the inner core ranged from 6,500 to 9,000°F.

Science uses remote sensing (bouncing sound waves through the earth and measuring how they return) to study the inner core. Remote sensing leads scientists to believe there are four layers within the earth:

Inner core (750 miles in diameter): the deepest part of the earth is a solid that contains both iron and nickel. It is because of this that the center of the earth is a magnet, a compass. It generates a magnetic field that protects the earth from flying out of orbit. Although the temperature may be 9,000°F, the inner core is solid due to the tremendous amount of pressure surrounding it.

Outer core (1410 miles): outside of the inner core is the outer core. The outer core is molten, like warm wax, and believed to consist of metals less dense than nickel.

Mantle (2224 miles): the mantle has a temperature of around 5400°F. Scientists believe the magma from this layer is the lava that erupts from volcanoes.

Crust (25 miles): This is the top layer of the earth, which is basically hardened mantle (magma). It contains two segments, the oceanic and continental crusts.

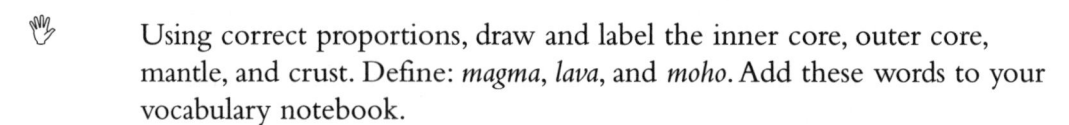

Using correct proportions, draw and label the inner core, outer core, mantle, and crust. Define: *magma*, *lava*, and *moho*. Add these words to your vocabulary notebook.

On the Internet, do research to find about the deepest mines in the world. What do they mine? What technological problems do they face in order to go deeper?

➤·❀·◦·❀·◄

Chapter 10

Vocabulary Words:

bulwark

jetty

nosegay

grotesque

gnome

marches (noun)

Vocabulary:

Look up the words in a dictionary before you read the chapter and write them, along with a definition, in your vocabulary notebook.

Using your vocabulary words, fill in the blanks. The answers may be found in the section entitled Answer Appendix.

1. You may have better luck fishing from the end of the _____ .

2. We will be safe as long as the _____ holds strong.

3. The knotted and gnarled trees appeared _____ in the darkness.

4. He picked a little _____ for his mother.

5. No one wanted to venture into the southern _____ of the country.

6. The _____ guarded this treasure carefully.

Read Chapter 10 of *The Silver Chair.*

✳ Assignments:

Art	✋	1. Draw some of the underground people. Make each one different.
Literature		2. The Prince looked a bit like Hamlet. Besides looking like Hamlet, he used the word **coil** which is also used in Hamlet's "To Be or Not to Be" soliloquy. "When we have shuffled off this mortal coil," refers to the turmoil in life.
	📖	Read "Hamlet" in *Tales From Shakespeare* by Charles and Mary Lamb and the soliloquy in the excerpt from *Hamlet,* Act III, Scene 1, in the Recommended Reading Appendix.

Watch a video of the play, *Hamlet*. The one starring Mel Gibson follows Shakespeare's play very closely. (Parents, please preview the story and any movie version you may choose to watch.)

---

3. "What coil are you keeping down there, Mulugutherum?" is an allusion to Shakespeare's *The Comedy of Errors*, Act III. It says, "What a coil is there, Dromio? Who are those at the gate?" **Coil** here means a disturbance.

   Literature

   Read "The Comedy of Errors" in *Tales from Shakespeare* by Charles and Mary Lamb.

---

4. Jill had no sympathy for Eustace's fear of heights (**acrophobia**). Now we find out she is afraid of small, enclosed places (**claustrophobia**). Of what are you afraid? Are you sympathetic to fears of others?

   Critical Thinking

   What do you think about Puddleglum's statement that there are no accidents?

   What phrase did the warden repeat?

---

5. The Prince said his lady was a "nosegay of all virtues." What virtues did he list?

   Bible

   Read Colossians 3:12–17. Do you see any similarities? Differences?

   Memorize these verses.

➤┼◆┼○┼◆┼◄

Chapter 11

Vocabulary Words:

vile

fie

tyrant

adjure

Vocabulary:

🗝 **Look up the words in a dictionary before you read the chapter and write them, along with a definition, in your vocabulary notebook.**

✏ Using your vocabulary words, fill in the blanks. The answers may be found in the section entitled Answer Appendix.

1. I _____ you to set him free.

2. "A prince, whose character is thus marked by every act which may define a _____ , is unfit to be the ruler of a free people." —Thomas Jefferson

3. The prince said, " _____ on gravity."

4. The way she behaved toward the beggar was _____ .

Read Chapter 11 of *The Silver Chair*.

✳ Assignments:

Bible	📖	1. Read Hebrews 5:14. We must have our senses trained in order to be able to discern good and evil. Who helps us to do this?
Art	✋	2. Draw a picture with a pool reflecting the picture.
English		3. The word **irony** has more than one meaning, although the two are closely related. It can mean the use of words to convey the opposite of their literal meaning, sarcasm; or, it can indicate incongruity between what might be expected and what actually happens.
	🗝	Find an example of the first meaning in this chapter. See Answer Appendix.
Critical Thinking	📕	4. Discuss the following questions with your instructor: • Aslan did not tell Pole what would happen. He only told her what to do. Can you think of any Biblical characters who were in the same position? Are you in the same position? • What was the "something wrong" that vanished from Rilian's face after he had destroyed the chair?

⋗⊷○⊶⋖

Vocabulary

☞ **Look up the words in a dictionary before you read the chapter and write them, along with a definition, in your vocabulary notebook.**

🖉 Using your vocabulary words, fill in the blanks. The answers may be found in the section entitled Answer Appendix.

1. The music she played on her _____ was hypnotic.

2. I will _____ his arms while you tie his legs.

3. _____ that which is evil.

4. I hereby _____ my throne!

Read Chapter 12 of *The Silver Chair*.

☀ Assignments:

📖 1. The Witch asked what the name Aslan meant. If someone asked you the same question about Jesus, what would your answer be? See Answer Appendix.

Bible

📖 Read Matthew 1:23 and Isaiah 9:6. Use a concordance or a Bible with references to find other names that are used to refer to Jesus.

✋ Make a banner using the names of Jesus.

🦁 Memorize one of the above Bible verses.

✋ 2. Draw Puddleglum, Eustace, and Rilian attacking the serpent.

Art

---

3. Puddleglum's speech, which begins to bring the others to their senses, almost sounds like one of the Psalms in which David lists the wonderful works of God.

Bible

📖 Read Psalms 104 and 146.

🖉 Write a paragraph praising the works and wonders of God that mean the most to you.

🦁 Memorize a Psalm of praise.

English		4. Go back to the definition of *irony* in the last chapter of *Further Up and Further In*. Find an example of the second meaning in Chapter 12 of *The Silver Chair*. The answer may be found in the Answer Appendix.

History		5. When Jill began to think of home she thought of ration books. This story is supposed to have taken place in 1942. What things were rationed? Why were these things rationed? Read about rationing during World War II. How long did the war last for the British? The Americans?
		For one week ration your food and gas:

- 2 oz of butter (some sources said 6 oz)
- 2 to 4 oz of cheese
- 1 to 2 eggs
- 4 oz bacon or ham
- 12 oz sugar

Art		6. Look at posters created during World War II.
		Make a poster supporting rationing.

Critical Thinking		7. Discuss the following questions with your instructor:

- Why do you think Puddleglum was able to hold out longer against the Witch than Rilian, Eustace, or Jill?
- The less you noticed the music the Witch was playing, the more it got into your brain and blood. If we are not on our guard, the world can do this to us. What other things besides music can get into our brains and blood more, the less we notice them?
- If we were in a war today, what types of things would be rationed? How would you need to change your life-style?

⊱—◆◆—O—◆◆—◆

⧗ PLANNING GUIDE – CHAPTERS 13-16

Gather These Items:

1. Items to make a model of the earth's inner layers, Chapter 13.

2. Recordings of different kinds of music, Chapter 15.

3. Items to make a banner, Chapter 16.

4. Recipes and ingredients to make the following items, Chapter 16:
   - Hot chocolate. See Activity Appendix.
   - Baked apples with raisins. See Activity Appendix.
   - A Centaur's breakfast: porridge, fish, meat (kidneys, bacon, or ham), omelet, toast, marmalade, and coffee.

Suggested Information to Gather:

Encyclopedia or books about:

1. Care of burns, Chapter 13 (Health/Safety).

   ....

2. Volcanoes, Chapter 13 (Science).

   ....

3. Salamanders, Chapter 14 (Science).

   ....

4. Flag care, Chapter 16 (History).
   - *Boy Scout Handbook.*

   ....

Suggested Videos:

Suggested Field Trips:

Suggested Memorization:

1. John 16:33 and Psalm 116:15, Chapter 14.

Notes:

Chapter 13

Vocabulary Words:

outstrip

sirrah

Vocabulary:

🔑 **Look up the words in a dictionary before you read the chapter and write them, along with a definition, in your vocabulary notebook.**

✏️ Skim the chapter for your vocabulary words. For each word, write one sentence from this chapter which contains the vocabulary word under its dictionary definition. Follow each sentence with a citation.

Read Chapter 13 of *The Silver Chair.*

☀ Assignments:

Reading Comprehension	📖	1. Answer this question orally: • Why had Scrubb and Pole not called each other by their Christian names?
Bible		2. What did Rilian mean when he said Aslan would be their good lord whether he meant for them to live or die?
	📖	Read Daniel 3:17–18 and Philippians 1:20–24.
Health/ Safety	🔑	3. How did they care for Puddleglum's burns? What is the proper treatment for burns? Was Puddleglum's foot treated correctly?
Critical Thinking	📖	4. Discuss the following question with your instructor: • The only things Rilian wanted to take with him when he left the Witch's house were the two horses. If you had to leave your house with only what you could carry, what would you take?
Literature		5. In *Surprised by Joy: The Shape of My Early Life*, C.S. Lewis talked about one of his favorite childhood authors, H.G. Wells. Wells and Jules Verne were both science fiction writers. It is rumored that Wells and the French novelist Jules Verne actually criticized each other's writing. Wells claimed "Verne couldn't write himself out of a paper sack," and Verne accused Wells of having "scientifically implausible ideas." Jules Verne wrote *Journey to the Center of the Earth.* Unlike C.S. Lewis, he was an evolutionist.

6. Devise a model of the earth's inner layers. — Science

If you cannot come up with your own idea for a model, try the
following:

Take a marble (inner core) and put it in a clear glass Christmas bulb
ornament. Fill the bulb with goop (outer core) three-quarters full
so the marble is left partially exposed. Cover three-fourths of the
ornament with play dough (the mantle). Cover the play dough with
paper maché (the crust).

7. Learn about volcanoes. — Science

Vocabulary:

**Look up the words in a dictionary before you read the chapter and
write them, along with a definition, in your vocabulary notebook.**

Using your vocabulary words, fill in the blanks. The answers may be found
in the section entitled Answer Appendix.

**Vocabulary
Words:**

squib

dazzle

mill-race

eloquent

1. The last time I let off a _____ was July 4th of last year.

2. We didn't think it was possible for him to survive the fall into
   the _____ .

3. He put on his sunglasses before emerging from the cave so the sunlight
   wouldn't _____ his eyes.

4. That was one of the most _____ speeches I've ever heard.

Read Chapter 14 of *The Silver Chair*.

☀ Assignments:

1. Rilian said Aslan would be their good lord whether they lived or died. — Bible

   Do Christians need to fear death? Do you have a favorite Bible verse that
   comforts you when you are afraid?

   Read John 14:1–4, 27 and Psalm 116.

   Memorize John 16:33 and Psalm 116:15.

2. Your perspective is your **point of view**—how you see things because
   of whom and where you are and what you have experienced. The — English

Earthmen could think of nothing worse than being forced to live on top of the ground in the open air. Most humans would feel just the opposite.

 Pretend you are a bug or an animal and write a story about the way that bug or animal would feel about something you, as a human, like. Or choose a foreign country and study the culture of the people there. If you were to go there, what would seem strange, uncomfortable, or wrong to you?

Science

3. On page 30 of his book, *Marco Polo—Overland to Medieval China*, Clint Twist writes:

> The salamander is an amphibian, which was widely believed to be fire-resistant and even to live inside fires. The belief arose because salamanders often hide beneath the bark of logs, and then rush out when the logs are placed on a fire.

 Read about salamanders.

 Write a paragraph about what you learned.

English

4. C.S. Lewis wrote a poem called, "The Salamander."

 You can read it in the book, *Poems*, edited by Walter Hooper. In the same book, you can also read Lewis' poem, "The True Nature of Gnomes," which was published in the magazine *Punch* in 1946, seven years before he wrote *The Silver Chair*.

⊱╌◈╌○╌◈╌⊰

Chapter 15

Vocabulary Words:

pert

disheveled

in league

phosphorescence

Vocabulary:

🔑 **Look up the words in a dictionary before you read the chapter and write them, along with a definition, in your vocabulary notebook.**

Using your vocabulary words, fill in the blanks. The answers may be found in the section entitled Answer Appendix.

1. We should have known that the dwarfs were _____ with the witch.

2. Grandma was offended by the little girl's _____ answer.

3. We could tell by her _____ appearance that she had been napping when we rang the doorbell.

4. In the darkness we could see the _____ of the rocks on the cave's walls.

Read Chapter 15 of *The Silver Chair.*

☀ Assignments:

---

1. When Jill was snatched away, Eustace immediately blamed Puddleglum for letting go of her. When did humans first begin placing blame on others for their problems and mistakes?

   Read Genesis 3.

Bible

---

2. Many times in *The Chronicles*, Lewis tried to describe what different kinds of music sound like.

   Listen to different kinds of music and write a paragraph describing the sounds.

English/ Music

---

3. Draw squirrels and owls coming out of trees in showers. Add badgers, hedgehogs, bears, and a panther if you like.

Art

---

4. Jill had to climb upon Puddleglum's shoulders in complete darkness. Try blindfolding yourself and another person. Give the other person instructions on how to do something safe and see what happens.

Games

---

5. Discuss the following questions with your instructor:
   • The oldest Dwarf told Rilian, ". . . those Northern Witches always mean the same thing, but in every age they have a different plan for getting it." What were the plans of the other witches in Narnia whose stories you have read?
   • Satan is always up to the same thing, too. What is he trying to do? What are some of the ways he tries to accomplish his plan? How can we resist him?

Critical Thinking

➤┥◆➤─O─◆┝◄

Chapter 16

Vocabulary Words:

humbug

doleful

disconsolate

vague

Vocabulary:

🔑 **Look up the words in a dictionary before you read the chapter and write them, along with a definition, in your vocabulary notebook.**

✏️ Using your vocabulary words, fill in the blanks. The answers may be found in the section entitled Answer Appendix.

1. Jill called Puddleglum a _____ because he acted sad but was really happy.

2. The young boy was _____ when he had to leave for summer camp; but when it was time to go home, he didn't want to leave.

3. After listening to the _____ music for a while, I began to feel sad.

4. The directions he gave me were so _____ that I soon became lost.

The word **leech** comes from a Middle English word for physician. What is the connection between a doctor and a bloodsucking parasite?

Read Chapter 16 of *The Silver Chair*.

☀ Assignments:

Critical Thinking

📖 1. Discuss the following questions with your instructor:
   • Caspian was given permission to come into our world once to help set things right. The end of the book is all about things being set right. How many things can you find that were made right?
   • When will things be set right in our world?

Bible

🔑 2. The Centaur told Jill and Eustace the nine names of Aslan and their meanings. Each different name used for God tells us something more about Him. Look up some of the names of God and their meanings. You may be able to find them in a reference Bible, a Greek/English study Bible, or by looking up *God* in *Strong's Exhaustive Concordance of the Bible*. El Elyon, Adonai, Elohim, El Shaddai, El Olam, Jehovah-jirah, Jehovah-rapha, Jehovah Sabaoth, and El Gibbor are some of His names.

✋ If you enjoyed making the banner with the names of Jesus, then make one using the names of God.

3. Lewis said it is the stupidest children who are the most childish. Jesus said, anyone who does not have faith like a little child will never get into the Kingdom of God, Luke 18:17. What is the difference between being childlike and being childish? — Bible

4. How is what happened to Caspian, when Aslan's blood splashed over his dead body, like what will happen to us after we die? — Bible

   Read I Corinthians 15 and Philippians 3:20–21. How is it different?

   Will Jesus' blood need to be shed anymore in order to change us?

   Read Hebrews 10:11–18.

5. C.S. Lewis comments on the sausages the Dwarfs cooked for Jill and Eustace. They were ". . . not wretched sausages half full of bread and soya bean." Why would anyone make sausages "half full of bread and soya bean"? (This story is supposed to have taken place in 1942. Remember they had rationing during World War II.) See Answer Appendix. — History

6. When Caspian died the Narnian flag was brought down to half-mast. Why was this done? What are some other flag signals? — History

   Find out about the proper way to care for an American flag. Your encyclopedia or the *Boy Scout Handbook* will probably have that information.

7. Make hot chocolate. Eat baked apples with raisins. Make a breakfast like the one the Centaurs ate. You may want to limit yourself to one kind of meat. Finish with oatmeal. See Activity Appendix for recipes. — Cooking

8. Review the list of Seven Deadly Sins found in *Further Up and Further In*, Chapter 15 of *The Magician's Nephew*. — Literature/Bible

   Of the remaining two sins, which sin did Jill display in *The Silver Chair*? Give examples of this. See Answer Appendix.

9. Do *The Silver Chair* Crossword Puzzle. — Vocabulary

Complete any unfinished assignments prior to going on to *The Last Battle*.

THE SILVER CHAIR CROSSWORD PUZZLE

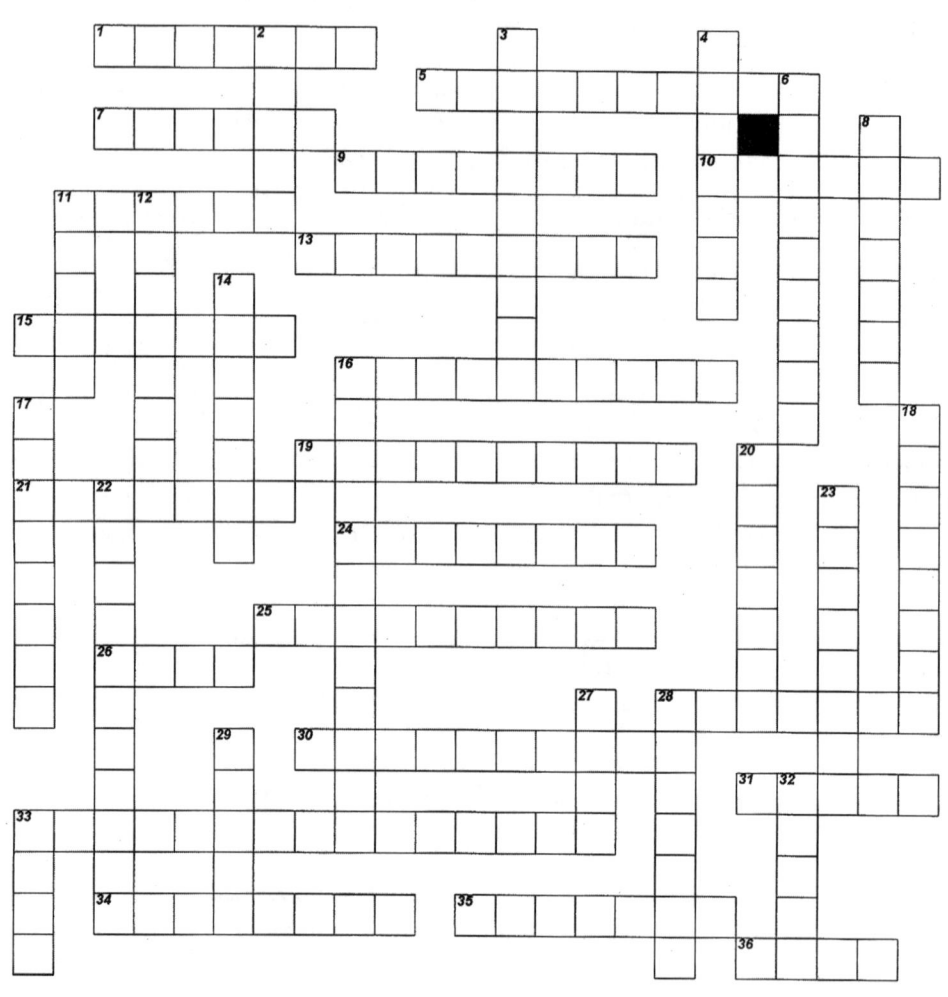

ACROSS

1 cheerless

5 supreme legislative body

7 baloney

9 treat

10 small gear

11 form of address for an inferior

13 fanciful

15 camp

16 disorderly

19 study of mind and behavior

21 posy

24 exceed

25 tormented

26 anchor

28 drinks of sweetened and hot spiced milk curdled by wine

30 low parapet

31 pier

33 heatless luminescence

34 gesturing without landing a blow

35 fruit, seed, or licorice candies

36 dour

DOWN

2 expression of disgust

3 meat pieces, stewed with white sauce

4 scorn

6 box used for tinder and flint

8 ceiling moulding

11 brief witty writing

12 recant

14 herb in the carrot family

16 downcast

17 in the lute family

18 protective barriers

20 tramps

22 yummy

23 fluent

27 fit

28 lapwings

29 loathe

32 eject

33 fresh

THE LAST BATTLE

⧗ PLANNING GUIDE – CHAPTERS 1-4

Gather These Items:

1. *The Last Battle* by C.S. Lewis.

2. Poster board and markers, Chapter 1.

3. *Genesis: Finding Our Roots* by Dr. Ruth Beechick, Chapter 2.

4. *1984* by George Orwell, Chapter 3. (Parents please preview this book. You may want to read aloud the suggested section of this book to your student instead of allowing them to read it without supervision.)

5. *American Dictionary of the English Language* (1828 Edition) by Noah Webster, Chapter 3.

6. *Little Town on the Prairie* by Laura Ingalls Wilder, Chapter 3.

Suggested Information to Gather:

Encyclopedia or books about:

1. Apes, Chapter 1 (Science).

   ....

2. Systems of government, Chapter 3 (Social Studies).

   ....

3. Islam religion, Chapter 3 (Bible/Social Studies).
   • *Learning About Islam* by LINK International.

   ....

4. Lions, Chapter 3 (Science).

   ....

Suggested Videos:

Suggested Field Trips:

Suggested Memorization:

1. Psalm 73, Chapter 1.

2. Genesis 2:7, Chapter 1.

Notes:

☙ WORKSHEET/CHAPTER 1
Parallel Character/Event List
Keep track of characters and events that parallel the Book of Revelation.

Event or Character

Book of Revelation

Event or Character

The Last Battle

_____

_____

_____

_____

_____

_____

_____

_____

_____

_____

APE WORKSHEET

FOR USE WITH CHAPTER 1

1) Description: _____

_____

_____

_____

2) Life Span: _____

3) Diet: _____

_____

_____

_____

4) Enemies: _____

_____

5) Habitat: _____

_____

_____

6) Behavior: _____

_____

_____

Draw a Picture

Draw a Track

Favorite Fact: _____

_____

_____

_____

_____

_____

Words to Learn:

opposable thumb

band

diurnal

Kingdom > Phylum > Class > Order > Family > Genus

Animalia > Chordata > Mammalia > Primates > Hominidae or Pongidae > Gorilla

LION WORKSHEET

FOR USE WITH CHAPTER 3

1) Description: _____

_____

_____

_____

2) Life Span: _____

3) Diet: _____

_____

_____

_____

4) Enemies: _____

_____

5) Habitat: _____

_____

_____

6) Behavior: _____

_____

_____

Draw a Picture

Draw a Track

Favorite Fact: _____

_____

_____

_____

_____

Words to Learn:

retractable claws

carnivores

pride

Kingdom > Phylum > Class > Order > Family > Genus > Species

Animalia > Chordata > Mammalia > Carnivoroa > Felidae > Panthera > Panthera leo

Study Guide – Chapters 1-4

Vocabulary:

Vocabulary Words:

panniers

caldron

🗝 **Look up the words in a dictionary before you read the chapter and write them, along with a definition, in your vocabulary notebook.**

✏ Skim the chapter for today's vocabulary words. For each word, write at least one sentence from this chapter which contains the vocabulary word under its dictionary definition. Follow each sentence with a citation.

✏ Under the definition of *caldron,* explain why it is a fitting name for the pool.

Read Chapter 1 of *The Last Battle*.

☀ Assignments:

1. Discuss the following questions:
   - Do the names Shift and Puzzle give you any idea of what the Ape and the Donkey will be like?
   - Puzzle and Shift said they were friends, but Shift treated Puzzle more like a slave. What are some qualities of a real friend?
   - Why do you think C.S. Lewis chose an ape for Shift's character?

   Critical Thinking

2. During the remainder of this study, read two chapters of the Book of Revelation daily.

   Bible

   ✏ As you read *The Last Battle* and the Book of Revelation, fill in the Parallel Character/Event List Worksheet found after this unit's Planning Guide.

3. The Donkey was ignorant and, therefore, susceptible to the trickery of the Ape. We have already studied wisdom and knowledge; what does the Bible say about being ignorant?

   Bible

   📖 Read Acts 17:30–31; Ephesians 4:17–19; I Peter 1:13–14; and Psalm 73:22.

   ✋ From the list of the above scriptures, make a warning poster utilizing your favorite verse.

Bible		4. Puzzle's ignorance could have been corrected by teaching, but Shift's ignorance seems to be willful. Romans 1:18–32 talks about those who choose to turn away from the knowledge of God. Take time to read and discuss these verses.
		Psalm 73 could be describing Shift. During the remainder of this study, memorize Psalm 73 and keep it in mind as you come to know Shift better.
		Read Acts 8:9–25. What warning did Simon receive? What similarities do you see between Simon and Shift? What differences?
Bible		5. The Ape felt secure in his deception because Aslan never did turn up in Narnia anymore anyway. Read II Peter 3:3–9.
		What does Colossians 2 say about being on guard against being led astray by the words of men?
Literature		6. Read Aesop's Fable, "The Ass in the Lion's Skin." This is included in the Recommended Reading Appendix. Do you think this fable might have stimulated C.S. Lewis' imagination?
Science		7. In what type of homes do apes live? How closely does Shift's home resemble the type of homes apes have in our world?
		Fill in the Ape Worksheet found after the Planning Guide.
Bible		8. Evolutionists attempt to classify man as a highly developed ape. All myths of the origin of mankind fall into two categories. Read about these in *Genesis: Finding Our Roots*, pages 39 and 40. Would you say these two beliefs still exist today?
		Read Genesis Chapters 1 and 2. How was man made? Does Scripture say we came from an ape?
		Memorize Genesis 2:7.
		God is a God of creativity. As an example of God's creativity, just look at the wide variety of plant and animal life on earth. He is also a God of order. By noting many of the similarities between humans and animals, man has improved his knowledge of the way God has ordered the world. Apes have been used in the medical study of human diseases and in behavioral, linguistic, and psychological studies. Through animal studies drug companies have found risks and benefits associated with certain medicines.

Vocabulary:

🔑 **Look up the words in a dictionary before you read the chapter and write them, along with a definition, in your vocabulary notebook.**

Vocabulary
Words:

✏️ Using your vocabulary words, fill in the blanks. The answers may be found in the section entitled Answer Appendix.

pomp

rash

sloth

conjunction

1. He was fired from his job because of his _____ .

2. I was impressed with the _____ with which the marriage of the prince was celebrated.

3. The superstitious people believed that the coming _____ of the planets would cause the end of the world.

4. Your _____ behavior will get you into trouble someday.

Read Chapter 2 of *The Last Battle.*

✳️ Assignments:

📖 1. Answer the following questions orally:
 • What was the Tree of Protection?
 • Who planted it?
 • What was Aslan's promise concerning it?

Reading
Comprehension

📖 2. In Narnia the truth was written in the stars. Read pages 97 and 98 of Dr. Ruth Beechick's *Genesis: Finding Our Roots.*

Bible

📖 What does she think about the truth being written in the stars above our world?

🔑 What is the difference between astronomy and astrology?

📖 3. Read Matthew 2:1–12. How did the wise men know about Jesus? Because of the way the wise men knew about Jesus, even some Christians have attempted to develop a doctrine of biblical astrology. The root meaning of the Greek word for *star* simply means radiance or brilliance. It is actually the *Shechinah* Glory rather than an astrologer's star. There are five things about this star which make it clear it cannot be a physical star.

Bible

✏️ Comparing your knowledge of astronomy and of Scripture, see if you can find these five things. See Answer Appendix.

Do you think any of the astrologers took note of Daniel's writings, especially since Daniel saved their lives? See Daniel 2:12–48. (Instructor, please explain the following answer to your student.)

How did the Gentile, Babylonian astrologers know about a Messianic King? The star did not tell them about the King of the Jews; Daniel's writings had. Daniel associated with Babylonian astrologers in Nebuchadnezzar's court. It was in Babylon that the Book of Daniel was written. Daniel dated the Messiah's First Coming in verses 24–27 of chapter 9 of the Book of Daniel.

Bible

4. Jewel and Tirian loved each other like brothers and each had saved the other's life in the wars. David and Jonathan had a similar friendship.

 Read about David and Jonathan's friendship in I Samuel. The main story of their friendship is told in Chapters 18–21, but their friendship continued until the death of Jonathan.

English   5. Write a paragraph comparing and contrasting the friendship of Jewel and Tirian to that of Puzzle and Shift.

Bible   6. Word was spreading in Narnia that Aslan had returned, and Narnians were coming from all over the country to see if it was true. Jesus told us that when He returns, we will not have to wonder if it is true.

 Read Matthew 24:21–28.

Bible   7. When Tirian heard the forests were being cut down and the logs sold to the Calormenes, he became too angry to think clearly and much evil came of what he did in his anger. Review what you learned about anger in Chapter 2 of *The Magician's Nephew*.

Chapter 3

Read Chapter 3 of *The Last Battle*.

☀ Assignments:

1. Answer the following questions orally:
   - What was Ginger the Cat beginning to understand?
   - Who is Tash?

   Reading Comprehension

2. Tirian asked Jewel how they could know what Aslan would do. He should at least have known what Aslan would not do. From Narnian history, write what you know about Aslan's character. Why do think Tirian did not know as much?

   English

3. What are some promises God has made which tell us what He will do and not do? The word *promise* is not used in every case where God made a promise, but if you need help finding some, try looking in a concordance under *promise* or *never*.

   Bible

4. The Ape keeps repeating he is not an Ape but a Man, as if repeating it over and over will make it so. Do we sometimes believe a lie is true just because we have heard it so many times?

   Critical Thinking

5. The Cat and the Calormene decided to say that Aslan is Tash and Tash is Aslan.

   Bible/ Social Studies

   Read Isaiah 5:20–21.

   Discuss times you have seen this happen.

   Many people say the God of Abraham, Isaac, and Jacob, the God of the Jews, is the same as Allah, the God of the Muslims.

   Find out about the Islam religion. Is their God the same as Jehovah? *Learning About Islam* by LINK International is an excellent source of information about this religion. See the Resource Appendix.

English		6. Read the appendix of George Orwell's *1984*, "The Principles of Newspeak." (Parents, please preview the book and the appendix.)

 Discuss the following questions:
- What would be the eventual effects of having fewer and fewer words in our language?
- In what ways are we controlled by language?
- What are some words you hear used today that are meant to cover up or soften what people really mean?
- What are some words that have lost their original meaning as a result of being used incorrectly?
- Do we use words to deliberately conceal the truth? Can we lie by only telling part of the truth?

English/
Social Studies

7. The Ape also said, "True freedom means doing what I tell you." What is true freedom?

 To discover the meaning of freedom, look up *freedom* in the 1828 Edition of Noah Webster's *American Dictionary of the English Language* or the dictionary of your choice. Also look *freedom* up in your Bible concordance. Be sure to read Galatians, Chapter 4. To further your understanding, read the chapter titled "Fourth of July" in Laura Ingalls Wilder's *Little Town on the Prairie*.

 After you have thought about this information, write a paragraph or poem on freedom.

Social Studies

8. The Ape told the animals their pay would all go into Aslan's treasury to be used for the good of everyone. What kind of government is this called? What are Socialism, Communism, Capitalism, and Democracy? What is a Republic? What kind of government does the United States have?

 Spend at least a day studying each of these forms of government. Younger children should learn the basics of each of these forms of government. Older children should learn more of the history of each one.

 Write one paragraph on each form of government. Older children write an additional paragraph on the history of each one.

 Discuss the effects of these forms of government in the countries where each is practiced.

Science   9. Learn about lions.

Complete the Lion Worksheet found after the Planning Guide.

>─┼◇─○─◇┼─<

Chapter 4

Read Chapter 4 of *The Last Battle*.

☀ Assignments:

1. Answer the following questions orally: Reading
   - How did Tirian figure out the truth about "Aslan" even though he   Comprehension
     had never seen a lion?
   - Name the seven people Tirian saw at the table.
   - Why do you think Peter, and not the old man, was the one
     to speak?

2. Tirian knew all of the stories about children coming from another world   Bible
   to help Narnia in times of trouble, but he did not believe things like that
   still happened. However, since he could no longer help himself, he cried
   out to Aslan; and even though nothing immediately happened, he felt
   better right away.

   Does God still hear us when we cry out to Him?

   How did David feel knowing God heard him cry out?

   Read Psalm 3, Psalm 30, and Psalm 138.

⧗ PLANNING GUIDE – CHAPTERS 5-8

Gather These Items:

1. Materials for making a telegraph, Chapter 5. (*World Book Encyclopedia* gives instructions for a simple telegraph. You may be able to find instructions online or in a book at the library.)

2. Items to make hardtack, Chapter 5. See Activity Appendix.

3. Items to make a turban, Chapter 5. See Activity Appendix.

4. Items to make an imitation scimitar, Chapter 5. See Activity Appendix.

5. *Bold Believers in Turkey* by LINK International, Chapter 5.

6. *Foxe's Book of Martyrs* by John Foxe, Chapter 8.

7. *Voice of the Martyrs* magazine, Chapter 8. See Resource Appendix.

8. *Poems* by C.S. Lewis, Chapter 8.

9. Materials for making soap, Chapter 8.

Suggested Information to Gather:

Encyclopedia or books about:

1. Soapmaking, Chapter 8 (History). See Resource Appendix.

Suggested Videos:

Suggested Field Trips:

1. Go rabbit hunting, Chapter 6.

Suggested Memorization:

1. Continue working on Psalm 73.

Notes:

Vocabulary:

Vocabulary Words:

perilous

prithee

firkin

sullen

rude (p. 62)

garrison

☞ **Look up the words in a dictionary before you read the chapter and write them, along with a definition, in your vocabulary notebook.**

✎ Using your vocabulary words, fill in the blanks. The answers may be found in the section entitled Answer Appendix.

1. The _____ shepherd's hut barely kept out the rain and wind.

2. Safely inside the walls of the _____ , the settlers slept soundly for the first time in weeks.

3. The _____ of water had to last the three travelers their entire journey.

4. She faced the _____ journey very bravely.

5. _____ , grant me a boon, your majesty.

6. If you continue to be _____ , you will have to go to your room.

Read Chapter 5 of *The Last Battle*.

✴ Assignments:

1. Answer these questions orally:
   - What two things did Tirian do to make tracking them difficult?
   - What made the old stories seem more real?
   - What showed Tirian the children were well-raised?
   - For what did each wish?
   - How do the Narnian night noises differ from what you hear at night where you live?

   This is the first time someone in Narnia, besides Aslan, has called for someone out of our world. Name the five other ways in which children from our world entered Narnia. See Answer Appendix.

Reading Comprehension

2. Eustace told Tirian that Peter had sent them a wire. What did he mean? How was this done? Is it still done today?

   Read about the telegraph in your encyclopedia or a book about the telegraph.

History

Science	3. Make a telegraph. The *World Book Encyclopedia* gives instructions for a simple telegraph.

History	4. To Tirian, Jill and Eustace were historical characters who had been in Narnia over two hundred years ago. If you could meet someone from history, whom would you choose? Why? What would you want to talk about? What do you think would interest that person the most about the present? Write about an imaginary meeting with the historical character of choice. Be sure to answer the above questions in your story.

Cooking	5. The children and Tirian ate some hard biscuit by breaking it into bits and making porridge. U.S. soldiers used something similar called hardtack. Hardtack was a type of perforated biscuit. It had a long shelf-life and was used by many soldiers, sailors, miners, and, yes, cowboys, as a replacement for bread, which went moldy very quickly. The only problem was hardtack is extremely (you guessed it) hard. In order to eat it, "you had to bust it up with your rifle butt or a handy rock; put it in your mouth and leave it there until it became soft(er)." Make hardtack. See Activity Appendix for recipe.

Geography	6. What are turbans? Which countries could one visit and see many people wearing turbans? Make a turban. Use the directions in the Activity Appendix or find directions on the Internet.

Art	7. Persians developed the scimitar. These swords are used by Arabs and Turks and are associated with the *Arabian Nights*. Make an imitation scimitar sword.

Social Studies	8. The contrast between the English/Narnian culture and the Arabic/Calormene culture can be seen throughout *The Last Battle*. The story would not have been very effective if there had not been a clear conrast between Aslan and Tash and their respective followers. C.S. Lewis is not around to ask why he chose to make Middle Eastern type people and their religions the embodiment of evil. Yet perhaps an analogy may be drawn from his letter to a boy. The boy asked C.S. Lewis if he did not like panthers because he had made some of them bad. In *Letters to Children*, Lewis said he thought panthers were beautiful and did not remember making them bad, but even if he did, that did not mean he did not like them any more than the fact Uncle Andrew is bad meant Lewis did not like men.

For a deeper understanding of this contrast, go through *Bold Believers in Turkey,* a LINK publication. See Resource Appendix.

Vocabulary:

Vocabulary Words:

miscarry

rive

malapert

mattock

Look up the words in a dictionary before you read the chapter and write them, along with a definition, in your vocabulary notebook.

Using your vocabulary words, fill in the blanks. The answers may be found in the section entitled Answer Appendix.

1. The animals fled as the giant began to _____ the trees of the forest.

2. If our original plan should _____ , we will have to resort to plan B.

3. No one wanted to have to speak to the _____ young man.

4. Would you rather use a _____ or a horse and plow?

Read Chapter 6 of *The Last Battle.*

Assignments:

1. The Donkey said he only did what he was told. What did Jesus say would happen to anyone who leads others astray? Read Matthew 18:5–10.	Bible
2. Hunt, kill, and skin a rabbit. (Cottontail is much better to eat than jackrabbit.) Make rabbit stew. Substitute rabbit for the usual beef.	Life Skills
3. Find the North Star.	Life Skills
4. How do you think it would be to sleep in chain-mail?	Critical Thinking

Chapter 7

Vocabulary Words:

manikin

miscreant

moke

churl

sagacious

scurvy

wood sorrel

belike

rally (p. 85)

Vocabulary:

🗝 **Look up the words in a dictionary before you read the chapter and write them, along with a definition, in your vocabulary notebook.**

✏ Using your vocabulary words, fill in the blanks. The answers may be found in the section entitled Answer Appendix.

1. At what time of year does the _____ bloom? _____ it blooms later at higher elevations.

2. His reputation for being a _____ made it difficult for him to make friends.

3. The _____ woman was often consulted before her children made important decisions.

4. By the time Scott was fourteen years old, he thought his grandmother should stop calling him a _____ .

5. Though he spoke pleasantly, his actions proved he was a _____ fellow.

6. The _____ scientist forged the evidence to support evolutionary propaganda.

7. He hoped many would _____ to the cause.

8. The _____ refused to climb any further up the hill.

Read Chapter 7 of *The Last Battle*.

✷ Assignments:

Bible	📖	1. Read the story of the ten lepers in Luke 17:11–19.

📜 In *The Last Battle*, which Dwarf was thankful? What effect did his thankfulness have on the children and Tirian? Share about a time you showed thankfulness when everyone else did not. Share about a time when you did not show gratitude, but should have.

✏ Write a note of thanks to Cadron Creek for publishing this study. Or write a note of thanks to your parent for choosing this study and assisting you with it.

Critical Thinking   📜   2. Go back to Chapters 7 and 12 of Prince Caspian and compare Nikabrik's attitude to that of the Dwarfs now. What is the difference?

3. Puzzle informed the King that Shift and the others would sometimes forget to give him water. — Bible

Read Proverbs 12:10. What insight does this verse give you into Shift's character?

⊱─◆─○─◆─⊰

Read Chapter 8 of *The Last Battle*.

☀ Assignments:

1. Answer these questions orally: — Reading Comprehension
   • Who brought Tirian and his party news of the fall of Narnia?
   • Do you agree with Roonwit that noble death is a treasure no one is too poor to buy?

2. Do you always feel better once you have made up your mind? — Critical Thinking

3. While Jewel was being held captive, he was threatened with death if he did not say he believed Aslan was in the stable. Name some Bible characters who were threatened with death or killed for what they believed. To learn about Christians throughout history who have been martyred, read *Foxe's Book of Martyrs* by John Foxe. See Resource Appendix or your local library. — Bible

Read some issues of the *Voice of the Martyrs* magazine. See Resource Appendix.

Read Colossians 2:2–4 and Ephesians 6:19–20.

Pray daily for one Christian who is being held captive or, as a family, choose to sponsor a minister of the gospel in a country where Christians are persecuted.

4. Jewel told Jill stories of the peaceful times in Narnia when no help from our world needed to be called. — English

Write a story about one of the characters mentioned: Swanwhite the Queen, Moonwood the Hare, or King Gale. Work on this story throughout the rest of this unit.

English		5. In this chapter Tirian hummed an old marching song. The refrain is from a poem, "Narnian Suite," which you can read in C.S. Lewis' book, *Poems*. Part I of the poem is a "March for Strings, Kettledrums, and Sixty-three Dwarfs." Part II is a "March for Drum, Trumpet, and Twenty-one Giants." Notice how the rhythm changes from Part I to Part II.
		What other literary devices were used to change the feeling of the marching of dwarfs to the feeling of giants marching? See Answer Appendix.
History		6. Tirian and the children washed off their disguises with a mixture of grease and ashes. Ashes were sometimes used in making soap because they were a source of lye. Working with lye made from ashes can be dangerous, but there are other ways to make soap.
		Read about how soap is made and try making some yourself if possible.
Bible		7. Jill said our world would end. Does Scripture say this? Use a Bible concordance to locate at least one verse which supports your answer.

⧖ PLANNING GUIDE — CHAPTERS 9-12

Gather These Items:

1. An iron and starch, Chapter 12.

Suggested Information to Gather:

Encyclopedia or books about:

1. Animal eyes, Chapter 9 (Science).

....

2. Cliches, Chapter 10 (English).

....

3. Maps of battles, Chapter 11 (History).

....

4. Permanent press fabric, Chapter 12 (Science).

....

Suggested Videos:

Suggested Field Trips:

Suggested Memorization:

1. Continue working on Psalm 73.

Notes:

Read Chapter 9 of *The Last Battle*.

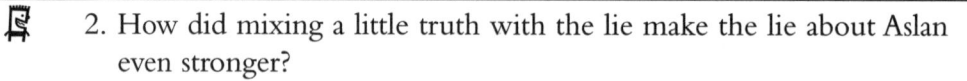

✳ Assignments:

Science	1.	Find out why an animal's eyes glow in the dark.

Critical Thinking	2.	How did mixing a little truth with the lie make the lie about Aslan even stronger?

One of the plans discussed for getting Narnia back from the Calormenes was to hide in the woods and wait until there were enough creatures on their side to sweep the Calormenes out of the country and revive Narnia as was done in the time of Miraz.

What are the differences between Miraz's time and now? Why would this not work? See Answer Appendix.

English	3.	Continue working on your story from Chapter 8.

➤┤◆─○─◆├◄

Vocabulary Words:

caterwaul

manifold

haughty

Emeth (Hebrew for faithful and true)

Vocabulary:

Look up the words in a dictionary before you read the chapter and write them, along with a definition, in your vocabulary notebook.

Skim the chapter for today's vocabulary words. For each vocabulary word, write at least one sentence from this chapter which contains the word under its dictionary definition. Follow each sentence with a citation.

Read Chapter 10 of *The Last Battle*.

☀ Assignments:

1. Answer this question orally:
   - Who said, "Whether we live or die, Aslan will be our good lord"?

Reading Comprehension

2. "Cool as a cucumber" is a simile. It is also a cliche—an overused expression. Can you think of some other cliches? Generally, cliches in writing should be avoided "like the plague."

English

3. The description of Ginger coming out of the stable is very vivid; we can almost see him and feel his panic. Include a description in your story of an animal or a person doing something that requires movement and emotion.

English

4. Ginger, the Calormene, and the Ape thought they were in control of the situation in the stable; but they were playing with something they did not understand. Read about what happened to the seven sons of Sceva when they tried to control something they did not understand, Acts 19:11–20. What happened to the seven sons?

Bible

5. What do you think is in the stable?

   Out of fear, the talking beasts did not want to see Aslan; they wanted Shift to go. Of what Old Testament story does this remind you?

Critical Thinking

Chapter 11

Vocabulary:

Vocabulary Words:

🔑 **Look up the words in a dictionary before you read the chapter and write them, along with a definition, in your vocabulary notebook.**

allegiance

✏ Skim the chapter for today's vocabulary words. For each vocabulary word, write at least one sentence from this chapter which contains the word under its dictionary definition. Follow each sentence with a citation.

despair

Read Chapter 11 of *The Last Battle*.

Assignments:

Bible 1. What the Ape had been threatening everyone else with finally happened to him. At the end of our world, what will happen to the false prophet and the beast? To find out, read Revelation 19:20.

History/
Reading
Comprehension

2. Pick your favorite battle in history. Find a map that charts the battle. Follow the flow of the battle with the map. What move decided the fate of the battle?

Carefully reread this chapter and draw a map showing how the battle went.

Critical
Thinking

3. Read the description of the Talking Dogs coming over to Tirian's side. Do you think C.S. Lewis liked dogs?

Vocabulary
Words:

starch

gravely

Vocabulary:

 Look up these words in a dictionary before you read the chapter and write them, along with a definition, in your vocabulary notebook.

Skim the chapter for today's vocabulary words. For each vocabulary word, write at least one sentence from this chapter which contains the word under its dictionary definition. Follow each sentence with a citation.

Read Chapter 12 of *The Last Battle*.

Assignments:

Reading
Comprehension

1. Answer the following questions orally:
   - What did Jewel mean when he said the door to the stable might be a door to Aslan's country?
   - What did it mean that Tirian's "only thought was to sell his life as dearly as he could"?
   - What did C.S. Lewis list as uncomfortable articles of clothing? Do you find them uncomfortable?

- Eustace had thought he and Jill were in a railway accident just before they came into Narnia. Do you know what really happened to them?
- What does Tash represent?

---

2. Tirian and those with him had found a trickle of water coming down from the rock around which they were gathered. What do you think this represents?   Bible

Using a Bible concordance, find as many verses as you can in which Jesus is referred to as our Rock. In how many verses does He offer water or is He called water?

---

3. Aslan had told the children they would have to learn to know him in their own world. What had happened to Susan? What things had become more important to her than being a friend of Narnia? In a letter written by C.S. Lewis to a boy on January 22, 1957, Lewis said it was not too late for her, there was plenty of time for Susan to mend (C.S. Lewis, *Letters to Children*). Why is it not too late for Susan?   Critical Thinking

---

4. Before the days of permanent press fabric, people ironed almost everything that was washed. Many people spent a whole day ironing what they had washed the day before.   Science

Find out how permanent press fabric works.

---

5. What is the purpose of starch in clothing? Iron an article of clothing which has been starched. How does it feel?   Life Skills

---

6. Continue working on your story from Chapter 8.   English

⧖ PLANNING GUIDE – CHAPTERS 13-16

Gather These Items:

1. *Letters to Malcolm: Chiefly on Prayer* by C.S. Lewis, Chapter 13.

2. Recipe and ingredients for trifle, Chapter 13. See Activity Appendix.

3. *Genesis: Finding Our Roots* by Dr. Ruth Beechick, Chapter 16.

4. Items to bind a book, Chapter 16.

Suggested Information to Gather:

Encyclopedia or books about:

1. Falling stars, Chapter 14 (Science).

....

2. Time and date of the next meteor shower, Chapter 14 (Science).

....

3. Plato, Chapter 15 (History).

....

4. Waterfalls, Chapter 16 (Geography).

....

5. Phoenix (mythical bird), Chapter 16 (Mythology).

....

6. Information on how to bind a book, Chapter 16 (Art).

....

Suggested Videos:

1. *Shadowlands*, Chapter 13.

Suggested Field Trips:

Suggested Memorization:

1. Continue working on Psalm 73.

Notes:

Study Guide – Chapters 13-16

Chapter 13

Vocabulary:

🔑 **Look up the word in a dictionary before you read the chapter and write it, along with a definition, in your vocabulary notebook.**

rugger

✏️ Skim the chapter for today's vocabulary word. Write at least one sentence from this chapter containing this word under its dictionary definition. Follow each sentence with a citation.

Read Chapter 13 of *The Last Battle*.

☀ Assignments:

1. Answer these questions orally:
   - Why did the Dwarfs not see the beauty around them?
   - What did Aslan mean by "taken in" and "taken out" when he said the Dwarfs were "so afraid of being taken in they could not be taken out"?
   - What happened to the young Calormene whom everyone liked?

   Reading Comprehension

2. Edmund said he remembered something hitting him while he was in the train but it did not hurt and his sore knee did not hurt anymore. What had happened? Will it be like that in our world?

   Read Revelation 21:4.

   Bible

3. Will we get to taste the fruit of the tree from which all of the Kings and Queens of Narnia were eating? Will it be like that in our world?

   Read Revelation 22:14.

   Bible

4. Aslan praised Tirian for standing firm in the darkest hour. What is promised to those on earth who are victorious?

   Read Revelation 2:7, 11, 17, 26; 3:5, 12, 21; and 21:7.

   Bible

5. **Digging Deeper:** Peter said he was sure they had gotten to a country where everything is allowed. C.S. Lewis said, "There is no morality in heaven." To find out what Lewis meant, read Chapter 21 of his book, *Letters to Malcolm: Chiefly on Prayer.*

   Critical Thinking

Cooking	✋	6. Make a trifle. See Activity Appendix for recipes. Invent your own Narnian trifle.

English	✏️	7. Complete your rough draft of the story started during Chapter 8.

History	👓	8. Watch the video *Shadowlands*.
	📖	Read the article, "How Hollywood Reinvented C.S. Lewis in the Film *Shadowlands*," by John G. West, Jr. A link to this article may be found at CadronCreek.com's Web site. To go to the link page, click on "Research Links" in the sidebar menu. At the page, select "Further Up and Further In" to find the listing of links for this study. Another way to find this article online is to do a search for it using the title as the keyword.

⊱—◆—○—◆—⊰

Chapter 14

Vocabulary Words:

rhubarb

tentacles

Vocabulary:

🗝️ **Look up the words in a dictionary before you read the chapter and write them, along with a definition, in your vocabulary notebook.**

✏️ Skim the chapter for *tentacles*. Write at least one sentence from this chapter containing this word under its dictionary definition. Follow each sentence with a citation.

Read Chapter 14 of *The Last Battle*.

☀️ Assignments:

Cooking/ English	✋	1. Eat some rhubarb.
	✏️	Write a paragraph to describe the taste and texture of rhubarb.

Reading Comprehension	📖	2. Answer these questions orally: • Who were the stars Edmund and Lucy had once met? See Answer Appendix. • Why did Digory and Polly recognize the dying sun? See Answer Appendix. • How did each of the group feel to see a Calormene in their new world?

3. When Father Time awoke, what do you think his name was?
See Answer Appendix.

Critical
Thinking

Digory saw Narnia begin, but he did not think he would live to see it
die. Digory went home shortly after the creation of Narnia and did not
see it again until it ended.

- Can you imagine how he would feel?
- Did he "live" to see it die?

4. It is interesting Peter had the key to lock the door of the old Narnia.

Bible

Read Matthew 16:17–19.

5. In this chapter we see the end of Narnia. What parallels did you find
between the Book of Revelation and *The Last Battle*?

Bible

Unlike many other Western mythologies, Norse mythology includes
an account of the end of the world. Teutonic (otherwise known as
Norse) mythology consists of the myths of Scandinavia and Germany.
The basic source written in the 1200's consist of two works, called
Eddas. According to Norse mythology there will be a great battle called
Ragnarok. This battle will be fought by the giants and the gods and
goddesses living in their home of Asgard. All will be killed and the earth
will be destroyed by fire. After the battle, Balder, the god of goodness
and harmony, will be reborn. He will form a new race of divinities. The
human race will also be recreated by the man and woman who took
refuge in the forest through the battle. The new world, cleansed of evil
and treachery, will endure forever.

Compare this mythological account with the Book of Revelation.

6. All of the creatures of Narnia came to Aslan and either loved him and
went to his right or hated him and went to his left and disappeared.

Bible

Read Matthew 25:31–46. Will something like this happen in our world?

7. What are falling stars?

Science

If you have never watched a meteor shower, find out when the next one
will occur and watch it. Using your favorite Internet search engine and
typing in *meteor* will help you do this.

8. Edit the rough draft of your story from Chapter 8.

English

Chapter 15

Vocabulary Words:	**Vocabulary:**
illuminate	🗝 **Look up the words in a dictionary before you read the chapter and write them, along with a definition, in your vocabulary notebook.**
delectable	✏ Skim the chapter for today's vocabulary words. For each vocabulary word, write at least one sentence from this chapter which contains the word under its dictionary definition. Follow each sentence with a citation.
constrain	

Read Chapter 15 of *The Last Battle*.

☀ Assignments:

Bible		1. Is it hard to understand why Emeth is in Aslan's country even though he had been seeking Tash all of his life?
	📖	Read Romans 2:12–16 and I John 2:29. Do either of these scriptures help you understand?
History	🗝	2. On page 195, Lord Digory was aghast that the children were not familiar with Plato. Find out about this famous Greek philosopher.
	✏	Write at least one paragraph about Plato.
	📖	With your instructor, read and discuss Plato's "Allegory of the Cave" from his book, *The Republic*. It may be found in the Recommended Reading Appendix.
Bible	📖	3. In light of the previous assignment, read and discuss I Corinthians 13:11–12; I Corinthians 10:1–11; and Ephesians 1–2:10. Has God used types to teach us before?
English	✏	4. Make a great title for your story from Chapter 8.
	✋	Include at least one illustration in your story.

>─◆─○─◆─<

Vocabulary:

Vocabulary Words:

helter-skelter

cascade (verb)

☞ **Look up the words in a dictionary before you read the chapter and write them, along with a definition, in your vocabulary notebook.**

✎ Skim the chapter for today's vocabulary words. For each vocabulary word, write at least one sentence from this chapter which contains the word under its dictionary definition. Follow each sentence with a citation.

Read Chapter 16 of *The Last Battle*.

✳ Assignments:

1. C.S. Lewis thought if you could run without getting tired you would not often want to do anything else.

   📖 Read Isaiah 40:31.

   Bible

2. Read *Genesis: Finding Our Roots*, pages 93–94, "History in Literature." Using the wide variety of mythology studied during *Further Up and Further In*, pick a different theme than the example given by Dr. Beechick and follow it through the generations or pick a mythological story and see if you can detect remnants of real history in it.

   Bible

3. What are the largest waterfalls in the world? In the U.S.? How much water passes over them per second?

   Geography

4. In your encyclopedia or a book on mythology, read the story of the Phoenix.

   Mythology

5. In Chapter 5, Eustace told Tirian how they had gotten the magic rings back and that he and Jill had not used them. How had they gotten into Narnia?

   When you get to heaven, which Bible heroes would you like to see? What would you talk about?

   Critical Thinking

6. Make a cover for your story from Chapter 8 and bind your book.

   English/ Art

Bible		7. Review all the scriptures you have learned.
Literature/ Bible		8. Review the list of Seven Deadly Sins found in *Further Up and Further In* in Chapter 15 of *The Magician's Nephew*.
		The remaining sin is envy. Give examples of this occurring in *The Last Battle*. See Answer Appendix.
Vocabulary		9. Complete *The Last Battle* Crossword Puzzle.
Party		10. Have a Narnia party. Wear the costume you made during *The Voyage of the Dawn Treader* study. Serve your favorite foods you learned to make during this study. Share your favorite activities from the study with your family or friends.
On-going Assignment		11. Learn to know Jesus so false prophets cannot fool you.

>—►—◦—◄—◄

THE LAST BATTLE CROSSWORD PUZZLE

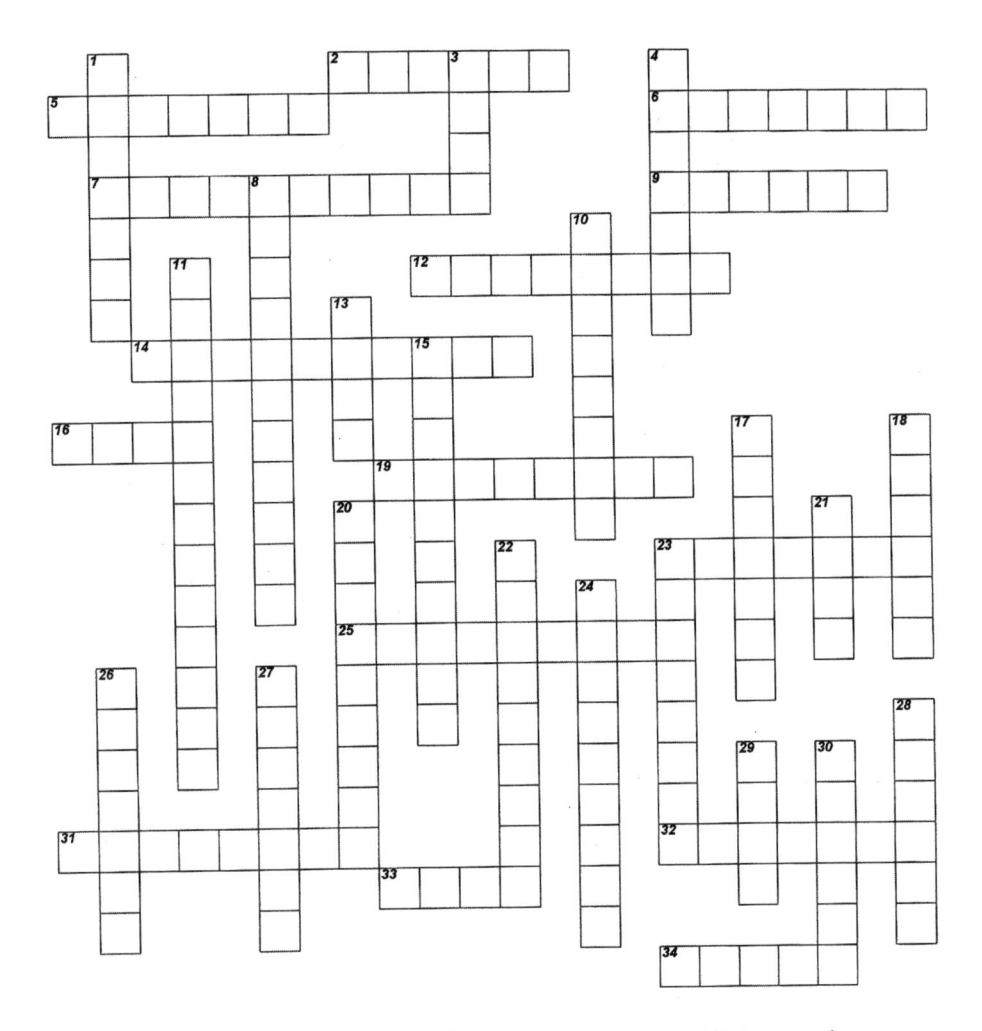

ACROSS

2 shirt stiffener

5 a dwarf

6 snooty

7 pleasing

9 probably

12 unsuccessful

14 edify

16 donkey (slang)

19 risky

23 pickaxe for loosening the soil

25 compel

31 saucy

32 abandon

33 chop down

34 to pull together or to recover one's health

DOWN

1 large kettle

3 unrefined

4 quarrel

8 association

10 fort

11 disorderly

13 split

15 loyalty

17 I pray thee

18 one-fourth of a barrel

20 vicious

21 splendor

22 cry of a cat

23 sundry

24 discerning

26 waterfall

27 solemnly

28 madcap

29 without deliberation

30 scarce

APPENDICES

SUBJECTS COVERED

Abbreviations used:

MN   *The Magician's Nephew*
LWW   *The Lion, the Witch and the Wardrobe*
HHB   *The Horse and His Boy*
PC   *Prince Caspian*
DT   *The Voyage of the* Dawn Treader
SC   *The Silver Chair*
LB   *The Last Battle*

Subjects Covered

Arts & Music

Bible

Bible Memory—According to Book

Cooking

English

English—Reading

ACTIVITY APPENDIX

Turkish Delight
(for use with *The Lion, the Witch and the Wardrobe*, Chapter 4, Activity 3)

VARIATION A
2 envelopes unflavored gelatin
1/2 cup cold water

Soften gelatin in cold water.

2 cups sugar
1/4 teaspoon salt
1-1/2 cups boiling water

In a large saucepan, heat sugar, salt and the 1-1/2 cups water to boiling point. Blend softened gelatin into hot syrup, stirring until dissolved. Boil slowly for 20 minutes.

1/4 cup orange juice (1 orange)
2 tablespoons lemon juice (1 lemon)
1 teaspoon mint or orange extract (optional)
Red or green food coloring, as desired

Add orange and lemon juices to hot mixture, then mint, if using, and food coloring. Allow to cool.

1/2 cup chopped nuts
1/2 cup raisins (optional)

When mixture starts to thicken, add nuts and raisins. Pour into a shallow pan (8 × 4-inch suggested) that has been rinsed in cold water. Let cool until firm.

1/4 cup confectioners' sugar
2 tablespoons cornstarch

In a shallow dish, sift together the confectioners' sugar and cornstarch. Using a wet, sharp knife, loosen candy around edges of pan; turn out on board lightly covered with confectioners' sugar mixture. Cut in 1-inch square cubes (kitchen shears may be easier than using a knife) and roll in confectioners' sugar mixture. (Placing the confectioners' sugar mixture in a small paper bag and adding a few squares at a time is an easy way to coat the cubes.) Dust off excess confectioners' sugar and place squares on wire racks to dry for at least 12 hours or up to 18 hours. To store, dust again with confectioners' sugar on all sides and pack in layers, separated by wax paper, in an airtight container. They will keep for up to 3 weeks.

VARIATION B
Source: Laurie W., London, UK

Laurie wrote: "Here in England, you can buy this sweet at almost any store. Ninety per cent of the Turkish Delight my husband has bought here has always been coated with dark chocolate. He has never in his life had it with nuts and fruits added to it. He says he doubts his parents have either. They are all Englishmen/women. This recipe allows you to make our own pink and white Turkish Delight."

9 cups confectioners' sugar
3 pints water
6 tablespoons cornstarch
3/4 pint cold water
Rose water
Lemon juice
Almond oil

Make a syrup of the icing sugar and 3 pints of water by boiling together in a heavy pan. Mix the cornstarch and the 3/4 pint of cold water, making sure the cornstarch is completely dissolved. Add the cornstarch mix to the boiling syrup and continue boiling until reduced by about two-thirds. The mixture will become very thick and stringy. Remove from heat. Pour half of the mixture into another saucepan. Flavour half with lemon and the other half with almond oil. Colour one with rose water. Grease two dishes with almond oil. Pour each mixture into its own dish. When set, turn both onto a board dredged with confectioners' sugar. Use kitchen paper to absorb any excess almond oil. Cut Turkish Delight into cubes and roll in confectioners' sugar. Store in a dry place.

Bird Suet
(for use with *The Lion, the Witch and the Wardrobe*, Chapter 6, Activity 3)
Source: *Portland Oregonian*

Suet makes a great diet supplement for insect eating birds during the winter when insects are harder to find. Bird feeding supply stores sell a wide range of suet cakes, some plain, some mixed with treats such as peanut butter, raisins or other dried fruit, nuts, or even peppers. You can make your own inexpensive mixture and freeze it to have on hand all winter. The Audubon Society originally published this recipe.

2 lb lard★
6 cups cornmeal
3 cups wheat flour
4 cups oatmeal
2 cups peanut hearts (optional), available at bird
 and feed stores

★DO NOT SUBSTITUTE SHORTENING
FOR LARD.

Soften the lard to room temperature. Stir in
the other ingredients a couple of cups at a time
until the mixture is quite thick. Freeze the
mixture in tuna cans or plastic tubs about 4
inches by 4 inches in size.

Note: The suet cakes can be hung frozen and
they fit nicely in wire suet cage feeders.

Summer Bird Suet Cakes
Recipe by: *Birds & Blooms*, June, 1997

1 cup lard★
1 cup crunchy peanut butter
1/3 cup sugar
1 cup whole wheat flour
2 cups oatmeal
2 cups cornmeal

★DO NOT SUBSTITUTE SHORTENING
FOR LARD

Melt lard and peanut butter. Stir in remaining
ingredients. Optional additions include raisins,
nuts, or birdseed. Pour mixture into a pan and
chill overnight. Then cut into squares to fit in
suet basket and store the unused portion in
refrigerator.

Marmalade Roll
(for use with *The Lion, the Witch and the Wardrobe*,
Chapter 7, Activity 4)

3 eggs
3/4 cup sugar
5 tablespoons milk
1-1/2 cups flour
1/4 teaspoon salt
1 teaspoon baking powder
1 tablespoon vanilla extract
1/2 cup orange marmalade
Powdered sugar

Beat the yolks of the eggs until light, then add
the sugar. Stir well and add the flour, salt, and

baking powder (sifted together), alternately with
the milk. Add flavoring. Grease a long shallow
pan of the size usually used in roasting meats. The
batter should be 1/4-inch deep; if it is thicker the
cake will not roll easily. Bake 6 to 8 minutes in
a moderate oven (350°F), watching closely, as it
bakes quickly.

When done, remove from the oven and cool.
When cool enough to handle, turn out on to a
cloth dusted with powdered sugar. Cut off the
side crusts, spread the jelly over the surface, roll
up and wrap the cloth about it to keep it in
shape. If the cake was spread too thick in the pan
and will not roll, cut it into three parts and lay
one upon the other, jelly between.

Make Your Own Modeling Clay
(for use with *The Lion, the Witch and the Wardrobe*,
Chapter 9, Activity 3 and *Prince Caspian*,
Chapter 7, Activity 2)
Source: <http://www.make-stuff.com>

VARIATION A
Mix together:
2-1/2 cups flour
1 cup water
1 cup salt
Food coloring (optional)

Store in refrigerator.

VARIATION B
Mix and cook over low heat until mixture
thickens:
1 cup salt
1 cup water
1 cup flour
Food coloring (optional)

Cool before using.

Plum Pudding
(for use with *The Lion, the Witch and the Wardrobe*,
Chapter 11, Activity 5)

An old Yorkshire tradition: In as many homes as
you eat plum pudding in the 12 days following
Christmas, so many happy months will you have
during the year.

Rather than a pudding, this is a steamed dessert
with a dense, cake-like texture.

1-1/3 cups flour
1 teaspoon soda
1/2 teaspoon cinnamon
1 teaspoon ground cloves
1/2 teaspoon salt
1/4 cup sugar
1 cup prunes (substitute raisins, nuts, or thinly
    sliced citron for prunes)
3/4 cup molasses
1/2 cup ground suet (This can be obtained
    from a butcher. The fat melts during cooking
    and moistens the pudding.)
1 egg
1/4 cup milk

In a bowl, combine dry ingredients and mix
in candied fruits. In separate bowl, beat wet
ingredients until well mixed. Add this mixture
to the dry ingredients and mix with a fork until
moistened. Pour into a well greased 2-quart
mold. Steam★ for 3 hours. Cool for 15 minutes
then remove. Serve with hard sauce.

★To steam the pudding: Take a large kettle
and put a vegetable steamer on the bottom.
The mold should not sit on the bottom of the
pan. Place the mold on the steamer, then add
water to approximately halfway up the mold
and cover the pan. Set the kettle on top of the
stove on a medium setting. Periodically check
the water level. Should you use a mold without
a cover, wrap the top with aluminum foil to
prevent the pudding from becoming watery.

Hard Sauce:
1/2 cup butter
1-1/2 cups confectioners' sugar
2 teaspoons vanilla

Cream the butter in a mixer or food processor,
blend in sugar and vanilla. Serve over the warm
pudding.

Fig Pudding
(for use with *The Lion, the Witch and the Wardrobe*,
Chapter 11, Activity 5)

VARIATION A
4 sweet potatoes, peeled and quartered
10 figs
2 cups milk, scalded
3 eggs
1/2 cup sugar

Boil sweet potatoes and figs in salted water for
about 25 to 30 minutes. Drain off water. Pass
potatoes and figs through meat chopper. Mix
together the eggs, sugar, and milk. Add this
mixture slowly to the potato and fig pulp. Pour
into a pudding dish. Set pudding dish in a pan
of hot water. Bake in moderate oven for about
25 minutes.

VARIATION B
8 oz figs
3/4 cup margarine or butter
3/4 cup sugar
3 eggs
1 teaspoon vanilla
1/4 cup molasses
4 slices bread
1 teaspoon cinnamon
1/2 cup cream sherry or concentrated
    orange juice
1 mold or coffee can

Stew figs for about 20 to 30 minutes. Drain
off liquid then chop figs. In large bowl, cream
margarine or butter with sugar. Add eggs and
vanilla and beat until smooth. Fold in molasses
and crumbed bread; fold in cinnamon, sherry or
orange juice concentrate and figs. Grease mold
or coffee can and sprinkle sugar all over the
inside. Pour in the fig mixture almost to the top
of mold. Cover with tin foil. Place on a rack in a
pan of water. The water should come up to the
middle of the mold. Cover pan. Bring water to
a boil. Reduce heat to medium or medium low
and steam for 3 hours. Then remove from pan
and cool on rack. When cooled, remove from
mold, wrap in foil, and place in refrigerator until
just before serving. Warm in the oven before
serving. Serve with hard sauce, foamy sauce, or
vanilla ice cream.

Foamy Sauce:
1 pint heavy cream
1 cup powdered sugar
1 teaspoon vanilla extract
1 teaspoon brandy extract

In mixing bowl, beat with an electric mixer the
heavy cream until almost stiff. Beat in sugar and
extracts and serve over the warm pudding.

VARIATION C (WITH LEMON SAUCE)

This fig pudding recipe is adapted from *The New York Times Cookbook*. The lemon sauce recipe is adapted from *The Joy of Cooking*.

Fig Pudding:
1 cup dried black figs
1-1/2 to 2 cups dried fruit (I used pineapple, golden raisins, and peaches)
1-1/4 cups flour
1 teaspoon baking soda
1 teaspoon cinnamon
1/2 teaspoon ground cloves
1/4 cup applesauce
1/2 to 3/4 cup brown sugar (I used 3/4, but next time I'll use 1/2.)
Egg substitute equivalent to 2 eggs (I used Eggbeaters.)
1 cup grated raw carrot
1 cup grated raw potato

Cover the figs with boiling water and let stand about 10 minutes. Drain and chop the fruit. Chop the other dried fruit in small pieces and combine.

Combine the flour with the soda and spices. Add 1/2 cup to the dried fruits and mix.

Beat the applesauce and the brown sugar together. Beat in the egg substitute. Add the grated vegetables. Gradually stir in the remainder of the flour mixture, beating until smooth. Mix in the dried fruits.

Fill a greased 1 1/2-quart mold about 2/3 full and cover with a lid or foil. Stand on a rack in an inch of boiling water in a pot with a tight cover. Steam 2 hours, adding more boiling water if necessary. Serve hot. Serve with lemon sauce.

Lemon Sauce:
1/4 cup sugar
1 tablespoon cornstarch
1 cup water
Grated rind of 1 lemon
1-1/2 tablespoons lemon juice

Combine sugar, cornstarch, and water in the top of a double boiler and stir over hot water until thickened. Remove from the heat. Add rind and juice. Serve warm. (I have also made it before dinner and reheated it gently in the double boiler.)

Meat Pasties from Karen's Kitchen

(for use with *The Horse and His Boy*, Chapter 2, Activity 4)

2 cups shortening, cut up in larger chunks
2 cups boiling water

Put shortening in a large pan and pour the boiling water over the shortening. Stir together until melted. Gradually stir in:

5-1/2 to 6 cups all purpose flour
2 teaspoons salt

Stir until a soft dough is formed. Cover and refrigerate 1 1/2 hours.

Filling:
12 large red potatoes, cut in smaller cubes
4 medium rutabagas, cut in smaller cubes (I assumed these were smaller rutabagas and used about 1/2 of a larger one.)
2 medium onions, chopped
2 pounds ground beef
2 pounds ground pork (I used all ground beef and they were great too.)
1 tablespoon salt
2 teaspoons pepper
2 teaspoons garlic powder
Butter

Divide dough into 12 large portions. Roll each, one at a time, into a 10-inch circle. Mound about 2 cups filling on half of each circle and dot with 1 teaspoon butter. Moisten edges of rounds with water, fold over and seal with a fork. Place on ungreased baking sheets. Cut several slits in the top of pasties. Brush with cream if desired. Bake at 350°F for 1 hour or until golden brown. Cool on wire racks. Serve hot or cold. Store in refrigerator. Makes 12 large pasties.

Note: When I made this recipe I halved everything and when I was cutting the rounds I used a small plate (5 to 6 inches) as a template for the circles I needed to cut from the dough. It worked quite well.

Gooseberry Fool

(for use with *The Horse and His Boy*, Chapter 5, Activity 2)
Source: *Great British Cooking: A Well Kept Secret* by Jane Garmey.

Gooseberry Fool is believed to date back to the 15th century. It is a blend of gooseberries, cream, and sugar.

1 lb gooseberries★
1 oz butter
2 tablespoons sugar
1-1/2 cups heavy cream

Pinch the ends off the gooseberries. Melt the butter in a heavy saucepan and add the gooseberries and sugar. Cover the saucepan and cook over the lowest heat possible until the gooseberries are soft and mushy (approximately 1/2 hour).

Remove the gooseberries from the pan and beat them to a pulp with a wooden spoon. Pass them through a sieve and discard the skins and pits. At this point you should taste the gooseberries; if they are too tart, add a little more sugar. Set them aside and allow to cool completely.

Whip the cream and fold it gently into the gooseberry pulp. Pour the fool into a glass serving dish or, if you prefer, divide it equally into small sherbet glasses. Chill for at least one hour before serving.

★If no gooseberries are available, rhubarb, fresh cranberries, or red currants all make good substitutes as they have the same kind of sharp, tart flavor that is absolutely essential for a good fool.

Childhood Games
(for use with *Prince Caspian*, Chapter 11, Activity 4)

Blind Man's Bluff
Step 1: Play this game in an easy-to-monitor area and be sure to clear away any toys or other objects the blindfolded player could trip on. Supervise carefully.

Step 2: The player who is "It" wears the blindfold. While he or she spins in place five times, all the other players run around the yard looking for a good spot to hide.

Step 3: When "It" finishes the fifth spin, he or she yells, "Stop," and all the other players must freeze in place.

Step 4: "It" then begins to search for the other players by yelling "Blind Man's. . . ." All other players must yell "Bluff," although they can disguise their voices. The searcher uses the vocal clues to track down the other players.

Variations:
Play without the verbal clues—the person who is "It" walks around the yard feeling for the players. The hiders must keep their feet in the same spot, but they can move the rest of their bodies in an effort to avoid getting tagged. The biggest challenge for the hiders? Don't giggle!

Stuck in the Mud—A Tig Game
Someone is "It." When caught, players stand still with their arms stretched out sideways and their legs apart. They can be released by another player passing between their legs. (Large groups may need a rule insisting on a one-way system between those legs, say back to front only, so as not to crack heads.)

Hoopla Tig
A tig game much the same as above, but when caught, players stand with their hands pointing to the sky. They can be released by a pair of other players getting together, holding hands, and hoopla-ing their "ring" of hands over the caught person, taking it down to the ground, so that the caught person can step out to freedom.

Chain Tig
When caught, the player joins hands with the one who is "It," and continues until everybody is caught and holding hands in one long line. Best played with only the people on the ends of the line being able to tig. This game does not work well if the group is too large or small for its space.

Snake Tig
One person has to try to tig other people—when tigged, player goes in front of first tigger, held by waist, and does the tapping, and so on.

Hunt the Slipper
All but one of the players sit in a circle. One sits in the middle, he closes his eyes and puts his hands over them. The players chant the following words:

Cobbler, cobbler mend your shoe,
Have it done by half past two.

During this chant, the players in the circle pass round a slipper behind their backs. The center player then chants:

Cobbler, cobbler tell me true,
Which of you has got my shoe?

When the last word is chanted, the circle stops passing the slipper and the player who has it makes sure it is hidden behind his back. The central player opens his eyes and has to guess who has the slipper just by looking at their faces. If he fails, he changes places with the person who holds the slipper.

Oatcakes

(for use with *Prince Caspian*,
Chapter 15, Activity 4)

There are several varieties of oatcakes. Some use baking powder while others use yeast. Some are baked while others are fried. Here are three different recipes you can choose from and two recipes which give ways to use them.

1 cup flour
1/2 teaspoon baking powder
1/2 teaspoon salt
1 teaspoon sugar
1-1/2 cups quick oats
1/2 cup butter or margarine
1 egg
2 tablespoons water

Mix flour, baking powder, salt, sugar, and oats in a bowl. Cut in the butter until mixture is crumbly. Beat egg with water and mix in dry ingredients. Work into a stiff dough. Sprinkle a few oats on a lightly floured board. Roll out dough as thinly as possible. Cut in circles or large triangles. Bake on greased cookie sheet in hot oven (400°F) about 12 minutes. Serve hot or cold with butter, cheese or jam. Makes 3 dozen.

Pictou County Oatcakes

Source: *Out of Old Nova Scotia Kitchens*

2 cups oatmeal
1 cup flour
1 cup brown sugar
1 teaspoon salt
3/4 cup shortening
1/4 cup boiling water
1/4 teaspoon baking soda

Combine dry ingredients (except baking soda) and cut in shortening. Dissolve baking soda in the boiling water and add, continuing to mix with a knife. Mold with the hands and shape into a long wedge. Slice off and bake in a 400°F oven for 10 minutes.

Derbyshire Oatcakes

Source: <http://www.high-lane-oatcakes.co.uk/recipies.html>

1 lb fine oatmeal★
1 lb flour
1 teaspoon salt
1 oz yeast
1 teaspoon sugar
2-1/2 pints warm water

Mix the oatmeal, flour, and salt in a warm bowl. Cream the yeast with the sugar and add 1/2 pint of the warm water. Pour the yeast mixture into the dry ingredients and add the rest of the water, mixing slowly until a thin batter is formed. Set aside in a warm place until well risen, about 30 minutes. Grease a large frying pan and heat. Pour cupfuls of the batter on to the hot pan and cook like thick pancakes for 4 to 5 minutes on each side. The oatcakes will keep for 2 to 3 days. Serve warmed up in a frying pan with bacon and eggs or with lemon juice and sugar or toasted with cheese or golden syrup. Makes 4 servings.

★If you cannot get fine oatmeal, use Quaker oats and grind fine in a food processor.

Savory Oatcakes

6 oatcakes
6 slices or more of bacon
6 oz cheddar cheese (grated)
4 oz mushrooms (thinly sliced)

Trim the rind from the bacon and grill until lightly crisp. Divide the cheese and mushrooms between the oatcakes and place under the grill until the cheese is melted. Put a rasher of bacon on each oatcake, roll up the oatcake, and serve. As an alternative, add cooked bacon, grated cheese, and mushrooms to oatcake, roll up oatcakes and microwave at 650 watts for approximately 1 minute per oatcake.

Sweet Oatcakes

6 oatcakes
3 bananas
3 oz soft brown sugar
1/4 pint orange juice
chopped walnuts (optional)

Grease a shallow ovenproof dish, large enough to hold 6 rolled oatcakes. Peel the bananas and cut each one in half lengthwise. Sprinkle 1 teaspoon of the brown sugar on an oatcake and put one of the halved bananas on the top of the sugared oatcake. Add some chopped walnuts if desired. Roll the oatcake around the banana and put the rolled oatcake into the baking dish, seam side down. Repeat the process with the remaining halved bananas and oatcakes. Combine the remaining brown sugar and the orange juice in a small saucepan. Put on low heat and stir until the sugar has dissolved. Remove from heat and pour the syrup evenly over the rolled oatcakes. Put the dish in a preheated oven (350°F) and bake for 15 to 20 minutes. Can be eaten plain or with cream or custard.

Easiest Loam

(for use with *Prince Caspian*,
Chapter 15, Activity 7)

1 box chocolate pudding
1 lb bag Oreo® cookies (regular)
1 bag gummy worms
Wax paper
Flowerpot (optional)

Mix pudding according to directions on box. While pudding sets, grind or smash Oreos until they are the consistency of dirt. Line flowerpots with wax paper, fill three-quarters full with pudding. Top with Oreos. Place gummy worms on top or hidden under the dirt. Preparation time, 15 minutes. Makes 8 servings.

Loam (A bit harder)

What you need:
Large package of Oreo® cookies
1/2 stick softened margarine or butter
8 oz softened cream cheese
3/4 cup powdered sugar
2 small packages instant French vanilla
    pudding
2-3/4 cups milk
12 oz Cool Whip® or other whipped
    topping

1 package gummy worms
8-inch flowerpot
Flowers
Gardening trowel

What you do:
1. Crush well the package of Oreo® cookies and set aside.
2. Cream together 1/2 stick of margarine or butter, 8 oz package cream cheese, and 3/4 cup powdered sugar. Set aside.
3. Mix together 2 packages pudding and 2-3/4 cups milk .
4. Combine #2 and #3. Mix well.
5. Fold in 12 oz Cool Whip®.
6. Plug the bottom of the 8-inch flowerpot with the lid from the Cool Whip®. Line the pot with wax paper or aluminum foil. Layer ingredients in pot, starting with cookie crumbs, then pudding mixture, and inserting the gummies. Repeat the process, using all the "layering material" and ending with cookie crumbs on top. Refrigerate overnight if possible.
7. Add flowers for decoration before serving. Serve with gardening trowel.

Somerset (Strawberry Delight)

(for use with *Prince Caspian*,
Chapter 15, Activity 7)

1 cup all-purpose flour
1/4 cup firmly packed brown sugar
1/2 cup chopped pecans
1/2 cup melted butter or margarine
1 (10 oz) package frozen
    strawberries, thawed, or 1-1/2 cups
    sliced fresh strawberries
1 cup sugar
2 teaspoons fresh lemon juice
2 egg whites
1/2 pint whipping cream, whipped

Combine the flour, brown sugar, pecans, and butter. Bake at 350°F for 20 minutes in a 9-inch square pan, stirring often. Let cool. Combine the strawberries, sugar, lemon juice, and egg whites; beat at high speed in an electric mixer for about 20 minutes or until light and fluffy. Fold the whipped cream into the strawberry mixture. Remove one-third of the crumb mixture from pan; pat remaining crumbs into a smooth layer. Pour the strawberry mixture over crumbs in pan and sprinkle the reserved crumbs over the top. Freeze.

Chalky Soil
(Hermie's Cheese Ball)
(for use with *Prince Caspian*,
Chapter 15, Activity 7)

Note: You will probably want to third this recipe.

3 - 8 oz packages of cream cheese
2 - 5 oz jars of old English cheese
2 tablespoons minced onions
3 tablespoons Worcestershire sauce
2 tablespoons parsley
3 garlic cloves
1/4 teaspoon cayenne

Combine all ingredients. Form a ball and roll in chopped nuts. Wrap in Saran Wrap plastic sacks.

Finest Gravels
(for use with *Prince Caspian*,
Chapter 15, Activity 7)

Rock candy or sugar coated nuts.

Silver Sand
(for use with *Prince Caspian*,
Chapter 15, Activity 7)

Powdered Sweetened Kool Aid®
or Jello® Gelatin

Suck up the powder with small straws similar to stirring spoons or lick your finger and dab!

Make Your Own Scratchboard
(for use with *The Silver Chair*,
Chapter 4, Activity 3)

What you need:
Oil pastel canvas
Oil pastels
Black ink
Paintbrush

What you do:
On a piece of oil pastel canvas, rub any color of oil pastel onto the canvas, pressing hard. Completely cover the canvas. Then with a paintbrush, spread on a coat of black ink. Let it dry. After it is completely dry, paint a second coat. If the canvas has curled, paint the second coat in the opposite direction of the first coat. The first coat of ink will not stick well to the oil pastel coating but the second coat will go on more easily than the first. After it is dry, you may scratch a picture into it.

Eel Pie
(for use with *The Silver Chair*,
Chapter 5, Activity 6)

Pie and Mash:
1 to 2 pounds of eel or firm fleshy fish
Salt to taste
Lemon
1/4 cup shallots
Puff pastry

Cut up the eel in half-inch chunks and boil it with the salt, lemon, and shallots. Put in a suitable baking dish or pan. Cover with puff pastry. Bake at 350° F for 35 to 40 minutes. For an authentic meal, serve with "green liquor," a parsley sauce (see recipe below), and mashed potatoes on the side.

Green Liquor or Parsley Sauce:
Chopped parsley
1 teaspoon butter
1 teaspoon flour
2-1/2 cups water★

Wash parsley. Melt butter in pan and stir in flour. Remove from the heat and stir in the water.

★You can use milk or potato or fish stock instead of water if you prefer.

Caraway Biscuits★
(for use with *The Silver Chair*,
Chapter 7, Vocabulary)

Only butter should be used when making shortbread—margarine does not give as good a result. The more butter the shortbread contains, the "shorter" and crumblier the shortbread.

110g or 4 oz Golden Caster sugar
   (substitute granulated sugar)
225g or 8 oz unsalted or sweet butter
350g or 12 oz plain flour, sifted
50g or 2 oz blanched almonds, chopped
1 tablespoon caraway seeds (optional)
25g or 1 oz candied peel, chopped

Knead the sugar and butter together. Gradually work in the flour, almonds, and caraway seeds until the mixture forms a soft dough. Shape into a thick round (the thickness is a matter of preference, but thicker will take longer to cook) and place on a lightly greased baking tray. Press the candied peel into the top and bake at 300°F for 30 to 60 minutes until cooked through.

★Since the English call cookies, *biscuits*, these "biscuits" are a type of shortbread and are served as a dessert.

Cock-a-leekie Soup

(for use with *The Silver Chair*, Chapter 8, Activity 1)

2 chicken fillets
1 tablespoon soy sauce
1 teaspoon butter
2 medium leeks, finely sliced
1 carrot, diced
1 medium potato, diced
8 cups chicken stock
Salt and freshly ground black pepper
1 cup corn kernels
2 tablespoons fresh parsley

Cut chicken into very small pieces and toss in a bowl with soy sauce. Heat butter in nonstick fry pan and stir-fry leeks for 2 minutes. Add carrot and stir-fry for 1 minute. Add potato and chicken stock and season with salt and pepper. Bring to a boil and cook on medium heat for 15 minutes. Blend half the soup to a puree and return the pureed soup to the pan. Add corn kernels and simmer for 5 minutes. Add chicken pieces to hot soup and leave on gentle heat for 5 minutes without boiling it. Stir in parsley and serve. Serves 6.

Posset

(for use with *The Silver Chair*, Chapter 8, Activity 4)

Substitute sparkling grape juice for the sherry.

1 pint milk
5 oz sweet sherry
Pinch grated nutmeg
1 tablespoon Demerara sugar
Lemon zest to decorate

Heat the milk, sherry, nutmeg, and sugar in a saucepan. Serve sprinkled with the lemon zest.

My Most Decadent Hot Chocolate

(for use with *The Silver Chair*, Chapter 16, Activity 7)
Source: <http://www.perfectentertaining.com/page1104.html>

Preparation Time: 5 minutes
Cooking Time: 15 minutes
Total Time: 20 minutes

1 cup milk
1 cup half-and-half
8 teaspoons sugar
1 oz semi-sweet chocolate, finely chopped
1 ounce unsweetened chocolate, finely chopped
1 tablespoon brown sugar
1/2 teaspoon pure vanilla extract

In a small heavy saucepan over medium heat mix together the milk, half-and-half, sugar, chocolates, and brown sugar. Heat until the chocolate melts and the sugar dissolves. Do not bring to a boil, but make sure the mixture gets steaming hot. Reduce the heat and keep the chocolate hot. Place half of the mixture in a blender and mix until frothy. Return to the pan, add the vanilla, and pour into cups. Serve immediately. Serves 2.

Hot Chocolate

You can make your own mix for hot cocoa.

Mix in a large bowl:
10-2/3 cups nonfat dry milk
6 oz powdered nondairy creamer
2 cups powdered sugar
16 oz can instant chocolate drink mix

Store in an airtight container that can hold about 17 cups and label it. Store in a cool, dry place. Add 3 tablespoons of the mix to 1 cup of hot water and stir to dissolve.

Baked Apples and Raisins

(for use with *The Silver Chair*, Chapter 16, Activity 7)
Source: <http://www.recipesource.com/misc/camping/00/rec0013.html>

4 green Granny Smith apples
1/3 cup sugar
1/2 cup sultana raisins (not golden raisins)
1 teaspoon ground cinnamon

Remove the cores of apples such that the apples are intact with a tube-like hole right through the center. Do not peel the apples. Mix the sugar, raisins, and cinnamon together. Stuff this raisin mixture into the cored apples in the tube-like hole. Compact well and wrap each whole apple in aluminum foil paper. Throw into embers at campfire. Wait 8 to 10 minutes. Remove foil and serve. Serves 4.

Baked Apples

Source: <http://www.virtualcities.com/ons/wv/gov/wvgvjr1.htm>

4 Granny Smith apples
2 tablespoons sugar
4 teaspoons margarine or butter
1/4 cup raisins
1/3 cup brown sugar, firmly packed
1 tablespoon flour
1/2 teaspoon cinnamon
1 tablespoon water

Preheat oven to 350 degrees. Take a small rectangular Pyrex dish and lightly grease the bottom with a little margarine or butter. Core apples, all the way through, and peel away the skin from around the top of the apple. Slice away a small piece from the bottom of the apple so it will stand up straight in the dish. Place the apples in the dish. Mix together the sugar and butter with the raisins and place in the cored out cavity of each apple. Place in the oven and bake for approximately 20 minutes. Meanwhile in a small bowl, combine the brown sugar, flour, and cinnamon along with the water. Spoon over the baking apples and continue to bake for another 10 minutes. Serve either warm or cool.

Hardtack

(for use with *The Last Battle*, Chapter 5, Activity 5)

2 cups flour
1/2 tablespoon salt (optional)
1/2 tablespoon sugar (optional)
1/2 cup water

Mix flour, salt (optional), sugar (optional), and water. Using hands or rolling pin, flatten dough on floured cloth until 1/4-inch thick. Score with a knife if desired. Bake on cookie sheet in 350°F oven for 30 minutes. Break into pieces as needed.

Hardtack Crackers

3 cups water or milk
8 cups plain flour
1/2 cup lard or shortening
3 teaspoons salt
1 teaspoon sugar (optional)
1 teaspoon molasses (optional)

Mix and knead to form workable dough. Flatten out or roll to 1/2 -inch thickness. Cut into 3-inch squares and punch holes with an ice pick or nail, three rows of three holes per square. Bake at 400°F for 45 minutes, or until jaw breaking hardness is achieved. Cool in open air and store in cloth or paper sack. Spoilage is not a problem.

Making a Turban

(for use with *The Last Battle*, Chapter 5, Activity 6)

What you need:
15 yards of light cotton about 20 inches wide (making strips out of an old cotton sheet is ideal)
Swimming cap (not essential, but very useful)

What you do:
Before starting to wind the turban, put on a swim cap. Its function is to keep your hair from getting wrapped into the turban and to make sure no hair shows through.

Start with one end of the cotton strip about six inches below the base of your neck; this will be the tail which one sees on some period turbans. The turban passes from there over your head to just above the forehead and then starts being wound. A single wind is a circle (clockwise seen from above) tilted somewhat from the horizontal. As you wind the turban, the low point should move around your head by about 90° each wind. If the low point is under your right ear the first time around, then the next time it is at the back of your head, then left ear, etc. (This is very approximate.) As you go, you can let the tilt increase, since the bottom of the circle will anchor itself below the bulge of cloth already there. When you are down to the last two yards or so, make a horizontal circle around the whole thing and tuck the end in. The result is the horizontal band that one often sees on period turbans. Tying a turban is more easily demonstrated than described. You may also want to look at some Web sites.

Trifle Cake

(for use with *The Last Battle*,
Chapter 13, Activity 6)
Source: <http://www.allsands.com/Food/
Recipes/trifflecakerec_sky_gn.htm>

A basic trifle cake consists of four elements:
cake, pudding, your choice of filling, and
whipped topping. It might sound overly simple,
but trifle cakes offer the opportunity to create a
dessert that can coordinate with any holiday or
event. They can be as simple as basic chocolate
or as extraordinary as pumpkin spice.

Basic Instructions

What you need:
Trifle dish or a punch bowl.
Cake mix
Pudding (choose a flavor that coordinates with
   the type of cake you chose)
Filling (fruit, candy, chocolate chips, etc.)
Cool Whip® or other whipped topping

What you do:
1. Bake the cake according to box directions.
2. Make pudding and chill for 1 to 2 hours.
3. Crumble about 1/3 to 1/2 of cake into
   bottom of bowl; layer with pudding; layer
   with filling; layer with whipped topping.
   Repeat until bowl is full.
4. Garnish with extra filling.

Now that you have the basic instructions
for creating a trifle, let's learn how to create
specialty trifles to coordinate with your life
events. How can a trifle cake become the perfect
addition to a holiday meal? Simple! Coordinate
your choices of cake fillings and flavors with the
time of year.

Spring Trifle

Use yellow cake, vanilla pudding, whipped
topping, peaches and strawberries. This is
popular for baby and bridal showers as well as
for Easter.

Autumn Trifle

This Autumn or Pumpkin Spice Trifle is a great
variation from the Thanksgiving tradition of
pumpkin pie. Use gingerbread, pumpkin mixed
with vanilla pudding, your choices of spices, and
whipped topping.

Chocolate Toffee Birthday Trifle

Use chocolate cake, chocolate pudding,
chocolate and English toffee chips, and whipped
topping.

Chocolate Peanut Butter Trifle

Use chocolate cake, chocolate pudding,
chocolate and peanut butter chips mixed with
peanut butter, and whipped topping. Note:
filling will be thick; drop by rounded spoonfuls
into bowl and gently spread.

Narnian Trifle

Make your own yummy combination!

Summer Trifle

Source: <http://www.lanierbb.com/recipes/
data/899.html>

This recipe is from the Allen House Victorian
Inn, Amherst, Massachusetts.

1 good quality pound cake
Good quality raspberry preserves
Pastry cream (see recipe below)
2 cups whipping cream with sugar to sweeten
   (whip to soft peaks)
4 cups mixed berries macerated in sugar

Pastry Cream:
4 cups half-and-half
1 cup sugar

Heat the half-and-half and sugar in a heavy pan.
Slowly temper 6 eggs into hot mix. Continue
whisking on low heat.

Mix 1/2 cup cornstarch with a little water. Add
to the hot mix and continue whisking. It will
get thick. Turn off heat.

Whisk in:
6 oz butter
1 teaspoon almond extract

Let cool.

1. Cut pound cake into thick slices
2. Thinly spread raspberry perserves, then cut
   into 4 squares.
3. Start to layer trifle: cake, pastry cream, berries,
   cake, whipped cream. Continue layering until
   all ingredients are used. End with whipped
   cream.

RECOMMENDED READING APPENDIX

SOUND WAVES

Many forms of energy exist as waves. Waves have these features:

- Crests—the high points on a wave

- Troughs—the low points on a wave

- Wavelength—the distance between two neighboring crests or troughs

- Amplitude—the height of a wave

- Frequency—the number of crests passing through a place per second

The International System SI (metric) unit for frequency is the hertz (Hz). The unit called megahertz is one million hertz. If one million crests pass a given place in one second, the frequency is one megahertz. Hertz is sometimes described as cycles per second.

Frequency is related to wavelength. The shorter the wavelength, the faster the frequency. The longer the wavelength, the slower the frequency.

Sound is a wave-form phenomenon which is produced by vibration. When you talk, your vocal cords vibrate, creating waves which travel through the air. When you whistle, your lips vibrate. Musical instruments have reeds or strings that vibrate. When you are sick or yell a lot, your vocal cords may become swollen so that they have difficulty vibrating. When this occurs, you have laryngitis and you lose your normal voice.

For sound waves to travel they need a conductor. All matter can conduct sound waves, but some matter conducts better than others. For example, air is a better conductor of sound waves than water.

A vacuum is a place that has no matter. Without matter, sound waves cannot occur. "In space no one can hear you scream." On the moon, verbal communication had to occur electronically.

Substances which trap sound waves are called insulators. Such things as carpet, furniture, acoustic tile, and drapes trap sound waves. If you have ever talked in an empty house, you have noticed that it sounds loud because there is almost nothing to trap your sound waves. An echo occurs because sound waves bounce off of something and return to your ears. If sound waves reach your ears, travel on and bounce off of something and return to your ears, you hear the sound again.

Sound waves take time to travel. The speed of sound is the speed at which sound waves travel. Sound does not travel at the same speed in all kinds of matter. In general, sound travels faster in a solid than in a liquid and faster in a liquid than in a gas. This is because the molecules are closer together in a solid than a liquid and closer together in a liquid than a gas. However, because more tightly packed molecules result in more friction, sound waves travel further in a gas than in a liquid and further in a liquid than in a solid. The speed of sound also depends on the temperature of the conductor. The warmer the conductor the faster sound waves can travel. Most guns shoot bullets at a speed greater than the speed of sound. So if someone was shot in the head and killed at the impact of the bullet, they would never hear the sound of the gun shot. In normal air, the speed of sound is 1,087 feet per second. This is equal to about 740 miles per hour.

When a moving object, such as an aircraft, reaches a speed where the molecules of the air can no longer be pushed aside, the air forms a barrier. If this barrier is broken, the compression of the air molecules produces heat which can cause the aircraft to burn up or disintegrate. This hot, compressed air acts like thunder and produces a shock wave known as a sonic boom. In 1947 the Bell X-1 became the first aircraft to successfully break the sound barrier. It did this at a high altitude where the air is thin. It had swept-back wings, and was constructed of heat resistant materials. A very small scale sonic boom occurs when you snap your fingers or clap your hands.

Not all sound waves can be perceived by people. We can only hear sound waves from 20 to 20,000 hertz. Vibrations slower or faster than this cannot be heard by people. However, animals such as dogs can hear vibrations that are faster than this. A dog whistle produces vibrations above 20,000 hertz.

Sound which can be heard has certain qualities. One such quality is pitch. Pitch refers to how high or low a sound is. The shorter the vibrating object, the higher its pitch.

Shorten a guitar or violin string and the pitch becomes higher. Strike a short string on a piano and it produces a high pitched sound. The thicker a vibrating object, the lower the pitch. The thick strings on a guitar or a piano produce low pitch sounds. Men have thicker vocal cords than women and their voices are usually lower in pitch. The tighter the vibrating object, the higher the pitch. Tighten a guitar string and the pitch will become higher. Helium tightens human vocal cords and causes people to talk in a higher pitch.

Another quality of sound is loudness. The greater the amplitude of the sound waves, the louder the sound. Loudness is measured in units called decibels (db). A sound of zero decibels is the quietest sound which can be heard by the human ear. A sound of 120 decibels is the loudest sound which can be heard by the human ear without producing pain. Prolonged exposure to any sound above 90 decibels can cause hearing loss. Normal conversation is 65 decibels; a rock concert, 120 decibels; a jet airplane, 140 decibels; a whisper, 20 decibels.

The external, fleshy portion of the ear which is trumpet-like in shape is called the pinna. Its purpose is to collect vibrations and channel them into the auditory canal. There they strike the tympanic membrane or ear drum which starts to vibrate. On the other side of the ear drum are the ossicles. The ossicles are the three smallest bones of the body, called the hammer, the anvil, and the stirrup. Their function is to amplify the vibrations of the ear drum. The stirrup exerts piston-like pressure against a structure called the oval window of the cochlea. The cochlea is a long, curled-up, fluid filled canal which is lined with millions of microscopic hair cells which are connected to nerve fiber. If the ripples caused by the piston-like pressure exerted by the stirrup bends certain hair cells, the connecting nerve fibers are activated. These nerve fibers feed into the auditory nerve which takes the sound message to our brain.

<http://www.homeschoolfun.com/unit.html>

COME, YE THANKFUL PEOPLE, COME

Sir George J. Elvey (1816–1893), organist at St. George's Chapel, Windsor Castle, for nearly fifty years, wrote the music to this well-loved Thanksgiving hymn about 1858. The lyrics were written by Henry Alford (1810–1871) in 1844.

Come, ye thankful people, come,
Raise the song of harvest home;
All is safely gathered in,
Ere the winter storms begin.
God our Maker doth provide
For our wants to be supplied;
Come to God's own temple, come,
Raise the song of harvest home.

All the world is God's own field,
Fruit unto His praise to yield;
Wheat and tares together sown
Unto joy or sorrow grown.
First the blade and then the ear,
Then the full corn shall appear;
Lord of the harvest, grant that we
Wholesome grain and pure may be.

For the Lord our God shall come,
And shall take His harvest home;
From His field shall in that day
All offenses purge away,
Giving angels charge at last
In the fire the tares to cast;
But the fruitful ears to store
In His garner evermore.

Even so, Lord, quickly come,
Bring Thy final harvest home;
Gather Thou Thy people in,
Free from sorrow, free from sin,
There, forever purified,
In Thy garner to abide;
Come, with all Thine angels come,
Raise the glorious harvest home.

THE BLIND MEN AND THE ELEPHANT
John G. Saxe

It was six men of Indostan
To learning much inclined,
Who went to see the Elephant
(Though all of them were blind),
That each by observation
Might satisfy his mind.

The First approached the Elephant,
And happening to fall
Against his broad and sturdy side,
At once began to bawl:
"God bless me! But the Elephant
Is very like a wall!"

The Second, feeling of the tusk,
Cried: "Ho! What have we here
So very round and smooth and sharp?
To me 'tis mighty clear
This wonder of an Elephant
Is very like a spear!"

The Third approached the animal,
And happening to take
The squirming trunk within his hands,
Thus boldly up and spake:
"I see," quoth he, "the Elephant,
Is very like a snake!"

The Fourth reached out an eager hand,
And felt about the knee.
"What most this wondrous beast is like

Is mighty plain," quoth he;
"'Tis clear enough the Elephant
Is very like a tree!"

The Fifth, who chanced to touch the ear,
Said: "E'en the blindest man
Can tell what this resembles most;
Deny the fact who can
This marvel of an Elephant
Is very like a fan!"

The Sixth no sooner had begun
About the beast to grope,
Than, seizing on the swinging tail
That fell within his scope,
"I see," quoth he, "the Elephant
Is very like a rope!"

And so these men of Indostan
Disputed loud and long,
Each in his own opinion
Exceeding stiff and strong,
Though each was partly in the right,
And all were in the wrong!

So oft in theologic wars,
The disputants, I ween,
Rail on in utter ignorance
Of what each other mean,
And prate about an Elephant
Not one of them has seen!

THE BELLS
Edgar Allan Poe

I

Hear the sledges with the bells -
Silver bells!
What a world of merriment their melody
foretells!
How they tinkle, tinkle, tinkle,
In the icy air of night!
While the stars that oversprinkle
All the heavens, seem to twinkle
With a crystalline delight;
Keeping time, time, time,
In a sort of Runic rhyme,
To the tintinnabulation that so musically wells
From the bells, bells, bells, bells,
Bells, bells, bells -
From the jingling and the tinkling of the bells.

II

Hear the mellow wedding bells -
Golden bells!
What a world of happiness their harmony
foretells!
Through the balmy air of night
How they ring out their delight!
From the molten-golden notes,
And all in tune,
What a liquid ditty floats
To the turtle-dove that listens, while she gloats
On the moon!
Oh, from out the sounding cells
What a gush of euphony voluminously wells!
How it swells!
How it dwells
On the Future! - how it tells

Of the rapture that impels
To the swinging and the ringing
Of the bells, bells, bells,
Of the bells, bells, bells, bells,
Bells, bells, bells –
To the rhyming and the chiming of the bells!

III

Hear the loud alarum bells –
Brazen bells!
What a tale of terror, now, their turbulency tells!
In the startled ear of night
How they scream out their affright!
Too much horrified to speak,
They can only shriek, shriek,
Out of tune,
In a clamorous appealing to the mercy of the fire,
In a mad expostulation with the deaf and frantic fire,
Leaping higher, higher, higher,
With a desperate desire,
And a resolute endeavor
Now – now to sit, or never,
By the side of the pale-faced moon.
Oh, the bells, bells, bells!
What a tale their terror tells
Of despair!
How they clang, and clash, and roar!
What a horror they outpour
On the bosom of the palpitating air!
Yet the ear, it fully knows,
By the twanging
And the clanging,
How the danger ebbs and flows;
Yet the ear distinctly tells,
In the jangling
And the wrangling,
How the danger sinks and swells,
By the sinking or the swelling in the anger of
the bells –
Of the bells,
Of the bells, bells, bells, bells,
Bells, bells, bells –
In the clamor and the clangor of the bells!

IV

Hear the tolling of the bells –
Iron bells!
What a world of solemn thought their monody
compels!
In the silence of the night,
How we shiver with affright
At the melancholy menace of their tone!
For every sound that floats
From the rust within their throats
Is a groan.
And the people – ah, the people –
They that dwell up in the steeple,
All alone,
And who tolling, tolling, tolling,
In that muffled monotone,
Feel a glory in so rolling
On the human heart a stone –
They are neither man nor woman –
They are neither brute nor human –
They are Ghouls:
And their king it is who tolls;
And he rolls, rolls, rolls,
Rolls
A paean from the bells!
And his merry bosom swells
With the paean of the bells!
And he dances, and he yells;
Keeping time, time, time,
In a sort of Runic rhyme,
To the paean of the bells,
Of the bells –
Keeping time, time, time,
In a sort of Runic rhyme,
To the throbbing of the bells,
Of the bells, bells, bells –
To the sobbing of the bells;
Keeping time, time, time,
As he knells, knells, knells,
In a happy Runic rhyme,
To the rolling of the bells,
Of the bells, bells, bells –
To the tolling of the bells,
Of the bells, bells, bells, bells,
Bells, bells, bells –
To the moaning and the groaning of the bells.

HAMLET'S SOLILOQUY
HAMLET, ACT III, SCENE 1
William Shakespeare

To be, or not to be: that is the question:
Whether 'tis nobler in the mind to suffer
The slings and arrows of outrageous fortune,
Or to take arms against a sea of troubles,
And by opposing end them. To die, to sleep—
No more—and by a sleep to say we end
The heartache, and the thousand natural shocks
That flesh is heir to! 'Tis a consummation
Devoutly to be wish'd. To die, to sleep—
To sleep—perchance to dream: ay, there's the rub,
For in that sleep of death what dreams may come
When we have shuffled off this mortal coil,
Must give us pause. There's the respect
That makes calamity of so long life:
For who would bear the whips and scorns of time,
Th' oppressor's wrong, the proud man's contumely,
The pangs of despis'd love, the law's delay,
The insolence of office, and the spurns
That patient merit of th' unworthy takes,
When he himself might his quietus make
With a bare bodkin? Who would these fardels bear,
To grunt and sweat under a weary life,
But that the dread of something after death,
The undiscover'd country, from whose bourn
No traveller returns, puzzles the will,
And makes us rather bear those ills we have,
Than fly to others that we know not of?
Thus conscience does make cowards of us all,
And thus the native hue of resolution
Is sicklied o'er with the pale cast of thought,
And enterprises of great pitch and moment,
With this regard their currents turn awry,
And lose the name of action. Soft you now,
The fair Ophelia!—Nymph, in thy orisons
Be all my sins rememb'red.

HAMLET, ACT III, SCENE 2
William Shakespeare

Hautboys play. The dumb-show enters.

Enter a King and a Queen very lovingly; the Queen embracing him, and he her. She kneels, and makes show of protestation unto him. He takes her up, and declines his head upon her neck: lays him down upon a bank of flowers: she, seeing him asleep, leaves him. Anon comes in a fellow, takes off his crown, kisses it, and pours poison in the King's ears, and exits. The Queen returns; finds the King dead, and makes passionate action. The Poisoner, with some two or three Mutes, comes in again, seeming to lament with her. The dead body is carried away. The Poisoner wooes the Queen with gifts: she seems loath and unwilling awhile, but in the end accepts his love.

Exit.

Ophelia: What means this, my lord?

Hamlet: Marry, this is miching mallecho; it means mischief.

Ophelia: Belike this show imports the argument of the play.

Enter Prologue.

Hamlet: We shall know by this fellow: the players cannot keep counsel; they'll tell all.

Ophelia: Will he tell us what this show meant?

Hamlet: Ay, or any show that you'll show him: be not you ashamed to show, he'll not shame to tell you what it means.

Ophelia: You are naught, you are naught: I'll mark the play.

Prologue.

For us, and for our tragedy,
Here stooping to your clemency,
We beg your hearing patiently.

Exit.

Hamlet: Is this a prologue, or the posy of a ring?

Ophelia: 'Tis brief, my lord.

Hamlet: As woman's love.

Enter two Players, King and Queen.

Player King: Full thirty times hath Phoebus' cart gone round
Neptune's salt wash and Tellus' orbed ground,
And thirty dozen moons with borrow'd sheen
About the world have times twelve thirties been,
Since love our hearts and Hymen did our hands
Unite commutual in most sacred bands.

Player Queen: So many journeys may the sun and moon
Make us again count o'er ere love be done!
But, woe is me, you are so sick of late,
So far from cheer and from your former state,
That I distrust you. Yet, though I distrust,
Discomfort you, my lord, it nothing must:
For women's fear and love holds quantity;
In neither aught, or in extremity.
Now, what my love is, proof hath made you know;
And as my love is sized, my fear is so:
Where love is great, the littlest doubts are fear;
Where little fears grow great, great love grows there.

Player King: 'Faith, I must leave thee, love, and shortly too;
My operant powers their functions leave to do:
And thou shalt live in this fair world behind,

Honour'd, beloved; and haply one as kind
For husband shalt thou—

Player Queen: O, confound the rest!
Such love must needs be treason in my breast:
In second husband let me be accurst!
None wed the second but who kill'd the first.

Hamlet: *[Aside]* Wormwood, wormwood.

Player Queen: The instances that second marriage move
Are base respects of thrift, but none of love:
A second time I kill my husband dead,
When second husband kisses me in bed.

Player King: I do believe you think what now you speak;
But what we do determine oft we break.
Purpose is but the slave to memory,
Of violent birth, but poor validity;
Which now, like fruit unripe, sticks on the tree;
But fall, unshaken, when they mellow be.
Most necessary 'tis that we forget
To pay ourselves what to ourselves is debt:
What to ourselves in passion we propose,
The passion ending, doth the purpose lose.
The violence of either grief or joy
Their own enactures with themselves destroy:
Where joy most revels, grief doth most lament;
Grief joys, joy grieves, on slender accident.
This world is not for aye, nor 'tis not strange
That even our loves should with our fortunes change;
For 'tis a question left us yet to prove,
Whether love lead fortune, or else fortune love.
The great man down, you mark his favourite flies;
The poor advanced makes friends of enemies.
And hitherto doth love on fortune tend;
For who not needs shall never lack a friend,
And who in want a hollow friend doth try,
Directly seasons him his enemy.
But, orderly to end where I begun,
Our wills and fates do so contrary run
That our devices still are overthrown;
Our thoughts are ours, their ends none of our own:
So think thou wilt no second husband wed;
But die thy thoughts when thy first lord is dead.

Player Queen: Nor earth to me give food, nor heaven light!
Sport and repose lock from me day and night!
To desperation turn my trust and hope!
An anchor's cheer in prison be my scope!
Each opposite that blanks the face of joy
Meet what I would have well and it destroy!
Both here and hence pursue me lasting strife,
If, once a widow, ever I be wife!

Hamlet: If she should break it now!

Player King: 'Tis deeply sworn. Sweet, leave me here awhile;
My spirits grow dull, and fain I would beguile
The tedious day with sleep.

Sleeps.

Player Queen: Sleep rock thy brain,
And never come mischance between us twain!

Exit.

My Shadow
Robert Louis Stevenson

I have a little shadow that goes in and out with me,
And what can be the use of him is more than I can see.
He is very, very like me from the heels up to the head;
And I see him jump before me, when I jump into my bed.

The funniest thing about him is the way he likes to grow—
Not at all like proper children, which is always very slow;
For he sometimes shoots up taller like an India-rubber ball,
And he sometimes gets so little that there's none of him at all.

He hasn't got a notion of how children ought to play,
And can only make a fool of me in every sort of way.
He stays so close beside me, he's a coward you can see;
I'd think shame to stick to nursie as that shadow sticks to me!

One morning, very early, before the sun was up,
I rose and found the shining dew on every buttercup;
But my lazy little shadow, like an arrant sleepy-head,
Had stayed at home behind me and was fast asleep in bed.

How They Brought the Good News from Ghent to Aix
Robert Browning

I sprang to the stirrup, and Joris, and he;
I gallop'd, Dirck gallop'd, we gallop'd all three;
"Good speed!" cried the watch, as the gate-bolts undrew;
"Speed!" echoed the wall to us galloping through;
Behind shut the postern, the lights sank to rest,
And into the midnight we gallop'd abreast.

Not a word to each other; we kept the great pace
Neck by neck, stride by stride, never changing our place;
I turn'd in my saddle and made its girths tight,
Then shorten'd each stirrup, and set the pique right,
Rebuckled the cheek-strap, chain'd slacker the bit,
Nor gallop'd less steadily Roland a whit.

'T was a moonset at starting; but while we drew near
Lokeren, the cocks crew and twilight dawn'd clear;
At Boom, a great yellow star came out to see;
At Duffeld 't was morning as plain as could be;
And from Mechelm church-steeple we heard the half chime,
So, Joris broke silence with, "Yet there is time!"

At Aerschot, up leap'd of a sudden the sun,
And against him the cattle stood black every one,
To stare thro' the mist at us galloping past,
And I saw my stout galloper Roland at last,
With resolute shoulders, each butting away
The haze, as some bluff river headland its spray:

And his low head and crest, just one sharp ear bent back
For my voice, and the other pricked out on his track;
And one eye's black intelligence,—ever that glance
O'er its white edge at me, his own master, askance!
And the thick heavy spume-flakes, which aye and anon
His fierce lips shook upward in galloping on.

By Hasselt Dirck groan'd; and cried Joris "Stay spur!
Your Roos gallop'd bravely, the fault's not in her,
We'll remember at Aix"—for one heard the quick wheeze
Of her chest, saw the stretch'd neck, and staggering knees,
And sunk tail, and horrible heave of the flank,
As down on her haunches she shuddered and sank.

So, we were left galloping, Joris and I,
Past Looz and past Tongres, no cloud in the sky;
The broad sun above laugh'd a pitiless laugh,
'Neath our feet broke the brittle bright stubble like chaff;
Till over by Dalhem a dome-spire sprang white,
And "Gallop," gasped Joris, "for Aix is in sight!"

"How they'll greet us!"—and all in a moment his roan
Roll'd neck and croup over, lay dead as a stone;
And there was my Roland to bear the whole weight
Of the news which alone could save Aix from her fate,
With his nostrils like pits full of blood to the brim,
And with circles of red for his eye-sockets' rim.

Then I cast loose my buff-coat, each holster let fall,
Shook off both my jack-boots, let go belt and all,
Stood up in the stirrup, lean'd, patted his ear,
Call'd my Roland his pet name, my horse without peer;
Clapp'd my hands, laugh'd and sung, any noise, bad or good,
Till at length into Aix Roland gallop'd and stood.

And all I remember is, friends flocking round,
As I sat with his head 'twixt my knees on the ground;
And no voice but was praising this Roland of mine,
As I pour'd down his throat our last measure of wine,
Which (the burgesses voted by common consent)
Was no more than his due who brought good news from Ghent.

THE ROAD NOT TAKEN
Robert Frost

Two roads diverged in a yellow wood,
And sorry I could not travel both
And be one traveler, long I stood
And looked down one as far as I could
To where it bent in the undergrowth;

Then took the other, as just as fair,
And having perhaps the better claim,
Because it was grassy and wanted wear;
Though as for that the passing there
Had worn them really about the same,

And both that morning equally lay
In leaves no step had trodden black.
Oh, I kept the first for another day!
Yet knowing how way leads on to way,
I doubted if I should ever come back.

I shall be telling this with a sigh
Somewhere ages and ages hence:
Two roads diverged in a wood, and I—
I took the one less traveled by,
And that has made all the difference.

A NARROW FELLOW IN THE GRASS
Emily Dickinson

A narrow fellow in the grass
Occasionally rides;
You may have met him,—did you not?
His notice sudden is.

The grass divides as with a comb,
A spotted shaft is seen;
And then it closes at your feet
And opens further on.

He likes a boggy acre,
A floor too cool for corn.
Yet when a child, and barefoot,
I more than once, at morn,

Have passed, I thought, a whip-lash
Unbraiding in the sun,—
When, stooping to secure it,
It wrinkled, and was gone.

Several of nature's people
I know, and they know me;
I feel for them a transport
Of cordiality;

But never met this fellow,
Attended or alone,
Without a tighter breathing,
And zero at the bone.

THE CHARGE OF THE LIGHT BRIGADE
Alfred, Lord Tennyson

Half a league, half a league,
  Half a league onward,
All in the valley of Death
  Rode the six hundred.
"Forward, the Light Brigade!
Charge for the guns!" he said:
  Into the valley of Death
  Rode the six hundred.

"Forward, the Light Brigade!"
  Was there a man dismay'd?
  Not tho' the soldier knew
  Some one had blunder'd:
  Their's not to make reply,
  Their's not to reason why,
  Their's but to do and die:
  Into the valley of Death
  Rode the six hundred.

Cannon to right of them,
  Cannon to left of them,
  Cannon in front of them
  Volley'd and thunder'd;
Storm'd at with shot and shell,
  Boldly they rode and well,
  Into the jaws of Death,
  Into the mouth of Hell
  Rode the six hundred.

Flash'd all their sabres bare,
  Flash'd as they turned in air
  Sabring the gunners there,
  Charging an army, while
  All the world wonder'd:
Plunged in the battery-smoke
Right thro' the line they broke;
  Cossack and Russian
  Reel'd from the sabre-stroke
  Shatter'd and sunder'd.
Then they rode back, but not
  Not the six hundred.

Cannon to right of them,
  Cannon to left of them,
  Cannon behind them
  Volley'd and thunder'd;
Storm'd at with shot and shell,
  While horse and hero fell,
They that had fought so well
Came thro' the jaws of Death,
Back from the mouth of Hell,
All that was left of them,
  Left of six hundred.

When can their glory fade?
O the wild charge they made!
  All the world wonder'd.
Honour the charge they made!
Honour the Light Brigade,
  Noble six hundred!

THE MIDNIGHT RIDE OF PAUL REVERE
Henry Wadsworth Longfellow

Listen, my children, and you shall hear
Of the midnight ride of Paul Revere,
On the eighteenth of April, in Seventy-five;
  Hardly a man is now alive
Who remembers that famous day and year.

He said to his friend, "If the British march
By land or sea from the town to-night,
Hang a lantern aloft in the belfry arch
Of the North Church tower as a signal light,—
  One if by land, and two if by sea;
  And I on the opposite shore will be,
Ready to ride and spread the alarm
Through every Middlesex village and farm,
For the country folk to be up and to arm."

Then he said "Good-night!" and with muffled oar
Silently rowed to the Charlestown shore,
Just as the moon rose over the bay,
Where swinging wide at her moorings lay
The Somerset, British man-of-war;
A phantom ship, with each mast and spar
Across the moon like a prison bar,
And a huge black hulk, that was magnified
By its own reflection in the tide.

Meanwhile, his friend through alley and street
Wanders and watches, with eager ears,
Till in the silence around him he hears
The muster of men at the barrack door,
The sound of arms, and the tramp of feet,
And the measured tread of the grenadiers,
Marching down to their boats on the shore.

Then he climbed the tower of the Old North Church,
By the wooden stairs, with stealthy tread,
To the belfry chamber overhead,
And startled the pigeons from their perch
On the sombre rafters, that round him made
Masses and moving shapes of shade,—
By the trembling ladder, steep and tall,
To the highest window in the wall,
Where he paused to listen and look down
A moment on the roofs of the town
And the moonlight flowing over all.

Beneath, in the churchyard, lay the dead,
In their night encampment on the hill,
Wrapped in silence so deep and still
That he could hear, like a sentinel's tread,
The watchful night-wind, as it went
Creeping along from tent to tent,
And seeming to whisper, "All is well!"
A moment only he feels the spell
Of the place and the hour, and the secret dread
Of the lonely belfry and the dead;
For suddenly all his thoughts are bent
On a shadowy something far away,
Where the river widens to meet the bay,—
A line of black that bends and floats
On the rising tide like a bridge of boats.

Meanwhile, impatient to mount and ride,
Booted and spurred, with a heavy stride
On the opposite shore walked Paul Revere.
Now he patted his horse's side,
Now he gazed at the landscape far and near,
Then, impetuous, stamped the earth,
And turned and tightened his saddle girth;
But mostly he watched with eager search
The belfry tower of the Old North Church,
As it rose above the graves on the hill,
Lonely and spectral and sombre and still.

And lo! as he looks, on the belfry's height
A glimmer, and then a gleam of light!
He springs to the saddle, the bridle he turns,
But lingers and gazes, till full on his sight
A second lamp in the belfry burns.

A hurry of hoofs in a village street,
A shape in the moonlight, a bulk in the dark,
And beneath, from the pebbles, in passing, a spark
Struck out by a steed flying fearless and fleet;
That was all! And yet, through the gloom and the light,
The fate of a nation was riding that night;
And the spark struck out by that steed, in his flight,
Kindled the land into flame with its heat.
He has left the village and mounted the steep,
And beneath him, tranquil and broad and deep,
Is the Mystic, meeting the ocean tides;
And under the alders that skirt its edge,
Now soft on the sand, now loud on the ledge,
Is heard the tramp of his steed as he rides.

It was twelve by the village clock
When he crossed the bridge into Medford town.
He heard the crowing of the cock,
And the barking of the farmer's dog,
And felt the damp of the river fog,
That rises after the sun goes down.

It was one by the village clock,
When he galloped into Lexington.
He saw the gilded weathercock
Swim in the moonlight as he passed,
And the meeting-house windows, black and bare,
Gaze at him with a spectral glare,
As if they already stood aghast
At the bloody work they would look upon.

It was two by the village clock,
When he came to the bridge in Concord town.
He heard the bleating of the flock,
And the twitter of birds among the trees,
And felt the breath of the morning breeze
Blowing over the meadow brown.
And one was safe and asleep in his bed
Who at the bridge would be first to fall,
Who that day would be lying dead,
Pierced by a British musket ball.

You know the rest. In the books you have read
How the British Regulars fired and fled,—
How the farmers gave them ball for ball,
From behind each fence and farmyard wall,
Chasing the redcoats down the lane,
Then crossing the fields to emerge again
Under the trees at the turn of the road,
And only pausing to fire and load.

So through the night rode Paul Revere;
And so through the night went his cry of alarm
To every Middlesex village and farm,—
A cry of defiance, and not of fear,
A voice in the darkness, a knock at the door,
And a word that shall echo for evermore!
For, borne on the night-wind of the Past,
Through all our history, to the last,
In the hour of darkness and peril and need,
The people will waken and listen to hear
The hurrying hoof-beats of that steed,
And the midnight message of Paul Revere.

THE VILLAGE BLACKSMITH
Henry Wadsworth Longfellow

Under a spreading chestnut tree
The village smithy stands;
The smith, a mighty man is he,
With large and sinewy hands;
And the muscles of his brawny arms
Are strong as iron bands.

His hair is crisp, and black, and long,
His face is like the tan;
His brow is wet with honest sweat,
He earns whate'er he can,
And looks the whole world in the face,
For he owes not any man.

Week in, week out, from morn till night,
You can hear his bellows blow;
You can hear him swing his heavy sledge
With measured beat and slow,
Like a sexton ringing the village bell,
When the evening sun is low.

And children coming home from school
Look in the open door;
They love to see the flaming forge,
And hear the bellows roar,
And watch the burning sparks that fly
Like chaff from a threshing-floor.

He goes on Sunday to the church,
And sits among his boys;
He hears the parson pray and preach,
He hears his daughter's voice,
Singing in the village choir,
And it makes his heart rejoice.

It sounds to him like her mother's voice,
Singing in Paradise!
He needs must think of her once more,
How in the grave she lies;
And with his hard, rough hand he wipes
A tear out of his eyes.

Toiling,— rejoicing,— sorrowing,
Onward through life he goes;
Each morning sees some task begin,
Each evening sees it close;
Something attempted, something done,
Has earned a night's repose.

Thanks, thanks to thee, my worthy friend,
For the lesson thou hast taught!
Thus at the flaming forge of life
Our fortunes must be wrought;
Thus on its sounding anvil shaped
Each burning deed and thought.

HEALTH AND SAFETY—ON ENCOUNTERING BEARS

Black bears may vary in weight from 125 to 450 pounds. When on all four legs, black bears measure about three feet high at the shoulders, but when upright on their hind legs they may approach five to six feet tall. Bears are most active in the late spring and summer. When in bear country it is always important to be aware of the potential of encountering bears and to take every precaution to reduce conflicts. Most conflicts between humans and black bears arise as the result of human food supplies.

Hiking at dawn or dusk may increase your chances of meeting a bear. Use extra caution in places where hearing or visibility is limited: in brushy areas, near streams, where trails round a bend, or on windy days. Avoid berry patches in fall. Reduce your chances of surprising a bear by making noise—talk or sing.

Make sure children are close to you or at least within your sight at all times. Leave your dog at home or have it on a leash. Watch ahead for bears. Look for tracks. Do not surprise bears. Hiking in groups is safer than hiking alone.

To enjoy a night in the wilderness without attracting bears to your camp: **Choose your campsite carefully**. DO NOT camp near a trail, salmon stream, animal carcasses or garbage, or any backcountry metal firepit (others may have left food odors). DO camp in a tent in an open quiet area where you can see and hear nearby wildlife, and where they can see and hear you. Keep a small, but sharp knife handy in your sleeping tent in the event that you need to make a new doorway.

Keep your camp odor free. DO NOT cook near your camp, cook smelly foods, sleep in clothes with food odors, or bring any food or lotions into your tent. DO cook at least 100 feet away from camp, downwind. Store food, pots, lotions and clothes with food odors away from camp. If there are trees, cache your food out of a bear's reach. If there are no trees, hang food off of a rock face or a bridge, or store it out of a bear's sight off the trail and downwind of camp. Pack out all trash. Do not cause trouble for those who will follow you.

Some campgrounds have electric fences around areas for storing coolers, dry boxes, and garbage overnight. Other places use food hoists. The food cache should be hung between two sturdy trees about 7 meters or 25 feet apart. About 30 meters or 100 feet of rope will suffice for this task. The food bag will need to be at least 5 meters or 16 feet above the ground once hanging. Remember the bag, if heavy, will sag below the rope level. To hang the bag, throw each end of the rope over a strong branch 6 meters or 20 feet above the ground. Tie the food bag into the middle of the rope and pull each end until the bag is suspended. Then tie each end of the rope around the trunk of the tree with a good knot. This allows one to hang the food without actually climbing a tree.

Close Encounters

Statistics have shown which ways of reacting to bears when you see them are safer.

IF YOU SEE A BEAR THAT IS FAR AWAY OR DOES NOT SEE YOU, turn around and go back, or circle far around. Do not disturb it.

IF YOU SEE A BEAR THAT IS CLOSE OR IT DOES SEE YOU, STAY CALM. Attacks are rare. Bears may approach or stand on their hind legs to get a better look at you. These are curious, not aggressive bears. Stop. Back away slowly while facing the bear. Avoid direct eye contact as bears may perceive this as a threat. Give the bear plenty of room to escape. Wild bears rarely attack people unless they feel threatened or provoked. Try not to show fear. If the bear follows, STOP.

BE HUMAN. Stand tall, wave your arms, and speak in a loud and low voice. (Other sources say to speak softly. This may reassure the bear that no harm is meant to it.) DO NOT RUN. Stand your ground or back away slowly and diagonally IF A BEAR IS CHARGING. (Almost all charges are "bluff charges.") DO NOT RUN. Olympic sprinters cannot outrun a bear, and running may trigger an instinctive reaction to chase. Do not try to climb a tree unless it is literally right next to you and you can quickly get at least 30 feet up.

STAND YOUR GROUND. Wave your arms and speak in a loud low voice. Many times charging bears have come within a few feet of a person and then veered off at the last second.

If a Bear Approaches Your Campsite
Aggressively chase it away. Make noise with pots and pans, throw rocks, and if needed, hit the bear. Do not let the bear get any food.

IF YOU HAVE SURPRISED A BEAR AND ARE ATTACKED, play dead. Playing dead is a last resort option and should be done after the bear has made contact. Struggling will encourage attack. Lie flat on your stomach, or curl up in a ball with your hands laced behind your neck. Lie still and be silent. Surprised bears usually stop attacking once you are no longer a threat or "dead."

IF YOU HAVE BEEN STALKED BY A BEAR, a bear is approaching your campsite, or an attack is continuing long after you have ceased struggling, fight back! Predatory bears are often young bears that can be successfully intimidated or chased away. Use a stick or rocks or your hands and feet.

Protection

Many people now carry pepper spray—a bear deterrent made from the juice of red-hot peppers. This incapacitating spray teaches bears a lesson without permanently maiming them. It is available at local sporting goods stores and at visitor centers. Be familiar with the characteristics of the brand you choose and its warnings. If you are allowed to carry a gun for protection and hunting, select a gun that will stop a bear—a 12-gauge shotgun or a .300 mag rifle.

LIMERICKS

I sat next the Duchess at tea.
It was just as I feared it would be:
Her rumblings abdominal
Were simply abominable,
And everyone thought it was me.

There was a young lady of Lynn
Who was so uncommonly thin
That when she essayed
To drink lemonade
She slipped through the straw and fell in.

There was an old man of Peru
Who dreamt he was eating his shoe.
He awoke in the night
In a terrible fright,
And found it was perfectly true!

A decrepit old gas man named Peter,
While hunting around for the meter,
Touched a leak with his light.
He arose out of sight,
And, as anyone can see by reading this, he
also destroyed the meter.

ANDROCLES AND THE LION
Aesop

A slave named Androcles once escaped from his master and fled to the forest. As he was wandering about there he came upon a Lion lying down moaning and groaning. At first he turned to flee, but finding that the Lion did not pursue him, he turned back and went up to him. As he came near, the Lion put out his paw, which was all swollen and bleeding, and Androcles found that a huge thorn had got into it, and was causing all the pain. He pulled out the thorn and bound up the paw of the Lion, who was soon able to rise and lick the hand of Androcles like a dog. Then the Lion took Androcles to his cave, and every day used to bring him meat from which to live. But shortly afterwards both Androcles and the Lion were captured, and the slave was sentenced to be thrown to the Lion, after the latter had been kept without food for several days. The Emperor and all his Court came to see the spectacle, and Androcles was led out into the middle of the arena. Soon the Lion was let loose from his den, and rushed bounding and roaring towards his victim. But as soon as he came near to Androcles he recognized his friend, and fawned upon him, and licked his hands like a friendly dog. The Emperor, surprised at this, summoned Androcles to him, who told him the whole story. Whereupon the slave was pardoned and freed, and the Lion let loose to his native forest.

Gratitude is the sign of noble souls.

THE FIRST PART OF HENRY THE FOURTH, ACT V, SCENE 4
William Shakespeare

On a field of battle.

The Prince spieth Falstaff on the ground.

Prince: What, old acquaintance? Could not all this flesh
Keep in a little life? Poor Jack, farewell!
I could have better spar'd a better man.
O, I should have a heavy miss of thee
If I were much in love with vanity!
Death hath not struck so fat a deer to-day,
Though many dearer, in this bloody fray.
Embowell'd will I see thee by-and-by;
Till then in blood by noble Percy lie.

Falstaff riseth up.

Falstaff: Embowell'd? If thou embowel me today,
I'll give you leave to powder me and eat me too tomorrow.
'Sblood, 'twas time to counterfeit,
or that hot termagant Scot had paid me scot and lot too.
Counterfeit? I lie; I am no counterfeit.
To die is to be a counterfeit;
for he is but the counterfeit of a man
who hath not the life of a man;
but to counterfeit dying when a man thereby liveth,
is to be no counterfeit, but the true and perfect image of life indeed.
The better part of valour is discretion;
in the which better part I have saved my life.
'Zounds, I am afraid of this gunpowder Percy, though he be dead.
How if he should counterfeit too, and rise?
By my faith, I am afraid he would prove the better counterfeit.
Therefore I'll make him sure;
yea, and I'll swear I kill'd him.
Why may not he rise as well as I?

Nothing confutes me but eyes,
and nobody sees me.
Therefore, sirrah
[stabs him], with a new wound in your thigh,
come you along with me.

To Build a Fire

Jack London

The following is the first version of this story, originally published in *Youth's Companion* in 1902. Another version, for an adult audience, was published in *The Century* Magazine in 1908. It is available online. Do a search for: "To Build a Fire" + "The Century Magazine."

For land travel or seafaring, the world over, a companion is usually considered desirable. In the Klondike, as Tom Vincent found out, such a companion is absolutely essential. But he found it out, not by precept, but through bitter experience.

"Never travel alone," is a precept of the north. He had heard it many times and laughed; for he was a strapping young fellow, big-boned and big-muscled, with faith in himself and in the strength of his head and hands.

It was on a bleak January day when the experience came that taught him respect for the frost, and for the wisdom of the men who had battled with it.

He had left Calumet Camp on the Yukon with a light pack on his back, to go up Paul Creek to the divide between it and Cherry Creek, where his party was prospecting and hunting moose.

The frost was sixty-degrees below zero, and he had thirty miles of lonely trail to cover, but he did not mind. In fact, he enjoyed it, swinging along through the silence, his blood pounding warmly through veins, and his mind carefree and happy. For he and his comrades were certain they had struck "pay" up there on the Cherry Creek Divide; and, further, he was returning to them from Dawson with cheery home letters from the States.

At seven o'clock, when he turned the heels of his moccasins toward Calumet Camp, it was still black night. And when day broke at half past nine he had made the four-mile cut-off across the flats and was six miles up Paul Creek. The trail, which had seen little travel, followed the bed of the creek, and there was no possibility of his getting lost. He had gone to Dawson by way of Cherry Creek and Indian River, so Paul Creek was new and strange. By half past eleven he was at the forks, which had been described to him, and he knew he had covered fifteen miles, half the distance. He knew that in the nature of things the trail was bound to grow worse from there on, and thought that, considering the good time he had made, he merited lunch. Casting

off his pack and taking a seat on a fallen tree, he unmittened his right hand, reached inside his shirt next to the skin, and fished out a couple of biscuits sandwiched with sliced bacon and wrapped in a handkerchief—the only way they could be carried without freezing solid.

He had barely chewed the first mouthful when his numbing fingers warned him to put his mitten on again. This he did, not without surprise at the bitter swiftness with which the frost bit in. Undoubtedly it was the coldest snap he had ever experienced, he thought.

He spat upon the snow,—a favorite northland trick,—and the sharp crackle of the instantly congealed spittle startled him. The spirit thermometer at Calumet had registered sixty below when he left, but he was certain it had grown much colder, how much colder he could not imagine.

Half of the first biscuit was yet untouched, but he could feel himself beginning to chill—a thing most unusual for him. This would never do, he decided, and slipping the packstraps across his shoulders, he leaped to his feet and ran briskly up the trail.

A few minutes of this made him warm again, and he settled down to a steady stride, munching the biscuits as he went along. The moisture that exhaled with his breath crusted his lips and mustache with pendent ice and formed a miniature glacier on his chin. Now and again sensation forsook his nose and cheeks, and he rubbed them till they burned with the returning blood.

Most men wore nose-straps; his partners did, but he had scorned such "feminine contraptions," and till now had never felt the need of them. Now he did feel the need, for he was rubbing constantly.

Nevertheless he was aware of a thrill of joy, of exultation. He was doing something, achieving something, mastering the elements. Once he laughed aloud in sheer strength of life, and with his clenched fist defied the frost. He was its master. What he did he did in spite of it. It could not stop him. He was going on to the Cherry Creek Divide.

Strong as were the elements, he was stronger. At such times animals crawled away into their holes and remained in hiding. But he did not hide. He was out in it, facing it, fighting it. He was a man, a master of things.

In such fashion, rejoicing proudly, he tramped on. After an hour he rounded a bend, where the creek ran close to the mountainside, and came upon one of the most insignificant-appearing but most formidable dangers in northern travel.

The creek itself was frozen solid to its rocky bottom, but from the mountain came the outflow of several springs. These springs never froze, and the only effect of the severest cold snaps was to lessen their discharge. Protected from the frost by the blanket of snow, the water of these springs seeped down into the creek and, on top of the creek ice, formed shallow pools.

The surface of these pools, in turn, took on a skin of ice which grew thicker and thicker, until the water overran, and so formed a second ice-skinned pool above the first.

Thus at the bottom was the solid creek ice, then probably six to eight inches of water, then the thin ice-skin, then another six inches of water and another ice-skin. And on top of this last skin was about an inch of recent snow to make the trap complete.

To Tom Vincent's eye the unbroken snow surface gave no warning of the lurking danger. As the crust was thicker at the edge, he was well toward the middle before he broke through.

In itself it was a very insignificant mishap,—a man does not drown in twelve inches of water,—but in its consequences as serious an accident as could possibly befall him.

At the instant he broke through he felt the cold water strike his feet and ankles, and with half a dozen lunges he made the bank. He was quite cool and collected. The thing to do, and the only thing to do, was to build a fire. For another precept of the north runs: Travel with wet socks down to twenty below zero; after that build a fire. And it was three times twenty below and colder, and he knew it.

He knew, further, that great care must be exercised; that with failure at the first attempt, the chance was made greater for failure at the second attempt. In short, he knew that there must be no failure. The moment before a strong, exulting man, boastful of his mastery of the elements, he was now fighting for his life against those same elements—such was the difference caused by the injection of a quart of water into a northland traveller's calculations.

In a clump of pines on the rim of the bank the spring high-water had lodged many twigs and small branches. Thoroughly dried by the summer sun, they now waited the match.

It is impossible to build a fire with heavy Alaskan mittens on one's hands, so Vincent bared his, gathered a sufficient number of twigs, and knocking the snow from them, knelt down to kindle his fire. From an inside pocket he drew out his matches and a strip of thin birch bark. The matches were of the Klondike kind, sulphur matches, one hundred in a bunch.

He noticed how quickly his fingers had chilled as he separated one match from the bunch and scratched it on his trousers. The birch bark, like the dryest of paper, burst into bright flame. This be carefully fed with the smallest twigs and finest debris, cherishing the flame with the utmost care. It did not do to hurry things, as he well knew, and although his fingers were now quite stiff, he did not hurry.

After the first quick, biting sensation of cold, his feet had ached with a heavy, dull ache and were rapidly growing numb. But the fire, although a very young one, was now a success; he knew that a little snow, briskly rubbed, would speedily cure his feet.

But at the moment he was adding the first thick twigs to the fire a grievous thing happened. The pine boughs above his head were burdened with a four months snowfall, and so finely adjusted were the burdens that his slight movement in collecting the twigs had been sufficient to disturb the balance.

The snow from the topmost bough was the first to fall, striking and dislodging the snow on the boughs beneath. And all this snow, accumulating as it fell, smote Tom Vincent's head and shoulders and blotted out his fire.

He still kept his presence of mind, for be knew how great his danger was. He started at once to rebuild the fire, but his fingers were now so numb that he could not bend them, and he was forced to pick up each twig and splinter between the tips of the fingers of either hand.

When he came to the match he encountered great difficulty in separating one from the bunch. This he succeeded in managing, however, and also, by great effort, in clutching the match between his thumb and forefinger. But in scratching it, he dropped it in the snow and could not pick it up again.

He stood up, desperate. He could not feel even his weight on his feet, although the ankles were aching painfully. Putting on his mittens, he stepped to one side, so that the snow would not fall upon the new fire he was to build, and beat his hands violently against a tree-trunk.

This enabled him to separate and strike a second match and to set fire to the remaining fragment of birch bark. But his body had now begun to chill and he was shivering, so that when be tried to add the first twigs his hand shook and the tiny flame was quenched.

The frost had beaten him. His hands were worthless. But he had the foresight to drop the bunch of matches into his wide-mouthed outside pocket before he slipped on his mittens in despair, and started to run up the trail. One cannot run the frost out of wet feet at sixty below and colder, however, as he quickly discovered.

He came round a sharp turn of the creek to where he could look ahead for a mile. But there was no help, no sign of help, only the white trees and the white hills, and the quiet cold and the brazen silence! If only he had a comrade whose feet were not freezing, he thought, only such a comrade to start the fire that could save him!

Then his eyes chanced upon another high-water lodgment of twigs and branches. If he could strike a match, all might yet be well. With stiff fingers which he could not bend, he got out a bunch of matches, but found it impossible to separate them.

He sat down and awkwardly shuffled the bunch about on his knees, until he got it resting on his palm with the sulphur ends projecting, somewhat in the manner the blade of a hunting-knife would project when clutched in the fist.

But his fingers stood straight out. They could not clutch. This he overcame by pressing the wrist of the other hand against them, and so forcing them down upon the bunch. Time and again, holding thus by both hands, he scratched the bunch on his leg and finally ignited it. But the flame burned into the flesh of his hand, and he involuntarily relaxed his hold. The bunch fell into the snow, and while he tried vainly to pick it up, sizzled and went out.

Again he ran, by this time badly frightened. His feet were utterly devoid of sensation. He stubbed his toes once on a buried log, but beyond pitching him into the snow and wrenching his back, it gave him no feelings.

He recollected being told of a camp of moose-hunters somewhere above the forks of Paul Creek.

He must be somewhere near it, he thought, and if he could find it he yet might be saved. Five minutes later he came upon it, lone and deserted, with drifted snow sprinkled inside the pine-bough shelter in which the hunters had slept. He sank down, sobbing. All was over, and in an hour at best, in that terrific temperature, he would be an icy corpse.

But the love of life was strong in him, and he sprang again to his feet. He was thinking quickly. What if the matches did burn his hands? Burned hands were better than dead hands. No hands at all were better than death. He floundered along the trail until be came upon another high-water lodgment. There were twigs and branches, leaves and grasses, all dry and waiting the fire.

Again he sat down and shuffled the bunch of matches on his knees, got it into place on his palm, with the wrist of his other hand forced the nerveless fingers down against the bunch, and with the wrist kept them there. At the second scratch the bunch caught fire, and he knew that if he could stand the pain he was saved. He choked with the sulphur fumes, and the blue flame licked the flesh of his hands.

At first he could not feel it, but it burned quickly in through the frosted surface. The odor of the burning flesh—his flesh—was strong in his nostrils. He writhed about in his torment, yet held on. He set his teeth and swayed back and forth, until the clear white flame of the burning match shot up, and he had applied that flame to the leaves and grasses.

An anxious five minutes followed, but the fire gained steadily. Then he set to work to save himself. Heroic measures were necessary, such was his extremity, and he took them.

Alternately rubbing his hands with snow and thrusting them into the flames, and now and again beating them against the hard trees, he restored their circulation sufficiently for them to be of use to him. With his hunting-knife he slashed the straps from his pack, unrolled his blanket, and got out dry socks and footgear.

Then he cut away his moccasins and bared his feet. But while he had taken liberties with his hands, he kept his feet fairly away from the fire and rubbed them with snow. He rubbed till his hands grew numb, when he would cover his feet with the blanket, warm his hands by the fire, and return to the rubbing.

For three hours he worked, till the worst effects of the freezing had been counteracted. All that night he stayed by the fire, and it was late the next day when be limped pitifully into the camp on the Cherry Creek Divide.

In a month's time he was able to be about on his feet, although the toes were destined always after that to be very sensitive to frost. But the scars on his hands he knows he will carry to the grave. And—"Never travel alone!" he now lays down the precept of the North.

THE ASS IN THE LION'S SKIN
Aesop

An ass, having put on the Lion's skin, roamed about in the forest and amused himself by frightening all the foolish animals he met in his wanderings. At last coming upon a Fox, he tried to frighten him also, but the Fox no sooner heard the sound of his voice than he exclaimed, "I might possibly have been frightened myself, if I had not heard your bray."

Clothes may disguise a fool, but his words will give him away.

ALLEGORY OF THE CAVE
Plato

And now, I said, let me show in a figure how far our nature is enlightened or unenlightened:— Behold! Human beings living in an underground cave, which has a mouth open towards the light and reaching all along the cave; here they have been from their childhood, and have their legs and necks chained so that they cannot move, and can only see before them, being prevented by the chains from turning round their heads. Above and behind them a fire is blazing at a distance, and between the fire and the prisoners there is a raised way; and you will see, if you look, a low wall built along the way, like the screen which marionette players have in front of them, over which they show the puppets.

I see.

And do you see, I said, men passing along the wall carrying all sorts of vessels, and statues and figures of animals made of wood and stone and various materials, which appear over the wall? Some of them are talking, others silent.

You have shown me a strange image, and they are strange prisoners.

Like ourselves, I replied; and they see only their own shadows, or the shadows of one another, which the fire throws on the opposite wall of the cave?

True, he said; how could they see anything but the shadows if they were never allowed to move their heads?

And of the objects, which are being carried in like manner, they would only see the shadows?

Yes, he said.

And if they were able to converse with one another, would they not suppose that they were naming what was actually before them?

Very true.

And suppose further that the prison had an echo which came from the other side, would they not be sure to fancy when one of the passers-by spoke that the voice which they heard came from the passing shadow?

No question, he replied.

To them, I said, the truth would be literally nothing but the shadows of the images.

That is certain.

And now look again, and see what will naturally follow if the prisoners are released and disabused of their error. At first, when any of them is liberated and compelled suddenly to stand up and turn his neck round and walk and look towards the light, he will suffer sharp pains; the glare will distress him, and he will be unable to see the realities of which in his former state he had seen the shadows; and then conceive some one saying to him, that what he saw before was an illusion, but that now, when he is approaching nearer to being and his eye is turned towards more real existence, he has a clearer vision,—what will be his reply? And you may further imagine that his instructor is pointing to the objects as they pass and requiring him to name them,—will he not be perplexed? Will he not fancy that the shadows which he formerly saw are truer than the objects which are now shown to him?

Far truer.

And if he is compelled to look straight at the light, will he not have a pain in his eyes which will make him turn away to take and take in the objects of vision which he can see, and which he will conceive to be in reality clearer than the things which are now being shown to him?

True, he said.

And suppose once more, that he is reluctantly dragged up a steep and rugged ascent, and held fast until he's forced into the presence of the sun himself, is he not likely to be pained and irritated? When he approaches the light his eyes will be dazzled, and he will not be able to see anything at all of what are now called realities.

Not all in a moment, he said.

He will require to grow accustomed to the sight of the upper world. And first he will see the shadows best, next the reflections of men and other objects in the water, and then the objects themselves; then he will gaze upon the light of the moon and the stars and the spangled heaven; and he will see the sky and the stars by night better than the sun or the light of the sun by day?

Certainly.

Last of he will be able to see the sun, and not mere reflections of him in the water, but he will see him in his own proper place, and not in another; and he will contemplate him as he is.

Certainly.

He will then proceed to argue that this is he who gives the season and the years, and is the guardian of all that is in the visible world, and in a certain way the cause of all things which he and his fellows have been accustomed to behold?

Clearly, he said, he would first see the sun and then reason about him.

And when he remembered his old habitation, and the wisdom of the cave and his fellow-prisoners, do you not suppose that he would felicitate himself on the change, and pity them?

Certainly, he would.

And if they were in the habit of conferring honors among themselves on those who were quickest to observe the passing shadows and to remark which of them went before, and which followed after, and which were together; and who were therefore best able to draw conclusions as to the future, do you think that he would care for such honors and glories, or envy the possessors of them? Would he not say with Homer,

Better to be the poor servant of a poor master,

and to endure anything, rather than think as they do and live after their manner?

Yes, he said, I think that he would rather suffer anything than entertain these false notions and live in this miserable manner.

Imagine once more, I said, such an one coming suddenly out of the sun to be replaced in his old situation; would he not be certain to have his eyes full of darkness?

To be sure, he said.

And if there were a contest, and he had to compete in measuring the shadows with the prisoners who had never moved out of the cave, while his sight was still weak, and before his eyes had become steady (and the time which would be needed to acquire this new habit of sight might be very considerable) would he not be ridiculous? Men would say of him that up he went and down he came without his eyes; and that it was better not even to think of ascending; and if any one tried to loose another and lead him up to the light, let them only catch the offender, and they would put him to death.

No question, he said.

This entire allegory, I said, you may now append, dear Glaucon, to the previous argument; the prison-house is the world of sight, the light of the fire is the sun, and you will not misapprehend me if you interpret the journey upwards to be the ascent of the soul into the intellectual world according to my poor belief,

which, at your desire, I have expressed—
whether rightly or wrongly God knows. But,
whether true or false, my opinion is that in the
world of knowledge the idea of good appears
last of all, and is seen only with an effort; and,
when seen, is also inferred to be the universal
author of all things beautiful and right, parent
of light and of the lord of light in this visible
world, and the immediate source of reason and
truth in the intellectual; and that this is the
power upon which he who would act rationally,
either in public or private life must have his eye
fixed.

I agree, he said, as far as I am able to understand
you.

Moreover, I said, you must not wonder that
those who attain to this beatific vision are
unwilling to descend to human affairs; for their
souls are ever hastening into the upper world
where they desire to dwell; which desire of
theirs is very natural, if our allegory may be
trusted.

Yes, very natural.

And is there anything surprising in one who
passes from divine contemplations to the
evil state of man, misbehaving himself in a
ridiculous manner; if, while his eyes are blinking
and before he has become accustomed to the
surrounding darkness, he is compelled to fight
in courts of law, or in other places, about the
images or the shadows of images of justice, and
is endeavouring to meet the conceptions of
those who have never yet seen absolute justice?

Anything but surprising, he replied.

Any one who has common sense will remember
that the bewilderments of the eyes are of two
kinds, and arise from two causes, either from
coming out of the light or from going into
the light, which is true of the mind's eye, quite
as much as of the bodily eye; and he who
remembers this when he sees any one whose
vision is perplexed and weak, will not be too
ready to laugh; he will first ask whether that soul
of man has come out of the brighter light, and is
unable to see because unaccustomed to the dark,
or having turned from darkness to the day is
dazzled by excess of light. And he will count the
one happy in his condition and state of being,
and he will pity the other; or, if he have a mind
to laugh at the soul which comes from below

into the light, there will be more reason in this
than in the laugh which greets him who returns
from above out of the light into the cave.

That, he said, is a very just distinction.

But then, if I am right, certain professors of
education must be wrong when they say that
they can put a knowledge into the soul which
was not there before, like sight into blind eyes.

They undoubtedly say this, he replied.

Whereas, our argument shows that the power
and capacity of learning exists in the soul
already; and that just as the eye was unable to
turn from darkness to light without the whole
body, so too the instrument of knowledge can
only by the movement of the whole soul be
turned from the world of becoming into that of
being, and learn by degrees to endure the sight
of being, and of the brightest and best of being,
or in other words, of the good.

Very true.

And must there not be some art which will
effect conversion in the easiest and quickest
manner; not implanting the faculty of sight, for
that exists already, but has been turned in the
wrong direction, and is looking away from the
truth?

Yes, he said, such an art may be presumed.

And whereas the other so-called virtues of the
soul seem to be akin to bodily qualities, for even
when they are not originally innate they can be
implanted later by habit and exercise, the virtue
of wisdom more than anything else contains a
divine element which always remains, and by
this conversion is rendered useful and profitable;
or, on the other hand, hurtful and useless. Did
you never observe the narrow intelligence
flashing from the keen eye of a clever rogue—
how eager he is, how clearly his paltry soul sees
the way to his end; he is the reverse of blind, but
his keen eyesight is forced into the service of
evil, and he is mischievous in proportion to his
cleverness.

Very true, he said.

But what if there had been a circumcision of
such natures in the days of their youth; and they
had been severed from those sensual pleasures,

such as eating and drinking, which, like leaden weights, were attached to them at their birth, and which drag them down and turn the vision of their souls upon the things that are below—if, I say, they had been released from these impediments and turned in the opposite direction, the very same faculty in them would have seen the truth as keenly as they see what their eyes are turned to now.

Very likely.

Yes, I said; and there is another thing which is likely, or rather a necessary inference from what has preceded, that neither the uneducated and uninformed of the truth, nor yet those who never make an end of their education, will be able ministers of State; not the former, because they have no single aim of duty which is the rule of all their actions, private as well as public; nor the latter, because they will not act at all except upon compulsion, fancying that they are already dwelling apart in the islands of the blest.

Very true, he replied.

Then, I said, the business of us who are the founders of the State will be to compel the best minds to attain that knowledge which we have already shown to be the greatest of all—they must continue to ascend until they arrive at the good; but when they have ascended and seen enough we must not allow them to do as they do now.

What do you mean?

I mean that they remain in the upper world: but this must not be allowed; they must be made to descend again among the prisoners in the cave, and partake of their labors and honors, whether they are worth having or not.

But is not this unjust? he said; ought we to give them a worse life, when they might have a better?

You have again forgotten, my friend, I said, the intention of the legislator, who did not aim at making any one class in the State happy above the rest; the happiness was to be in the whole State, and he held the citizens together by persuasion and necessity, making them benefactors of the State, and therefore benefactors of one another; to this end he created them, not to please themselves, but to be his instruments in binding up the State.

True, he said, I had forgotten.

Observe, Glaucon, that there will be no injustice in compelling our philosophers to have a care and providence of others; we shall explain to them that in other States, men of their class are not obliged to share in the toils of politics: and this is reasonable, for they grow up at their own sweet will, and the government would rather not have them. Being self-taught, they cannot be expected to show any gratitude for a culture which they have never received. But we have brought you into the world to be rulers of the hive, kings of yourselves and of the other citizens, and have educated you far better and more perfectly than they have been educated, and you are better able to share in the double duty. Wherefore each of you, when his turn comes, must go down to the general underground abode, and get the habit of seeing in the dark. When you have acquired the habit, you will see ten thousand times better than the inhabitants of the cave, and you will know what the several images are, and what they represent, because you have seen the beautiful and just and good in their truth. And thus our State which is also yours will be a reality, and not a dream only, and will be administered in a spirit unlike that of other States, in which men fight with one another about shadows only and are distracted in the struggle for power, which in their eyes is a great good. Whereas the truth is that the State in which the rulers are most reluctant to govern is always the best and most quietly governed, and the State in which they are most eager, the worst.

Quite true, he replied.

And will our pupils, when they hear this, refuse to take their turn at the toils of State, when they are allowed to spend the greater part of their time with one another in the heavenly light?

Impossible, he answered; for they are just men, and the commands which we impose upon them are just; there can be no doubt that every one of them will take office as a stern necessity, and not after the fashion of our present rulers of State.

Yes, my friend, I said; and there lies the point. You must contrive for your future rulers another and a better life than that of a ruler, and then you may have a well-ordered State; for only in the State which offers this, will they rule who are truly rich, not in silver and gold, but in virtue and wisdom, which are the true blessings of life. Whereas if they go to the administration of public affairs, poor and hungering after their own private advantage, thinking that hence they are to snatch the chief good, order there can never be; for they will be fighting about office, and the civil and domestic broils which thus arise will be the ruin of the rulers themselves and of the whole State.

Most true, he replied.

And the only life which looks down upon the life of political ambition is that of true philosophy. Do you know of any other?

Indeed, I do not, he said.

And those who govern ought not to be lovers of the task? For, if they are, there will be rival lovers, and they will fight.

No question.

Who then are those whom we shall compel to be guardians? Surely they will be the men who are wisest about affairs of State, and by whom the State is best administered, and who at the same time have other honours and another and a better life than that of politics?

They are the men, and I will choose them, he replied.

And now shall we consider in what way such guardians will be produced, and how they are to be brought from darkness to light,—as some are said to have ascended from the world below to the gods?

By all means, he replied.

The process, I said, is not the turning over of an oyster-shell, but the turning round of a soul passing from a day which is little better than night to the true day of being, that is, the ascent from below, which we affirm to be true philosophy?

Quite so.

Plato. *The Republic*. Trans. Benjamin Jowett. Vintage, 1991, Book VII: 253–261.

RESOURCE APPENDIX

To reduce costs as much as possible, the library and the Internet are recommended as the primary sources for materials. Comparable books and sources are fine to use. This list of homeschool suppliers is not meant to replace your usual retailer. Please check with them first.

★★★ Books or materials that are used several times or more in this curriculum.

★★ Books or materials used for an ongoing activity.

★ Books or materials used for one activity.

Alpha Omega Discover Creation
P. O. Box 4343
Grand Junction, CO 81502
(903) 523-9943
<http://discovercreation.org>

★ Video–*Grand Canyon Catastrophe: New Evidence of the Genesis Flood.* (High School to Adult)

★ Video–*Grand Canyon: Monument to the Flood.* (High School to Adult)

Cadron Creek Christian Curriculum
4329 Pinos Altos Road
Silver City, NM 88061
(505) 534-1496
<http://www.CadronCreek.com>

★★★ *Genesis: Finding Our Roots* by Dr. Ruth Beechick. Arrow Press. ISBN 0-940319-11-X.

★★★ *Surprised By Joy: The Shape of My Early Life* by C.S. Lewis. Harcourt, Brace, Jovanovich. ISBN 0-15-687011-8.

★★★ *Poems* by C.S. Lewis, edited by Walter Hooper. Harcourt, Brace and Company. ISBN 0-15-672248-8.

★★ Audiocassette–*More True Tales from the Times of Ancient Civilizations and the Bible* by Diana Waring.

★ *American Dictionary of the English Language* (1828 Edition) by Noah Webster.

★ *Of Other Worlds: Essays and Stories* by C.S. Lewis, edited by Walter Hooper. Harcourt, Brace, Jovanovich. ISBN 0-15-667897-7.

★ *Shurley Grammar Grades 1–8* by Brenda Shurley.

Spelling Power by Beverly L. Adams-Gordon.

Canon Press and Book Service
P. O. Box 8729
Moscow, ID 83843

★★ *Introductory Logic* by Douglas J. Wilson and James B. Nance. Canon Press. ISBN 1-885767-36-6. (This is one of several logic books you can choose.)

Christian Book Distributors
P. O. Box 7000
Peabody, MA 01961-7000
(800) 247-4784
<http://www.christianbook.com>

★★★ *Chronicles of Narnia* by C.S. Lewis.

★★★ *Genesis: Finding Our Roots* by Dr. Ruth Beechick. Arrow Press. ISBN 0-940319-11-X.

★★★ *Tales from Shakespeare* by Charles and Mary Lamb. (This is also available online.)

★ Audiocassette–*Bonhoeffer: The Cost of Freedom.*

★ *Foxe's Book of Martyrs* by John Foxe.

★ *Letters to Malcolm* by C.S. Lewis.

★ Audiocassette or book–*Miracles* by C.S. Lewis. (High School to Adult)

★ *Perelandra* by C.S. Lewis. (High School to Adult)

★ Video–*Shadowlands*, 1993, with Anthony Hopkins. (See if your local video store has it first.)

★ Audiocasette or book–*Till We Have Faces* by C.S. Lewis. (High School to Adult)

Farm Country

412 North Fork Road
Metamora, IL 61548
Questions: (309) 367-2844
Orders: (800) 551-3276
<http://www.homeschoolcgs.com>

★★★ *Chronicles of Narnia* by C.S. Lewis.

★★★ *Genesis: Finding Our Roots* by
   Dr. Ruth Beechick. Arrow Press.
   ISBN 0-940319-11-X.

★★★ *Tales from Shakespeare* by Charles and Mary
   Lamb. (This is also available online.)

★ *The Boy's King Arthur* edited by
   Sidney Lanier.

★ *Write Source 2000: A Guide to Writing,
   Thinking and Learning* by Patrick Sebranek,
   et al. (For writers 5th to 8th grade)

★ *Shurley Grammar* by Brenda Shurley.

★ *First Book of the Recorder Kid Kit* with
   Hohner Recorder.

★ *Soap Making,* A Unit of Study.

Francesco Sirene, Spicer

P. O. Box 1051
Peachland, British Columbia
Canada V0H 1X0

★ Comfits at <http://www.silk.net/sirene/
   comfits.htm>

Home Science Tools

546 S 18th Street W, Suite B
Billings, MT 59102
(800) 860-6272
(406) 256-0990
<http://www.hometrainingtools.com>

★ Owl pellets.

Mantle Ministries

228 Still Ridge
Bulverde, TX 78163
(830) 438-3777
<http://www.mantleministries.com>

★ Video–*The Kit Carson Story: Lessons in
   Atonement.*

Memoria Press

P. O. Box 5066
Louisville, KY 40255-0066
(502) 458-5001
<http://www.memoriapress.com>

★★ *Traditional Logic I: Introduction to Formal Logic*
   by Martin Cothran. Memoria Press.
   ISBN 19309531000. (This is one of several
   logic books you can choose.)

Rainbow Resource Center

50 N 500 East Road
Toulon, IL 61483
Questions: (309) 695-3200
Orders: (888) 841-3456
Fax: (800) 705-8809
<http://www.rainbowresource.com>

★★★ *Chronicles of Narnia* by C.S. Lewis.

★★★ *Genesis: Finding Our Roots* by Dr. Ruth
   Beechick. Arrow Press.
   ISBN 0-940319-11-X.

★★★ *Tales from Shakespeare* by Charles and Mary
   Lamb. (This is also available online.)

★★ *Traditional Logic I: Introduction to Formal Logic*
   by Martin Cothran. Memoria Press.
   ISBN 19309531000. (This is one of several
   logic books you can choose.)

★ *The Boy's King Arthur* edited by
   Sidney Lanier.

★ *Foxe's Book of Martyrs* by John Foxe.

★ *Perelandra* by C.S Lewis. (High School to
   Adult)

★ *Into the Forest Game.*

★ *Write Source 2000: A Guide to Writing,
   Thinking and Learning* by Patrick Sebranek,
   et al. (For writers 5th to 8th grade)

★ *Shurley Grammar* by Brenda Shurley.

★ *Sundials and Timedials to Cut Out & Make.*

★ You will find a selection of recorders
   and books about recorders at Rainbow
   Resource Center's Web site: From their
   shopping menu, select the subject, "Music";
   then select, "Recorder."

Tobin's Lab

P. O. Box 725
Culpepper, VA 22701
(540) 937-7173
<http://www.tobinslab.com>

* Solargraphics paper kit.

The Voice of the Martyrs

P. O. Box 54
Caney, KS 67333-9980
(800) 747-0085
<http://www.persecution.com>

* *Learning About Islam* by LINK International.
  (For students eight and older)

* *Bold Believers in Turkey* by LINK
  International. (For students eight and older)

* *Voice of the Martyrs* magazine.

Resources Available in Canada

Canadian Home Resources

7 Stanley Cres SW
Calgary, Alberta
Canada T2S1G1
(403) 243-9727

Resources Available Online

Great Search Engine: Google.com
Great Bible Concordance:
    bible.gospelcom.net
Merriam Online Dictionary: m-w.com

If you have Internet access, almost any poem
may be found simply by searching under the
title of the poem in quotation marks. You may
also find many poems at the following Web sites:
    <http://www.everypoet.com>
    <http://www.bartleby.com/authors>
    <http://www.online-literature.com/
    author_index.php>

All of Aesop's Fables may be found on the
Internet by searching under "Aesop's Fables"
or at the above listed sites. "The Village
Blacksmith" by Henry Wadsworth Longfellow;
"The Rime of the Ancient Mariner" by Samuel
Taylor Coleridge; "The Road Not Taken" by
Robert Frost; and *Paradise Lost* by John Milton
may also be found at these sites.

The texts for *Tales from Shakespeare* by Charles
and Mary Lamb may be found online at
sites such as <http://shakespeare.palomar.
edu/lambtales/LAMBTALE.HTM>. This
site, <http://www.ibiblio.org/eldritch/cml/
au.html>, has a number of texts including:
Charles Lamb's *The Adventures of Ulysses* with
"The House of Circe" in Chapter II and "The
Song of the Sirens" in Chapter III; Nathaniel
Hawthorne's *A Wonder Book for Girls and Boys*
and *Tanglewood Tales* with "Circe's Palace" and
"The Golden Touch," the story of King Midas.

Answer Appendix

P.Martirosian 2000

The Magician's Nephew

Chapter 1

Answers:

1. immigrant
2. pantomime
3. vain
4. feeble
5. bachelor
6. cistern
7. emigrant

Chapter 2

Answers:

1. indignant
2. pluck
3. godmother
4. chivalry
5. preposterous
6. jaw
7. adept

Chapter 4

Sound Study Worksheet Answers:

1. Frequency	9. yes	17. Pitch
2. crest	10. solids	18. lower
3. trough	11. gases	19. higher
4. Amplitude	12. liquids	20. yes
5. wavelength	13. Insulators	21 liquids
6. Hertz	14. decibel	22. faster
7. megahertz	15. vacuum	23 20 to 20,000
8. higher	16. ossicles	24. higher

25. 90

26. to amplify the vibrations of the ear drum

27. to collect vibrations and channel them into the auditory canal

28. tympanic membrane

29. cochlea

30. pinna

31. echo

32. 740

Activity 3 Answer: Foreshadowing. (See *The Magician's Nephew*, Chapter 2, Activity 4.)

Chapter 6

Answers:

1. distinguished

2. pax

3. treachery

4. vain

5. sham

6. dabble

7. scorn

Chapter 7

Answers:

1. bow-window

2. hansom

3. minion

Chapter 8

Activity 1 Answers: Digory, Polly, and the Cabby were happy. Strawberry felt younger. Uncle Andrew wanted to get away. Jadis hated the voice and wanted to smash the world. She looked as if she understood better than any of them.

Activity 6a Answers: Answers may vary. Uncle Andrew was an old magician who was thoughtless of others, selfish, proud, untrustworthy, whiny, and foolish.

Activity 6b Answers: Answers may vary. Cabby was a brave horse owner who was thoughtful of others.

Chapter 15

The Magician's Nephew **Crossword Puzzle Answers:**

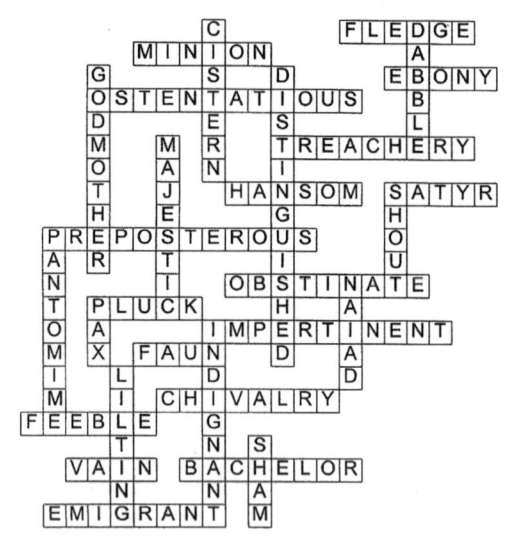

THE LION, THE WITCH AND THE WARDROBE

Chapter 3

Answers:

1. spiteful

2. gilded

3. sulk

Chapter 4

Answers:

1. dryad's

2. courtier

Chapter 5

Answers:

1. snigger

2. row

3. disposal

Chapter 6

Answers:

1. prig

2. camphor

3. chatelaine

4. fraternize

Chapter 7

Answers:

1. oilcloth

2. festoon

Activity 1 Answer: Mr. Beaver.

Chapter 9

Answers:

1. cat-a-mountain

2. sledges

3. turret

4. eerie

Chapter 10

Activity 5 Answers:

a. Had I guessed it was ***they***, I would have hurried.

b. The visitors sat beside ***us*** boys.

c. Mom blamed ***us*** for the mess.

d. I thought the culprit to be ***she***.

e. The youngest member of the band was ***he***.

f. It wasn't ***I*** who whispered.

g. No one but ***he*** knew the answer.

More information about personal pronouns: A **subjective pronoun** is used as the subject of a sentence. The **subject** is the person/place/thing the sentence is about. Most of us know instinctively which pronouns are subjective. Think about this simplest sentence form:

> ***I*** *ran.*

Who is the sentence about? The sentence is about ***I*** (subject). What did ***I*** do? ***I*** *ran* (verb). You could rewrite that sentence using any of the subjective pronouns: ***You*** *ran.* ***He*** *ran.* ***She*** *ran.* ***It*** *ran.* ***We*** *ran.* ***They*** *ran.* These "people" are the ones being discussed in each sentence.

But you would never say: *Me ran. Him ran. Her ran. Us ran. Them ran.*

Now add an **object**.

> *I ran with* **him**.

I is still doing the running and the talking, but now we know with whom *I* ran: **him**.

You could say: *I ran with* **her**. *I ran with* **them**. But not: *I ran with he. I ran with she. I ran with they.* **Her** and **them** are **objective pronouns** and can be used as the object of a sentence; **he, she,** and **they** are **subjective pronouns** and cannot be used as the object of a sentence.

They could run with **me**, but *they* could not run with *I*.

Look at sentence **c** in the exercise:

> Mom blamed (**we, us**) for the mess.

Do not be confused by the rest of the sentence, *for the mess.* The sentence is about **Mom.** What did she do? She **blamed.** Did she blame **us** or **we**? The people she blamed cannot be the subject of the sentence because Mom already has that privilege. They have to be the object, so they have to be **us**.

In exercise sentence **f**, *it* and **I** are both the subject. *It wasn't* **I**. *I wasn't* **it**. *It* and **I** are the same person.

Turning sentences around like this can be a good way to figure out these things. In exercise sentence **e**, the sentence is about **he**. Try saying: *The youngest member of the band was* **him**. Then turn it around: **Him** *was the youngest member of the band.* **He** *was the youngest member of the band.* Your ear knows the second sentence is correct, even if you do not know how to explain it.

The youngest member of the band was **him**, may sound better to you than, *The youngest member of the band was* **he**, because we are used to a certain amount of laziness with our grammar. Speech that sounds too correct seems a bit snobbish.

Some people use **I** exclusively where they should use **me** because they do not know how to figure out what is correct; **I** apparently sounds more educated than the lowly **me**. Consider the sentence, *She went skating with Lucy and* **me/I**. Most people who have to choose either **me** or **I** without thinking about it would probably think **I** sounds better, but not if you break the sentence down to, *She went skating with* **I**.

 # Chapter 11

Answers:

1. traitor
2. repulsive
3. vermin
4. indulgence
5. Gluttony

 # Chapter 12

Answers:

1. Alsatian
2. pavilion
3. standard

Chapter 13

Answers:

1. audience
2. forfeit
3. crave

Activity 3 Answer: Peter

 # Chapter 14

Answers:

1. gibber
2. siege
3. whet

 # Chapter 15

Answers:

1. skirling
2. rabble
3. gorse bush
4. cavern
5. vile
6. stead

 # Chapter 16

Answers:

1. plumage
2. indigo
3. prodigious
4. saccharine
5. din
6. ransack
7. liberate

Chapter 17

Answers:

1. quarry

2. score

3. signification

4. valiant

5. revelry

6. alight

7. quest

8. feat

9. foreboding

Activity 8 Answer: Like Eve's, Edmund's gluttonous desire has deadly ramifications. Later in the tale, after he has betrayed his brother and sisters in order to obtain more and more Turkish Delight (which, ironically, he does not receive), Jadis demands his life by invoking Deep Magic, an ancient Narnian law that entitles her to the blood of any traitor. And while Edmund is saved by the intervention and intercession of Aslan, the cost is deadly to the latter. C.S. Lewis' point in emphasizing Edmund's **gluttony** is to illustrate vividly the effects of sins in general and this sin in particular; overindulgence blinds us to the truth, turning us inward, making us slaves to our own insatiable desires. —Dr. Don W. King, "Narnia and the Seven Deadly Sins." A version of this essay first appeared in *Mythlore* 10 Spring 1984: 14–19.

The Lion, the Witch and the Wardrobe Crossword Puzzle Answers:

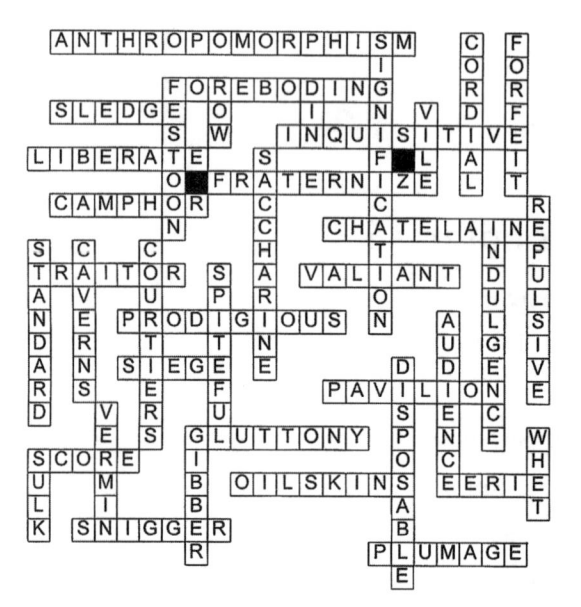

THE HORSE AND HIS BOY

Chapter 1

Answers:

1. loquacious
2. august
3. indigence, hovel, beneficent
4. jargon
5. dappled
6. scimitar
7. wheedle
8. apace
9. carbuncles
10. paddock

Chapter 2

Answers:

1. copse
2. booty
3. spoil
4. cob, downs

Chapter 3

Answers:

1. feign
2. inexorable
3. pith
4. rite
5. dowry
6. inquisitive

Chapter 4

Answers:

1. luxurious, treat
2. arcades
3. Colonnades
4. pinnacle
5. minarets
6. brazen
7. truant
8. dazzle
9. avouch
10. scapegrace
11. refuse

Chapter 5

Answers:

1. closefisted
2. chafed
3. oasis
4. flagon
5. bazaar
6. embark
7. stoup
8. tilt

Chapter 7

Answers:

1. divan
2. talisman
3. punt
4. fortnight

Activity 2 Answer: Answers may vary. Some names for this trait in Lasaraleen are vanity, conceit, immodesty, and egotism.

Chapter 8

The Horse and His Boy **Crossword Puzzle Answers:**

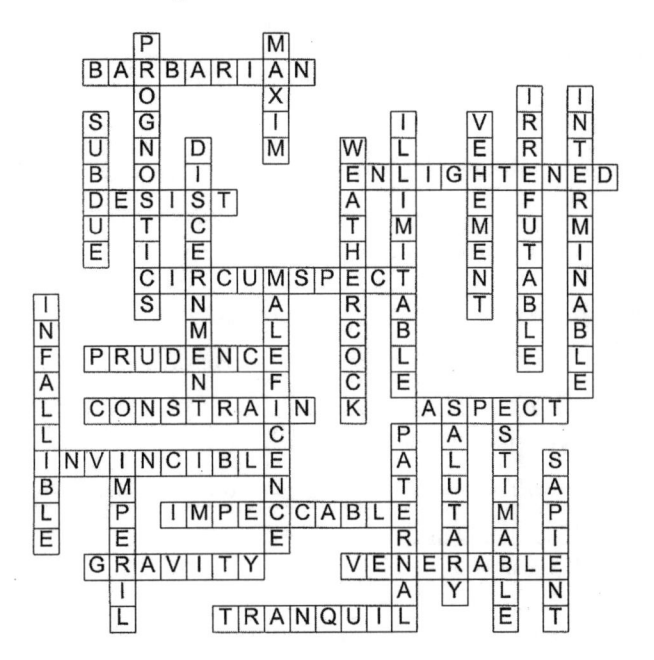

 # Chapter 9

Answers:

1. cataract
2. grovel
3. scullion
4. prim
5. hummocks
6. faugh
7. quailed

Activity 3 Answer: Deserts occur where rainfall is less than 50 cm/year.

Chapter 11

Activity 6 Answer. Answers may vary.

Alliteration: using the same sound two times or more in a line of speech.

Example from "How They Brought the Good News from Ghent to Aix" by Robert Browning.

> **Line 1:**   I **s**prang to the **s**tirrup

Example from "My Shadow" by Robert Louis Stevenson.

> **Line 15:**   But my **l**azy **l**ittle shadow,
> **l**ike an arrant sleepy-head

Simile: comparing two unlike things using "like" or "as."

Example from "My Shadow" by Robert Louis Stevenson.

> **Line 7:**   For he sometimes shoots up
> taller **like** an India-rubber ball

Example from "How They Brought the Good News from Ghent to Aix" by Robert Browning.

> **Line 44:**   Rolled neck and croup over,
> lay dead **as** a stone

Metaphor: comparing two unlike things not using the words "like" or "as."

Example from "My Shadow" by Robert Louis Stevenson.

> **Line 11:**   He stays so close beside me,
> **he's a coward** you can see

The whole poem, "The Road Not Taken," is an example of a metaphor between the choices in life and traveling a road.

Imagery: descriptions used in writing to create mental images in the reader or listener.

Example from "My Shadow" by Robert Louis Stevenson.

> **The fourth stanza*, first two lines:**
> **One morning, very early, before the sun was up,**
> **I rose and found the shining dew on every buttercup**

Example from "How They Brought the Good News from Ghent to Aix"

> **The first stanza:**
> **I sprang to the stirrup, and Joris, and he;**
> **I gallop'd, Dirck gallop'd, we gallop'd all three;**
> **"Good speed!" cried the watch, as the gate-bolts undrew;**
> **"Speed!" echoed the wall to us galloping through;**
> **Behind shut the postern, the lights sank to rest,**
> **And into the midnight we gallop'd abreast.**

*Definition of **stanza**: One of the divisions of a poem, composed of two or more lines usually characterized by a common pattern of meter, rhyme, and number of lines.

Chapter 12

Answers:

1. valiant
2. Lintels
3. extremity
4. excruciating
5. lief

Chapter 13

Answers:

1. portcullis
2. defiance
3. sortie

Chapter 14

Answers:

1. brick
2. cambric
3. embezzling
4. heraldry
5. halberds

Chapter 15

Answers:

1. boudoir
2. lapsed
3. phantasms
4. gentilesse
5. cheer
6. pajock
7. lay

Activity 6 Answers: Answers may vary. Examples: "When pigs fly" or "When chicken have teeth."

Activity 8 Answer: Pride characterizes three key characters in *The Horse and His Boy*. Bree, a talking Narnian war horse, is acutely conscious of how he looks; as he travels towards Narnia, he does all he can to make sure he acts and looks the part. Avaris, an escaped princess of Calormene, holds an extremely high opinion of herself and her position; she is royalty and demands respect, in spite of her runaway status. Most indicative of her pride is her tendency to use others regardless of the consequences for them. However, Prince Rabasash, the evil heir of Calormene, is Lewis' supreme example of pride. In him Lewis creates a comic episode appropriate to the sin of pride. Rabadash, whose pride makes him act like an ass, gets turned into one. In Rabadash, Lewis reminds us that "pride goes before destruction, and a haughty spirit before stumbling."

—Dr. Don W. King, "Narnia and the Seven Deadly Sins." A version of this essay first appeared in *Mythlore* 10 Spring 1984: 14–19.

The Horse and His Boy **Crossword Puzzle Answers:**

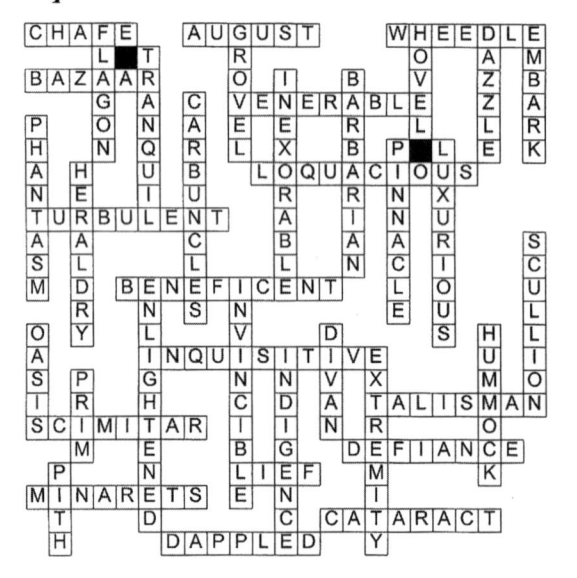

PRINCE CASPIAN

Chapter 1

Answers:

1. inhabited

2. boarding school

3. errant

4. promontory

5. junction

Chapter 2

Answers:

1. dais
2. brooch
3. coronet
4. perish

Activity 5a Answer:

1. The hall was the same size and shape as Cair Paravel.
2. The castle well was in the same place and the same size and shape as at Cair Paravel.
3. Susan had found a chess piece exactly like one they used to play with.
4. There was an orchard in the same place where they had planted one when they had been kings and queens.

Activity 5b Answer: They found the door to the treasure chamber where it had been in their castle and there were sixteen steps from the door to the treasure chamber just as there had been in Cair Paravel.

 # Chapter 4

Answers:

1. buskins
2. battlements
3. turret
4. tutor
5. leads

Activity 7d Answer: Answers may vary. Example: Not everyone believes the poet Homer, named as the author of *The Iliad* and *The Odyssey*, was a real person.

Activity 7e Answer: Answers may vary. Example: The world being flat was once believed to be true.

 # Chapter 5

Answers:

1. truffles
2. theorbo
3. usurp
4. treason
5. pother

Chapter 6

Answers:

1. gorge	6. glen	11. rooks	16. anvil
2. rapier	7. descendants	12. ravine	17. bellows
3. glade	8. Subterranean	13. foxglove	
4. rabble	9. martial	14. smithy	
5. contempt	10. hedgerow	15. tongs	

Vocabulary Answer: *Sub* means under and *terra* means earth.

Activity 11 Answers: Answers may vary. Examples: Abraham had a son by Sarah's handmaiden. This son and Israel have fought for centuries. Saul consulted a medium. He lost his kingdom.

Chapter 7

Answers:

1. contingent

2. lair

3. sortie

4. bivouac

Chapter 8

Answers:

1. seneschal

2. Jinn

3. offense

4. jibe (gibe)

5. pelted, pelt

6. pompous

7. grueling

8. scanty

Activity 5 Answers: Answers may vary. Examples: Jonah, Doubting Thomas, Mary Magdalene.

Chapter 9

Answers:

1. bracken
2. twilight
3. rueful
4. precipice

 # Chapter 11

Answers:

1. vixen
2. tinker
3. grousing
4. blown
5. grape
6. rum

 # Chapter 13

Answers:

1. avenge
2. parley
3. fell
4. dictate
5. dastard
6. effrontery
7. herald, herald
8. dappled
9. levy
10. prescription

Chapter 15

Answers:

1. fray

2. gilt

3. canny

4. mazer

5. woebegone

6. loam

Activity 8 Answer: King Miraz's downfall is the sin of **luxury**. In the tale, Prince Caspian's uncle, King Miraz, is clearly guilty of profiteering in his desire to gain power, wealth, and position. This led to the death of Caspian's father, Belisar, Uvilas, Arlian, and Eriman as well as many others. While Miraz rules, truth is suppressed; talking Narnian creatures are outlawed as well as tales about them. There is little trust between the members of society and even Narnian creatures are affected.

—Dr. Don W. King, "Narnia and the Seven Deadly Sins." A version of this essay first appeared in *Mythlore* 10 Spring 1984: 14–19.

Prince Caspian Crossword Puzzle Answers:

THE VOYAGE OF THE DAWN TREADER

Chapter 1

Answers:

1. exquisite
2. curt
3. briny
4. teetotaler
5. courtly
6. assonance
7. sentiment
8. vulgar
9. prow
10. poop
11. port, starboard

Chapter 2

Answers:

1. tribute
2. carrack
3. regent
4. dromond
5. disposition
6. supple
7. boatswain
8. galleon
9. cog
10. poltroon
11. oars, kitchen

Chapter 3

Answers:

1. rigmarole

2. languish

3. carrion

4. liege

5. consul

6. fief

Activity 2 Answer: *The Horse and His Boy.*

Chapter 4

Answers:

1. vagabond

2. galling

3. languid

4. victuals

5. postern

6. slovenly

7. bilious

8. dossier

Chapter 5

Answers:

1. fiend

2. appalling

3. scree

4. jerkin

5. fathoms

Activity 5 Answers: There are 16 ounces or 2 cups in a pint. There are 8 pints in a gallon. There are 2 pints in a quart. There are 4 quarts in a gallon. There are 16 cups in a gallon.

Chapter 6

Answers:

1. ingots

2. import

3. shamming

4. descent

5. lithe

6. ascent

7. export

 # Chapter 7

Answers:

1. ghastly

2. prosperity

3. quoits

4. unmitigated

5. ejaculations

 # Chapters 9, 10 & 11

Matching Answers:

1. astrolabe   *c. altitude of celestial bodies*

2. orrery   *a. solar system*

3. chronoscope   *b. time*

4. theodolind   *d. horizontal or vertical angles*

Vocabulary Answers:

5. enmity	9. inaudible	12. crestfallen
6. grimace	10. conspicuous	13. courtyard
7. infallible	11. mead	14. monopods
8. flagged		

Activity 6a Answer: Answers may vary. The less you say, the less you will have to apologize for later. Sometimes talking about things blows them out of proportion and can require awkward explanations later.

Activity 6b Answer: "This is an ugly furrow to plow," means this is not going to be easy.

Activity 6c Answer: "Time out of mind" and "since time immemorial" are phrases which mean since before anyone can remember.

Activity 10 Answer: The "invisible ink" chars at a lower temperature than the paper, so the writing appears faint and brown.

Chapter 12

Answers:

1. impeachment

2. extremity

3. poltroonery

4. lurid

5. compose

Chapter 13

Answers:

1. heather

2. device

3. luminous

4. turf

5. botany

Chapter 15

Answers:

1. abdicate

2. coronation

3. falconing

4. keelhaul

5. kraken

6. maroon

Chapter 16

Activity 8 Answer: In *The Voyage of the Dawn Treader* C.S. Lewis emphasizes **greed**, pictured in the thoroughly obnoxious Eustace Clarence Scrubb. Eustace, besides being entirely egocentric and totally selfish, is greedy beyond bounds. His greed and its consequences provide the central episode of the tale. In Eustace, Lewis illustrates the negative, egocentric effect greed has upon an individual. Such a person is useless (Eustace) to himself and to society. The greedy person is only interested in elevation of self and is more than willing to use others for his own advantage. Fortunately for Eustace he "sees" the light and is transformed, though only through an extremely painful experience. Unable to shed his dragon skin himself, Eustace submits to the fierce claws of Aslan and is reborn a new, whole person. —Dr. Don W. King, "Narnia and the Seven Deadly Sins." A version of this essay first appeared in *Mythlore* 10 Spring 1984: 14–19.

The Voyage of the Dawn Treader **Crossword Puzzle Answers:**

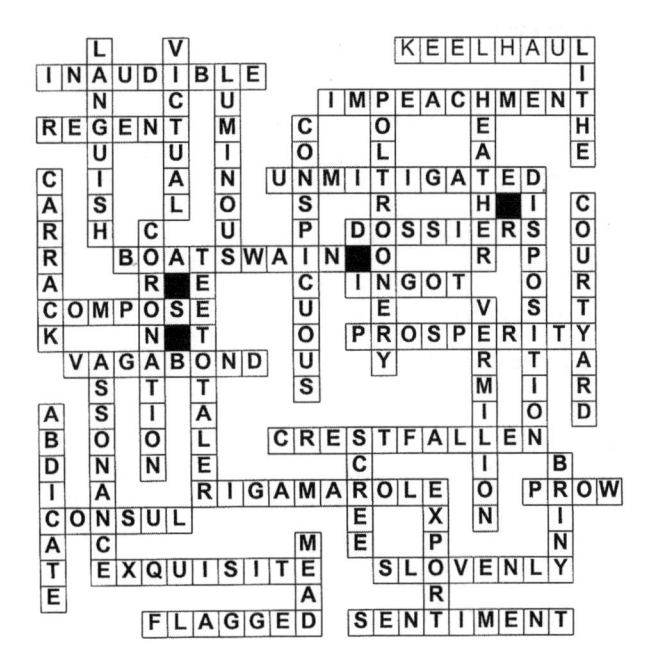

THE SILVER CHAIR

Chapter 1

Answers:

1. psychology

2. despise

3. moor

4. expel

Chapter 4

Answers:

1. avenge

2. distraught

3. fusty

4. parliament

5. physic

Chapter 5

Answers:

1. wigwam
2. belfry
3. bastion
4. funk
5. glum
6. reeds, rushes
7. tinderbox
8. fricassee
9. sparring
10. cockshy

 # Chapter 6

Answers:

1. cairn
2. balustrade
3. scrumptious
4. kirtle

 # Chapter 7

Answers:

1. eddy
2. loiter
3. crag
4. guffaw
5. wet blanket
6. cornice
7. caraway

 # Chapter 8

Answers:

1. poppet
2. posset
3. comfits

Chapter 9

Answers:

1. shingle

2. delicacy

3. mantle

4. scullery

5. bipeds

6. prattle

Chapter 10

Answers:

1. jetty

2. bulwark

3. grotesque

4. nosegay

5. marches

6. gnome

Chapter 11

Answers:

1. adjure

2. tyrant

3. Fie

4. vile

Activity 3 Answer: "Sounds a very nice lady indeed," said Puddleglum.

Chapter 12

Answers:

1. mandolin

2. pinion

3. Abhor

4. renounce

Activity 1 Answer: Jesus is a transliteration of the Hebrew name, "Joshua." It means, Jehovah is Salvation. It was a common Jewish name.

Activity 4 Answer: The Witch had told Rilian if he were not in the silver chair when his fit came on him, he would change into a horrible serpent. She is the one who turned into a horrible serpent.

Chapter 14

Answers:

1. squib

2. mill-race

3. dazzle

4. eloquent

Chapter 15

Answers:

1. in league

2. pert

3. disheveled

4. phosphorescence

Chapter 16

Answers:

1. humbug

2. disconsolate

3. doleful

4. vague

Activity 5 Answer: They were attempting to stretch the meat, due to rationing.

Activity 8 Answer: *The Silver Chair* portrays the dangerous effects of **sloth**, a disgust with the spiritual because of the physical effort involved. Jill Pole is confronted by Aslan early in the tale and commanded to set to memory four important signs that will aid her and Eustace as they quest for a lost prince of Narnia. The importance of remembering the signs is paramount as Aslan indicated repeatedly.

Jill fails, as do many of us, because of sloth. That is, her sloth is not so much overt laziness or reckless disregard as it is gradual wearing away of devotion, ever creeping numbness regarding the spiritual tasks set before her. Indeed, at first she is keenly aware of the signs and tells Eustace about them; however, within a matter of hours after her arrival in Narnia, "she had forgotten all about the Signs and the lost prince for the moment" (37). Consequently, they stumble along on their quest and as the going gets rougher, her diligence to remembering the signs fades: "They never talked about Aslan, or even about the lost prince now. And Jill gave up her habit of repeating the Signs over to herself every night and morning. She said to herself, at first, that she was too tired, but she soon forgot all about it" (79–80).

In Jill, C.S. Lewis portrays all who fail to persevere, who fail to keep the vision. Like Jill, many are susceptible to the weary grind, the dull repetition of routine, the easy slide into self-fulfillment at the cost of spirituality. Yet like Jill too, Lewis suggests we can break the chains of sloth; we too can regain a spiritual vision.   —Dr. Don W. King, "Narnia and the Seven Deadly Sins." A version of this essay first appeared in *Mythlore* 10 Spring 1984: 14–19.

The Silver Chair Crossword Puzzle Answers:

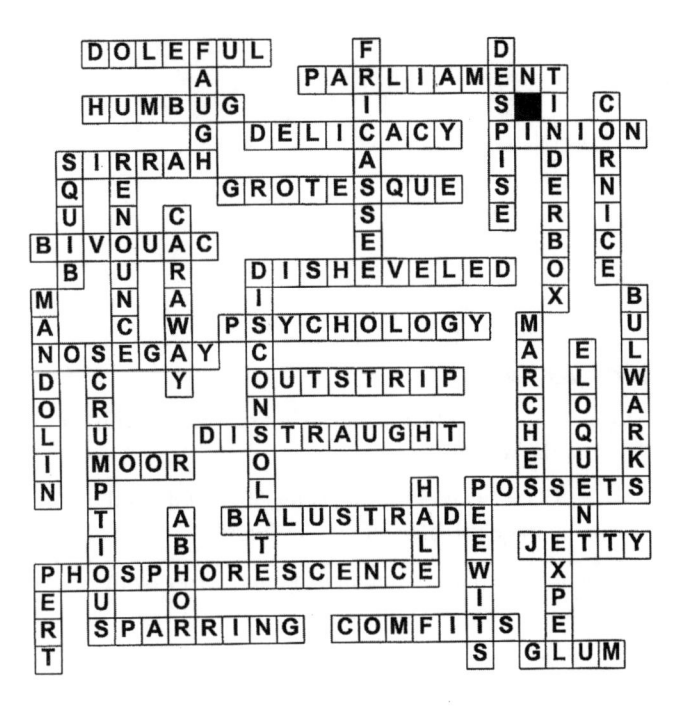

THE LAST BATTLE

Chapter 2

Answers:

1. sloth

2. pomp

3. conjunction

4. rash

Activity 3 Answer:

1. It is the personal star of the King of the Jews.

2. It appears and disappears.

3. It moves from east to west.

4. It moves from north to south.

5. It literally hovers over a single house in Bethlehem. Any literal star, as we know it, that hovered or stayed in one place for any time could destroy the entire planet.

Chapter 5

Answers:

1. rude

2. garrison

3. firkin

4. perilous

5. Prithee

6. sullen

Activity 1 Answer:

In *The Magician's Nephew*, Digory and Polly first entered with the rings by way of the pools in the Wood Between the Worlds.

In *The Lion, the Witch and the Wardrobe*, Peter, Susan, Edmund, and Lucy discovered the wardrobe in Professor Kirke's house was a doorway into Narnia.

In *Prince Caspian*, the children were pulled into Narnia by the sounding of the horn which legend said would summon help in a time of great need.

In *The Voyage of the Dawn Treader*, Edmund, Lucy, and Eustace fell into Narnia through a painting.

In *The Silver Chair*, Lucy and Eustace entered Narnia through the gate of their school grounds after having called to Aslan.

Chapter 6

Answers:

1. rive

2. miscarry

3. malapert

4. mattock

Chapter 7

Answers:

1. wood sorrel, Belike

2. churl

3. sagacious

4. manikin

5. scurvy

6. miscreant

7. rally

8. moke

Chapter 8

Activity 5 Answer: Answers may vary. In Part I, Lewis used words with softer sounds and gentler connotations than in Part Two. Phrases like "point'll tickle 'em" and "trick'll trouble 'em" help create a feeling of dwarfs tripping along. Although the dwarfs are threatening violence, there is a lighter feel to the first part. Words like "stumping," "lumpish," "ramparts," "bludgeon," and "blunder," in Part II, have harsh, abrupt sounds and the repetition of the words "tramp," "thunder," and "rumble" help the reader feel the reverberation of the giants' heavy tread. The giants, who are usually characterized as rude and not too smart, seem to have an even simpler vocabulary and are more insulting.

Chapter 9

Activity 2 Answer: In the time of Miraz the talking animals had gone into hiding. No one really believed in them anymore, so they were not being actively hunted. Now the Calormenes are hunting and killing anyone who will not obey them. Now, also, Tash has come to Narnia so there are powerful lies and supernatural forces working against the Narnians.

In *Prince Caspian*, the talking animals and dwarfs had the advantage of surprise and Miraz's men were afraid of the woods. Now the Narnians have been taken by surprise.

They are completely unprepared to defend themselves and the Calormenes are not afraid.

Chapter 14

Activity 2 Answer: Edmund and Lucy had once met the stars during *The Voyage of the Dawn Treader*. The stars were the wizard on the Duffelpuds' island and Ramandu at their last stop where they found the sleepers.

Digory and Polly recognized the dying sun because they had the seen the dying sun of Charn in *The Magician's Nephew*.

Activity 3 Answer: Eternity.

Chapter 16

Activity 8 Answer: The **envy** of Shift does much disservice to Aslan and the cause of truth. Innocent lives are taken and a world is destroyed. Once more, C.S. Lewis illustrates the destructive power of a deadly sin in the context of a Narnian tale.

—Dr. Don W. King, "Narnia and the Seven Deadly Sins." A version of this essay first appeared in *Mythlore* 10 Spring 1984: 14–19.

The Last Battle Crossword Puzzle Answers:

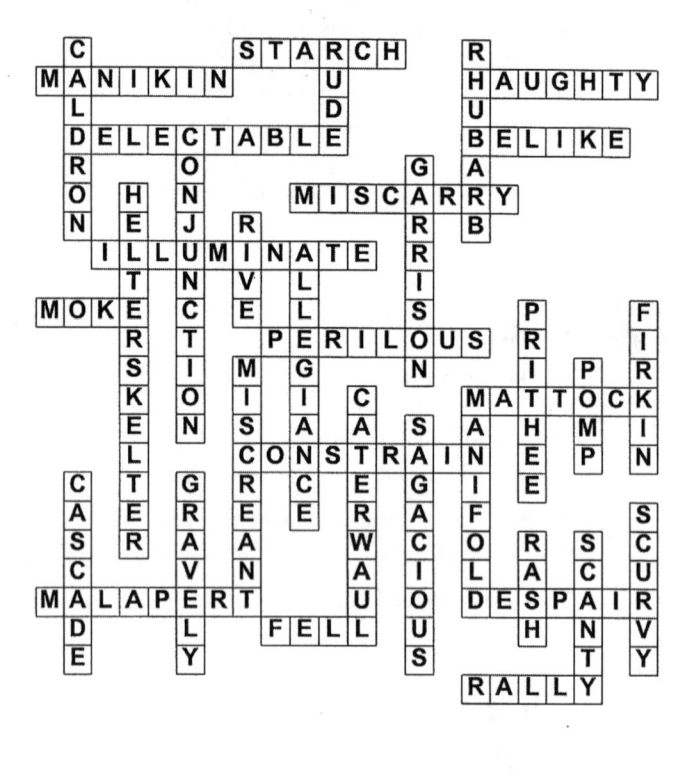

Sold To: (Please Print)

Name: _____

Address: _____

City/State/Zip: _____

Phone: _____

Three ways to order:

1 **Online** catalog @ www.CadronCreek.com
2 **Mail** this order form with check or money order made payable to:
   Cadron Creek Christian Curriculum or CCCC
   4329 Pinos Altos Road
   Silver City, NM 88061
3 **Phone** (505) 534-1496

Quantity	Item	Price	Total
	The Prairie Primer — Literature-based unit study utilizing the Little House series	$ 50.00	
	Further Up and Further In — Literature-based unit study utilizing *The Chronicles of Narnia* (spiral)	56.00	
	Surprised by Joy: The Shape of My Early Life by C.S. Lewis (paperback)	13.00	
	Poems by C.S. Lewis (paperback)	13.00	
	Genesis: Finding Our Roots (hardback)	17.50	
	Of Other Worlds: Essays and Stories by C.S. Lewis (paperback)	12.00	
	Companion to Narnia — A complete guide to the world of *The Chronicles of Narnia* (paperback)	18.00	
	More True Tales: Ancient Civilizations and the Bible (audiocassette)	8.95	
	Further Up and Further In Basic Pack —*Books included in Basic Pack — Save 15%	85.00	
	Where the Brook and River Meet — Literature-based unit study utilizing *Anne of Green Gables*	65.00	
	Anne's Anthology — Poetry that Anne would have studied during the Victorian Era	29.95	
	The Annotated Anne of Green Gables (hardback)	40.00	
	The Green Gables Letters (paperback)	19.50	
	Writers INC (paperback)	20.95	
	American Dictionary of the English Language (1828 edition) by Noah Webster (hardback)	60.00	
	Spelling Power (paperback)	TBA	
		SHIPPING 12.5% (MINIMUM $4.50)	
		TAX (NM RESIDENTS 5.9375%)	
		TOTAL DUE	

We accept the following credit cards:

Prices and availability subject to change. Above prices guaranteed through 2006.